CREATIVE COMMUNICATION
PRINCIPLES & APPLICATIONS

Craig E. Johnson
George Fox College

Michael Z. Hackman
University of Colorado—Colorado Springs

WAVELAND
PRESS, INC.
Prospect Heights, Illinois

Robert E. Denton, Jr.
Consulting Editor

For information about this book, write or call:

Waveland Press, Inc.
P.O. Box 400
Prospect Heights, Illinois 60070
(708) 634-0081

Credits:

p. 1: M. C. Escher, *Swans,* Cornelius Van S. Roosevelt Collection, © 1955. National Gallery of Art, Washington.

p. 36: Figure from *Modes of Thinking in Young Children: A Study of the Creativity-Intelligence Distinction* by Michael A. Wallach and Nathan Kogan, copyright © 1965 by Holt, Rinehart and Winston, Inc. and renewed 1993 by Michael A. Wallach and Nathan Kogan, reproduced by permission of the publisher.

p. 117: M. C. Escher, *Day and Night,* Cornelius Van S. Roosevelt Collection, © 1937. National Gallery of Art, Washington.

Printed in the United States of America

7 6 5 4 3 2 1

To my parents, Harold and Harriet Johnson,
who have supported me in all of my creative efforts.

To four generations of creative achievers
who modeled the way for me—
Marie Phillips, Anita Hackman,
Tammy Barthel-Hackman and Jane Hackman

Craig Johnson is an Associate Professor of Communication and chair of the department of Communication Arts at George Fox College, Newberg, Oregon. In addition to teaching courses in communication theory, interpersonal communication, public speaking, leadership, and nonverbal communication, he serves as faculty director of the college's leadership studies minor. Dr. Johnson's research interests include powerful/powerless forms of speech, creativity and innovation, and leadership education. He has published articles in such journals as *Communication Quarterly, Communication Reports, Communication Education, Journal of the International Listening Association,* and *The Speech Communication Teacher.* Between 1991–1993 he served as chair of the faculty at George Fox College and in 1994 received the school's faculty achievement award for teaching.

Michael Z. Hackman is an Associate Professor of Communication at the University of Colorado-Colorado Springs. His research focuses on a wide range of communication issues, including the impact of gender-role behaviors on leadership, humor and communication, mediated instruction, communication competency assessment, and creativity. Dr. Hackman's research has appeared in such journals as *Communication Education, Communication Quarterly, Distance Education, Perceptual and Motor Skills,* and the *Southern Speech Communication Journal.* While on leave during the academic year 1991–1992 and Fall semester 1994, Dr. Hackman served as a Visiting Senior Lecturer at the University of Waikato in Hamilton, New Zealand. There, he developed and taught graduate courses in leadership, management communication, and public speaking. He has conducted over two hundred workshops on more than twenty topics related to management and communication for a variety of public and private sector organizations in both the United States and New Zealand. His clients have included AARP, Hewlett-Packard, Telecom New Zealand, and the United States Olympic Training Center.

Drs. Johnson and **Hackman** co-authored *Leadership: A Communication Perspective,* published by Waveland Press, Inc.

Contents

3   The Creative Process   61

4   Creativity and Language   91

![bar]

PART II Creative Applications   117

Preface

Creativity is discussed in a variety of communication courses ranging from organizational and group communication to public relations, persuasion, advertising, and scriptwriting. Unfortunately, many communication scholars and textbook writers have neglected the study of creativity, forcing communication students and instructors to rely on sources authored by experts in other disciplines. *Creative Communication: Principles and Applications* is written for those interested in learning about creativity from a communication perspective. This book can be used as a supplemental text in communication classes which include units on creativity, or it can serve as the primary text in a course devoted entirely to creativity and communication.

Two themes run throughout this text. The first is the notion that creating is a symbolic process. Our capacity as symbol users makes creative thinking possible; through our symbols we create environments which nurture creativity and promote the spread of new ideas. The second is the belief that we can become more productive creative thinkers by learning more about creativity, honing our communication skills, and developing effective, creative problem-solving strategies. For this reason, *Creative Communication: Principles and Applications* has an applied focus. We describe important theories and research findings and then suggest ways to put these concepts into action. Special chapter features called Creative Profiles and Creative Dilemmas introduce significant creators and provide problem-solving practice. Application exercises at the end of each chapter also encourage active learning.

Part I lays the foundation for understanding the relationship between creating and communicating. Chapter 1 introduces the study of creativity from a communication vantage point. Chapter 2 surveys important theories of creativity which focus on cognitive processes, creative individuals, and creative motivation. Chapter 3 examines the creative process in detail. Chapter 4 discusses the connection between language and creativity. Part II extends the principles discussed in the first four chapters to important communication contexts. Chapters 5 and 6 describe creative group problem solving and creative organizational communication. Chapters 7 and 8 focus on creative writing and creative persuasion.

We couldn't have written this book without the support of colleagues, our families, and students. Thanks to Bruce Dixon and Shirley Leitch for assisting us in obtaining the grant that brought us together to work on the early stages of this project in Hamilton, New Zealand. Joanne Desrochers, Ed Higgins, Beth LaForce and John Wish directed us to a number of valuable sources. The library staffs at George Fox College and the University of Colorado-Colorado Springs patiently processed hundreds of interlibrary loan requests for books and articles. Tammy Barthel-Hackman spent many hours editing portions of the manuscript and producing the mind map in Chapter 3. Students enrolled in our courses provided us with valuable feedback on chapter content and exercises. Student assistants Mitzi Tunison, Peg Hutton and Jennifer Shoemaker gathered information, photocopied materials and carried out many other important tasks essential to completing this project. Our appreciation goes to all of these people and to Neil and Carol Rowe at Waveland Press who demonstrated their willingness to take creative risks by publishing this text.

Craig E. Johnson
George Fox College

Michael Z. Hackman
University of Colorado-Colorado Springs

PART I

Principles of Creative
Communication

1 | Understanding Creativity

> Surprise is at the core of existence. It's true. You never ever really know what's coming next.
>
> Robert Fulghum

PREVIEW

- ► The Growing Importance of Creativity
- ► Creativity From A Communication Perspective
    Humans as Symbol Users
    Communicating and Creating
- ► Defining Creativity
    Definitional Elements
    Dispelling the Myths
- ► Creativity Roadblocks
- ► The Ethical Dimension of Creativity
    Ethical Guidelines
- ► Summing Up
- ► Application Exercises

3

The Growing Importance of Creativity

Creativity is the driving force in human history. Over the centuries, progress has been fueled by creative ideas. Every product, building, painting, social program, musical composition, medical treatment, poem, mathematical theorem, philosophical belief and political system is a human invention. Although creativity has always been essential to human survival, systematic attempts to measure and to promote creative thinking emerged primarily after World War II. Since that time, interest in creativity has exploded. Experts in nearly every walk of life now study the creative process in an attempt to encourage the generation of new ideas. Scientists, engineers, doctors, managers, manufacturers, advertisers, public relations professionals, composers, writers and others realize that creativity is the key to success in any endeavor.

Creativity is likely to attract even more attention in the years to come because the pace of change is accelerating.[1] As the rate of change increases, so does the need for creative ideas. Consider, for example, the demands that rapid political and economic developments in Eastern Europe make on decision makers. Leaders from both the East and West must respond to the overthrow of Communism, a shift to capitalist economies, and the disintegration of the Union of Soviet Socialist Republics and Yugoslavia. If Eastern bloc countries are going to survive the transition to democracy and capitalism, creative solutions must be found to such problems as ethnic violence, food and currency shortages, unemployment, control of nuclear arms, and the collapse of traditional authority.

The proliferation of new products is another indication that creative thinking is more important than ever. When it comes to getting new products to market, "Speed is Life."[2] Companies like Hewlett-Packard, Lockheed and Westinghouse have shortened product development times by 50–96 percent.[3] Over thirteen thousand new consumer products (food, beverages, household cleaners, etc.) appear in one year. The typical grocery store now carries 18,000 items, up from 7,800 in 1970.[4] The introduction of any new product sets off a creative chain reaction. New ways must be found to manufacture, package, advertise and ship the item. Competitors then respond with new products of their own, which prompts another round of creative problem solving.

Rapid change also makes creativity increasingly important in our careers and relationships. As a student, you may need to find creative ways to balance the demands of school with the demands of your job, as tuition hikes and new limits on federal aid push college costs higher. As a dating or marriage partner, you may seek creative solutions to conflicts generated by the changing roles of men and women. As a parent, you may explore creative, nontraditional strategies for disciplining your children.

There is a growing sense of urgency to the study of creativity. We need more creative ideas in a shorter period of time than ever before. Those who think creatively will play a significant role in small groups, organizations and society; they will also enjoy productive interpersonal relationships. This text is a response to the increasing demand for creative problem solvers. Our goal is to help you become a more creative communicator. In this chapter we lay the groundwork for reaching this objective. We'll examine creativity from a communication perspective, define creativity, identify creative blocks, and then talk about how ethical choices influence creative communication.

Creativity from a Communication Perspective

Humans as Symbol Users

We noted earlier that experts in nearly every discipline study creativity. With so many scholars already interested in the topic, why view creativity from a communication perspective? Because the creative process is a communication process. To demonstrate how creativity relates to communication, we'll rely on the insights of Kenneth Burke, one of the most influential communication theorists of this century. Among Burke's most important contributions is his communication-based definition of human:

> *[Hu]man is the symbol-using (symbol-making, symbol-misusing) animal; inventor of the negative (or moralized by the negative); separated from his[her] natural condition by instruments of his[her] own making (maker of technology); goaded by the spirit of hierarchy (or moved by the sense of order); and rotten with perfection.*[5]

This definition provides a foundation for 1) understanding what makes humans unique and 2) understanding creativity from a communication perspective. Burke builds his definition much like a bricklayer constructs a wall. The earliest sections of the definition act like the bottom layers of brick in a wall, supporting the phrases that are added later.

[Hu]Man is the symbol-using (symbol-making, symbol-misusing) animal

Burke begins his definition with his most important assertion: we are unique because we are symbolic communicators. Symbols substitute for (take the place of) the actual objects, emotions, events or ideas we want to discuss. Language, for example, enables us to talk about things that aren't physically present, past occasions or future plans, and such abstract ideas as "democracy" and "communism." In addition, one symbol or set of symbols can be exchanged or substituted for another. Many such symbolic substitutions take place when Americans visit Canada. When they cross the border, American visitors exchange currencies, switch to the metric system, and learn the meaning of new words like "loonies" (Canadian silver dollars).

Abbreviation is an important attribute of substitution. Symbols are shorthand or abbreviated ways to refer to reality. Whenever a word is used to label someone or something, many important details are left out. For instance, if you tell a friend you own a dog, you've said nothing about the animal's breed, size or personality. If you tell your friend you own a pet, you've taken an even bigger shortcut since this term could refer to a cat, bird, hamster or other creature.

Symbol using is such a part of our nature as humans that we often forget just how much we depend on symbols to understand the world. According to Burke:

> Take away our books, and what little do we know about history, biography, even something so "down to earth" as the relative position of seas and continents? What is our "reality" for today (beyond the paper-thin line of our own particular lives) but all this clutter of symbols about the past combined with whatever things we know mainly through maps, magazines, newspapers, and the like about the present?. . . And however important to us is the tiny sliver of reality each of us has experienced firsthand, the whole overall "picture" is but a construct of our symbol systems.[6]

Museums remind us that symbols play a central role in human life. Museums contain artifacts (symbolic products) of past and present societies. These tools, carvings, drawings, buildings and paintings were created by groups of people bound together by common symbol systems. Museum curators use the symbols they share in common with museum visitors (language) to explain what the objects on display meant to their creators.

Burke uses the label "terministic screens" to describe how the language we use determines what we see.[7] The words or terms that we learn, often in specialized fields of study like psychology, sociology or communication, focus our attention or observations on some features of the world around us while diverting our attention from others. Someone learning how to flyfish will discover the impact of terministic screens. When fishing with nightcrawlers, one pays little attention to "bugs" on the stream. After learning the specialized language of fly fishing, the same angler peers into the water to determine if the emerging insects are "caddis flies," "mayflies," or "midges."

Symbol use can easily lead to abuse. While symbols enable us to express love, coordinate our actions and inspire others, this same symbolic capacity empowers us to lie, cheat and make racial slurs. For this reason, Burke is quick to point out that humans are also symbol *misusing* animals.

Inventor of the negative

As a result of our symbolic capacity, only humans can talk about what is *not*. We can say, for example, that a chair is not a table, a lamp, a map, a person and so on. This ability, coupled with the fact that we can make up messages about messages, can lead to some very complicated statements about things that never happened. Consider this statement: "If it had rained today, I would not have gone to the park and would not have gotten into trouble." Implied here is that the day was dry which meant that the speaker did visit the park and then did something that got him/her into trouble![8]

By inventing (creating) the negative through language we set up a contrast between what is and what ought to be. This dichotomy is a major source of dissatisfaction because reality frequently doesn't meet our expectations—as when we get a C grade instead of the A we expected. The negative is the foundation for morality and religion. These systems of laws and beliefs clearly identify positive and negative thoughts and behaviors. With religious belief in mind, Burke notes that we are "moralized by the negative." Guilt comes from engaging in such negative behaviors as breaking biblical commandments against lying or stealing.

Separated from his[her] natural condition by instruments of his[her] own making (maker of technology)

Like symbol using, toolmaking (technology) is an integral part of human nature. Burke argues that the ability to create tools depends on the ability to make and to use symbols. Toolmaking is impossible without conceptualizing; conceptual thinking, in turn, is impossible without symbols. While some animals use tools (chimpanzees use sticks to draw ants from holes, for example), they don't use tools to create other tools. Phillip Tompkins describes the difference this way: "I have seen films of Goodall's chimps using saliva-moistened sticks to draw ants out of their holes. I did not see the chimps create what we humans call a knife in order to fashion these ant-catchers with the efficiency of mass production."[9]

Technology is such a significant part of our daily lives that we sometimes go to great lengths to make contact with our "natural condition." Many people take up camping, backpacking and other outdoor activities in order to escape from television, radio, air conditioning, refrigerators and other technological developments. But even the most ardent outdoor enthusiast is typically dependent on such human inventions as sleeping bags, portable stoves, backpacks and tents.

Goaded by the spirit of hierarchy (or moved by the sense of order)

Through our use of symbols, we determine who is wealthy or poor, stylish or outdated, powerful or powerless. The presence of these distinctions fosters guilt because those who are "down" feel guilty about not being "up" and those who are "up" often feel that they don't deserve their high standing. To illustrate how much influence status considerations have on our everyday decisions, think about the type of jeans you wear. Your decision to buy Levis, Wranglers, Guess jeans, Calvin Kleins or some other jean may have been based in large part on the image or status associated with the brand name.

Rotten with perfection

Humans are the only living creatures who strive for perfection. The principle of perfection, like the other components of Burke's definition, has its origin in symbol using. Certain terms encourage perfectionism. For example, for many with religious training, the ultimate good is perfectly captured by the term "God," while the term "Devil" represents ultimate or perfect evil. Language moves or motivates us to action. The motivating force of language is particularly apparent in times of war. Before Operation Desert Storm, Saddam Hussein was an "ally" of the United States. During the conflict he became a "madman" and "brutal dictator" who had to be defeated. Even the names of the weapons used in the Gulf encouraged the war effort. The Iraqis fired "Scud" missiles; the United States fired "Patriots."

Perfection becomes "rotten" when we make others the victims or scapegoats for the frustration we feel when we don't reach the perfection we seek. A student of the rhetoric of Hitler, Burke was keenly aware of the destructive force of scapegoating. Hitler and his followers blamed the Jews for Germany's economic, political and social problems. As a result, they sent millions of Jewish men, women and children to their deaths in concentration camps.

Communicating and Creating

Kenneth Burke's definition of human provides us with some important insights into the relationship between communication and creation. First, *symbolic ability is the basis for creative ability.* Creativity involves abstract or conceptual thinking which is based on symbol using. Creative ideas nearly always take a particular symbolic form—as mathematical formulas, sentences, slogans, computer programs and so on. Further, "symbolic environments" (relationships and structures created through the use of symbols) either encourage or discourage the generation of creative ideas. Innovative small groups, for example, stimulate the flow of creative ideas by promoting a cooperative, supportive climate while less productive groups are marked by defensiveness and destructive conflict (see chapter 5). Innovative organizations promote creative thinking by reducing levels of hierarchy, empowering employees and rewarding creative ideas, while traditional organizations stifle creativity through excessive bureaucracy and red tape (see chapter 6). Symbols also play a significant role in the dissemination of creative ideas. Successful creators know how to use team-building and persuasion skills in order to promote their ideas (see chapter 8).

We've entitled this text *Creative Communication: Principles and Applications* because we recognize that symbols play an important role not only in generating ideas but also in nurturing and spreading them. Although our primary focus will be on creative thinking, we'll also suggest ways to build symbolic environments which foster creativity. We will identify important communication strategies which promote innovations. In the chapters to come, we will discuss such key creative communication skills as asking provocative questions and using metaphors (chapter 4), fostering a cooperative climate and managing conflict (chapter 5), challenging mental models and coalition building (chapter 6), writing (chapter 7), and bargaining and negotiation (chapter 8).

Second, *creativity is a distinctly human characteristic*. If creativity is a symbolic process, as Burke suggests, then creative thinking is a uniquely human phenomenon. Other animals may generate novel solutions to problems. Yet, because humans alone create and manipulate symbols, only they have the conceptual abilities necessary for creative problem solving.[10] W. Barnett Pearce contrasts the communication patterns of honey bees and wolves to the communication abilities of humans to demonstrate that animal communication is instinctual, not symbolic. Pearce notes that honey bees can "talk" about distant food sources through sophisticated dance movements. But a dancing bee cannot dance for the fun of it, improvise, or change the subject; the result would be dead bees. Wolves establish the order of the pack and hunt through scents, posture and sounds. A wolf's understanding of the world, however, is much more limited than ours. A wolf walks in the woods to seek prey, to mark territory, or to meet some other physical need. A human may walk in the woods, according to Pearce, as "a restful respite from the day's labors, a spiteful withdrawal from human company, a fearful ordeal, a spiritual quest, a shortcut to a destination."[11]

> . . . The koala bear does not limit its diet to leaves from certain eucalyptus trees because of neurotic food faddish. The crested flycatcher does not incorporate a cast-off snake skin in its nest because of a superstitious or fetishistic hang up. The wolverine does not enter a cabin and befoul the stores of food there as an act of revenge against any specific trapper. The lion does not decorate its den with horns of the impala it has slain. Animals are entrapped in acting, reacting, enacting and re-enacting a limited and circumscribed repertoire of behavior closely tied to their immediate physical and physiological needs.
>
> George S. Welsh

Third, *symbols limit our creative capacity*. This conclusion might seem to contradict our earlier assertion that creativity is impossible without the manipulation of symbols. However, symbols can also derail the creative process if we're not careful. Because symbols are shorthand or abbreviated ways of referring to reality; no symbol completely captures all of the important details about an object, person, feeling or idea. A creative idea often comes from information that has been omitted or abstracted. If we're locked into one way of describing a problem (bound by our terministic screens), we lose sight of the fact that there may be many other ways to refer to reality that suggest creative solutions. When synthetic paint brushes were first introduced, for example, they didn't work as well as natural ones. They were reshaped and improved when inventors no longer thought of them as "brushes" but as "pumps" which force paint into channels between the bristles.[12] (More information on semantic barriers to creativity can be found in chapter 4.)

The relationship between symbols and creativity is a two-way street. Although creativity is based on symbol using, we can become the victims of our own symbolic creations. Groups, organizations and individuals rely on rules, systems, ideas and products (which were creative solutions to earlier problems) long after they've outlived their usefulness. Clinging to past successes can have disastrous consequences. For instance, typewriter manufacturers who concentrated on building better typewriters lost their market share when consumers switched to word processors and computers.

Fourth, *creativity is a response to the negative—the difference between what is and what ought to be.* Creative thinking is often directed at correcting imperfections or problems. In fact, actively seeking problems to solve ("problem finding") can be one way to stimulate creative thinking. Stanford creativity expert James Adams encourages his engineering students to develop inventions by asking class members to make a "bug" list—a list of minor details in life that bother them. Among the items annoying Stanford students are cleaning the oven, noisy clocks, vending machines that take your money, and stamps that won't stick.[13] (To see if identifying minor irritations can stimulate your thinking, create your own "bug" list in Application Exercise 1 on page 28). Human obsession with hierarchy also stimulates creativity. Status and wealth often go to those who introduce a new product, manufacturing process, theory or other idea. However, as we noted earlier, hierarchical environments can impede the generation and dissemination of creative ideas.

Fifth, *creativity involves moral (ethical) choices.* Burke's somber reminder that we are symbol *mis-users* who are *obsessed* with hierarchy and *rotten* with perfection should focus our attention on the importance of making reasoned ethical choices about the uses of creative ideas. Generally we think of creativity as a positive attribute, but creative solutions can be used to hurt as well as to help others. Creative processes were responsible for both the development of penicillin and the invention of the atomic bomb and nerve gas. Every creative idea must come under close ethical scrutiny. For this reason, we'll discuss the ethical dimension of creativity later in this chapter.

Defining Creativity

Definitional Elements

Defining creativity is no easy task. At last count there were well over 100 definitions to choose from.[14] Compounding the confusion is the fact that researchers approach creativity with different orientations. Some focus on creative products—the end results of creative thinking. Others examine the nature of the creative process itself or study habits and motivations of creative persons. Still others concentrate on the setting or place for creative thinking and are most interested in how culture, organizational structure, group norms and other environmental factors influence the generation of creative ideas.[15] Yet, most definitions of creativity share certain elements in common. These elements include originality (novelty), relevance and lateral (divergent) thinking.

Originality (Novelty).   Creative thinking is, first and foremost, original thinking. The goal of creative communication is to produce advertising slogans, songs, musical compositions, formulas, manufacturing processes and other symbolic products which are new and different. Perhaps the simplest definition of creativity is "the ability to bring something new into existence."[16] According to this definition, an idea is creative as long as it is novel to its creator. Other definitions go further, suggesting that ideas are new because they combine existing elements into new configurations:

> The creative act is not an act of creation in the sense of the Old Testament. It does not create something out of nothing; it uncovers, selects, re-shuffles, combines, synthesizes already existing facts, ideas, faculties, skills. The more familiar the parts, the more striking the new whole.[17]

> . . . human creativity uses what is already existing and available and changes it in unpredictable ways.[18]

> . . . putting old things into new combinations and new things into old combinations.[19]

Because creativity involves the association of existing elements, creators must have a solid grasp of old ideas before they can develop new ones. Creativity begins with careful preparation. Composers, for example, average ten years of study before they produce their first major compositions, and professional dancers often perform six years before they develop creative new routines.

Relevance. Much of our creative communication is goal-directed. As we noted earlier, creative thinking is often prompted by irritations or problems. In addition, we create in order to meet such needs as our desire to feel competent or to influence others. If creativity is a response to problems or needs, then novel ideas must have relevance to the goals we seek. This suggests that while all creative thinking is original, not all original thinking is creative. While spontaneous thoughts produced by schizophrenia or other mental illnesses may be highly original, for instance, we would not label these ideas as creative since they are not in touch with reality. Note the emphasis on relevance in these definitions of creativity:

> the fresh and relevant association of thoughts, facts, ideas, etc. in a new configuration.[20]

> the forming of associative elements into new combinations which either meet specified requirements or are in some way useful.[21]

> . . . must serve to solve a problem, fit a situation, or accomplish some recognizable goal."[22]

Introducing relevance to a definition of creativity acknowledges the role that group consensus plays in creative communication. Ultimately the group (whether it be a small group, organization or society) decides if the idea can be applied to the problem at hand.

Lateral (Divergent) Thinking. Creativity is also characterized by *how* it generates new ideas. As the definitions cited above suggest, creative thinking results in new combinations and associations. These novel products come from taking a variety of perspectives and generating a variety of solutions. Creative ideas often come from linking concepts which seem totally unrelated at first. For example, Alastair Pilkington, a British engineer, got the idea for a new glass manufacturing process while washing his dinner dishes. Plate glass had traditionally been made by running molten glass through a set of rollers and then polishing any imperfections. While looking at soap and grease floating in his dishwater, Pilkington decided that the same concept could be applied to glassmaking. Now plate glass is floated in an oven on molten tin and then transferred to the finishing stage without the need for grinding or polishing. This greatly reduces production costs.[23]

Creative thinking is frequently referred to as divergent or lateral thinking. In contrast, convergent thinking (also known as vertical thinking) seeks to converge on a single solution and is directed at evaluating and developing ideas. According to Edward de Bono, the leading proponent of lateral thinking, vertical thinking digs the same hole deeper while lateral thinking involves digging a hole in another place.[24] (For more information on lateral and vertical thinking, see chapter 3.) De Bono offers the puzzle, the Merchant's Daughter's Problem, presented below to illustrate the differences between vertical and lateral thought processes.

The Case of the Merchant's Daughter

Many years ago when a person who owed money could be thrown into jail, a merchant in London had the misfortune to owe a huge sum to a moneylender. The moneylender fancied the merchant's beautiful teenage daughter. He proposed a bargain. He said he would cancel the merchant's debt if he could have the young woman instead.

Both the merchant and his daughter were horrified at the proposal. So the cunning moneylender proposed that they let Providence decide the matter. He told them that he would put a black pebble and a white pebble into an empty moneybag, and then the young woman would have to pick out one of the pebbles. If she chose the black pebble, she would become his wife and her father's debt would be cancelled. If she chose the white pebble, she would stay with her father and the debt would still be cancelled. But if she refused to pick out a pebble her father would be thrown into jail and she would starve.

Reluctantly the merchant agreed. They were standing on a pebble-strewn path in the merchant's garden as they talked, and the moneylender stooped down to pick up the two pebbles. As he picked up the pebbles, the daughter noticed that he picked up two black pebbles and put them into the moneybag. He then asked the young woman to pick out the pebble that was to decide her fate and that of her father.

Imagine that you are standing on that path in the merchant's garden. What would you have done if you had been the unfortunate daughter? If you had to advise her what would you have advised her to do?

Instructions

Take ten minutes to solve this problem on your own or in a group. When you have reached a decision, turn to page 16 for the correct answer.

Despite his fondness for lateral thinking, de Bono argues that both divergent and convergent thinking play a role in the creative process. "Lateral thinking generates the ideas," he notes, "and vertical thinking develops them."[25] A creative idea generated through lateral thinking is refined through careful analysis, evaluation and other convergent thought processes. Alastair Pilkington conducted thousands of experiments in order to perfect his floating glass process. Full-scale production did not begin until twelve years after Pilkington first noticed the similarity between his soap suds and molten glass.

The term "critical thinking" has also been applied to convergent thought processes. Critical thinking programs encourage participants to recognize their assumptions and to challenge personal inferences and biases in order to become clearer vertical thinkers. These same skills are important in the creative process as well. Learning to think critically can help develop creative thinking habits. In the same way, learning to think creatively can sharpen critical thinking abilities. Successful critical and creative thinkers are self-reflexive—they think about (reflect on) their thinking in order to improve.[26]

Putting the three definitional elements described above together with our previous discussion of creativity and communication, we come up with the following definition of creativity:

Creativity is human (symbolic) communication which generates new and relevant combinations or associations of existing elements (materials, words, ideas, facts, sounds, movements, colors, lines, mathematical notations, procedures, etc.) through lateral (divergent) thinking.

Dispelling the Myths

Before we finish the task of defining creativity, we need to dispel some of the misperceptions or myths surrounding the topic. These myths can seriously hinder our attempts to become more creative problem solvers. One such myth is the belief that creativity is limited to the gifted few, such creative "giants" as Thomas Edison, Albert Einstein, Mozart, Marie Pasteur, physicist Stephen Hawking, artist Georgia O'Keefe or Steven Jobs of Apple Computer. From this perspective, the rest of us either lack creative thinking ability or have a fixed amount of creativity; therefore, we can do little to improve our creative thinking skills. Another misperception is that creativity is a mystery. According to this myth, creative ideas

---

Solution: Merchant's Daughter Case.

According to de Bono, vertical thinkers concentrate on the fact that the daughter has to take a pebble. This leads them to conclude that the daughter should a) refuse to take a pebble, b) show that there are two black pebbles in the bag and reveal that the moneylender is dishonest, or c) take a black pebble and sacrifice herself for the sake of her father. If she follows any of these courses of action, her father goes to jail or she has to marry the moneylender. In contrast, lateral thinkers focus on the pebble that is left behind. They explore many different angles rather than accepting only the most promising idea and developing it. In the story, the daughter put her hand into the moneybag and drew out a pebble which she dropped on the path where it was indistinguishable from all the others.

"Oh, how clumsy of me," she said, "but never mind—if you look into the bag you will be able to tell which pebble I took by the color of the one that is left."

Unwilling to admit that he was dishonest, the moneylender must act as if the daughter picked the white pebble since the remaining pebble is black. Through lateral thinking the daughter remains with her father and cancels his debt. What could have been a disastrous choice actually turned out to be a better option than the original proposition. After all, if the moneylender had been honest, the daughter would have had only a 50–50 chance of a favorable outcome.

---

appear as sudden flashes of insight which defy explanation. Since creativity is beyond our understanding, little time should be spent on learning about the creative process. Still another common myth suggests that creative thinking requires minimal effort and results in a series of exhilarating breakthroughs. Those with this perspective overlook the preparation that provides the foundation for creative thinking and become disillusioned when creative breakthroughs are few and far between.

It's easy to see how each of these myths got started. Much has been written about creative geniuses; sudden insights and dramatic breakthroughs do occur during the creative process. Nonetheless, each of these myths distorts the true nature of creativity. First, everyone engages in creative problem solving on a regular basis, not just the fortunate few. Every time we complete a term paper, embark on a new dating relationship, or work out a new fund raising idea we exercise our creative thinking abilities. (See the Creative Profile on page 18 for a sample of creative ideas produced by "ordinary" people.) Each of us, however, can improve our creative thinking skills by learning more about creativity and developing effective, creative problem-solving strategies. Second, creativity (though complex) is no mystery. Thousands of books and articles have been written on the subject. Third, creativity involves more labor than glamour. Generating creative ideas and developing them takes sustained effort. Shortly before his death, psychologist Abraham Maslow complained that many creativity trainers "deify" the exciting side of creativity—the "great insight, the illumination"—while understating the fact that lots of hard labor is needed to make something useful out of the idea. "Bright ideas really take a small proportion of our time," he noted. "Most time is spent on hard work."[27] Developing creative thinking skills requires both sacrifice and courage. Creating takes time, energy and resources, and even the best new ideas are often rejected at first. The most successful creators are those with the courage to persist in the face of adversity.[28]

Creativity Roadblocks

Even though we all have the potential to be prolific creative thinkers, we often have trouble coming up with creative ideas. Creativity consultants use such terms as "blocks," "barriers" and "mental locks" to describe those factors which inhibit creative thinking. James Adams suggests that there are four major blocks or mental walls that keep us from accurately perceiving problems or generating solutions.[29] Recognizing these conceptual blocks reduces their power over our thinking and is the first step in becoming a more productive creative problem solver.

1. ***Perceptual Blocks.***   Perceptual blocks cloud our vision both of the problem itself and of the information we need to help us solve the problem. Significant perceptual blocks include:
   - seeing only what we expect to see, relying on preconceived ideas.
   - having difficulty in isolating a problem due to limited or misleading information.
   - putting too many constraints or limits on a problem which excludes possible solutions.
   - not being able to see a problem from different viewpoints.
   - being so close to a problem that we forget important details or can't recall them when needed.
   - failing to use all the senses in solving problems.

Creative Profile: Ordinary People/Extraordinary Ideas

People in the Pacific Northwest have created a number of widely adopted ideas and products. As you'll see, in most cases the ideas have become much more famous than the individuals who created them. Ordinary Northwesterners have used creative thinking to solve every kind of problem. Here are some of the creative ideas generated in the Northwest over the past century.

The Happy Face
Developed in 1967 by advertising executive David Stearn for a bank advertising campaign, the smiley face became one of the best known symbols of the 1970s. Unfortunately, Stearn didn't copyright his idea, so he never profited from the popularity of this national symbol for "Have a Nice Day!"

Microsoft
Bill Gates and Paul Allen rewrote the BASIC operating system for the personal computer and started a multi-billion dollar company.

Kwik-Lok Plastic Bag Ties
The first Kwik-lok was made out of plexiglas by high school drop out Floyd Paxton in 1954. More than four billion of these ties are used by bread companies every year.

Down Parkas
Using down feathers originally imported for fly tying and badminton shuttlecocks, outdoorsman Eddie Bauer marketed the first down parka in 1936. Bauer supplied down sleeping bags and flight suits to the military in World War II.

The Gas Station
Motorists used to fill up using five-gallon cans until John McLean, a sales manager for Standard Oil of California, installed a thirty-gallon barrel with a feed line in Seattle in 1907.

The Conibear Stroke
The Conibear stroke (named after the University of Washington crew coach) is the most efficient way to power a rowing shell. Conibear borrowed a skeleton from the college's medical school in 1908 and moved its arms and legs to determine the most effective movement. Later a colleague of Conibear's designed sliding seats for racing shells in order to ease the back-and-forth movement of rowers.

Hacky Sack
This game, in which a player keeps leather ball in the air with the feet, was invented by John Stalberger Jr. as a way to rehabilitate his knee after an injury.

Slinky Pull Toy
Helen Malsed put wheels on the Slinky toy after her son Rick, who got a slinky for his birthday in 1952, said "it would really go" if it had wheels.

Quick-Release Ski Binding
Mechanical draftsman Hjalmar Hvam sketched the design for this safer ski binding in a hospital bed in 1937 after breaking his leg in a ski accident.

The Electric Guitar
The first electric guitar, made by Paul Tutmarc in 1931, consisted of parts from an old radio, telephone and Hawaiian steel guitar.

Source: Woog, A. (1991, March 3). Making things up. *Northwest Magazine*, pp. 8 + .

Discussion Questions

1. Are people in any region of the United States more creative than people in other regions of the country? Why or why not? What social and environmental factors encourage creativity?

2. Do you know any ordinary people who have come up with extraordinary ideas? What characteristics do creative thinkers have in common?

3. What steps can we take to improve our own creative thinking skills? The creative thinking skills of others?

2. ***Emotional Blocks.*** Fear of making a mistake/taking a risk is the most common emotional barrier to creativity. We may have a general fear of failure or worry that even the most minor mistake will have catastrophic consequences. Other common emotional blocks include: 1) the inability to tolerate the uncertainty and disorder associated with solving complex problems; 2) judging ideas rather than generating them; 3) the inability to relax, to let problems incubate; 4) being unmotivated (which makes it hard to tackle a problem); 5) being too motivated (which tempts us to accept the first, not the best, solution); and 6) inadequate control over our imaginations.

3. ***Cultural and Environmental Blocks.*** Cultural roadblocks are unproductive attitudes and values that we acquire as members of society. In American culture, such barriers include taboos against certain solutions (an idea may be rejected, for instance, if it is perceived as immoral), a bias against fantasy and playfulness, the belief that humor has no place in problem solving, putting more value on reason than intuition, and a

reliance on tradition. Each of these cultural patterns can delay or derail the creative thinking process.

Environmental blocks are imposed on us by physical and social conditions. Overcrowding, excessive noise and distractions are physical barriers to creativity. Criticism, distrust and lack of support for new ideas characterize social environments which discourage divergent thinking.

4. ***Intellectual and Expressive Blocks.***   Intellectual blocks are the result of choosing the wrong problem-solving tactics or "a shortage of intellectual ammunition."[30] Generally we don't give much thought to the particular strategy we should use when we tackle a problem. Out of habit, we use words and mathematical symbols as our problem-solving tools. However, these symbolic codes or languages aren't always the most efficient mental strategies. Visualization and drawing are better tools for solving problems which require the creation and arrangement of physical objects and spaces, such as engineering a new product or completing an interior design assignment. (For more information on alternative thinking languages, see chapter 4.) Not having enough accurate information is another intellectual stumbling block. If a creative solution eludes us, it may be that we haven't gathered enough facts or that the information we have gathered is inaccurate.

Expressive blocks interfere with our ability to express our thoughts to ourselves or to others. Sometimes our poor verbal skills prevent us from describing problems clearly and concisely. At other times we communicate in the wrong code. Adams suggests the following exercise to demonstrate how using an inappropriate language can block the transmission of ideas. Build a simple object with an unfamiliar shape and put the object into a bag. Ask an audience to draw whatever is in the bag based on a description provided by a volunteer. The audience generally can't complete this assignment if the volunteer uses words because coordinates or geometric/mathematical symbols better describe shapes. Even when the volunteer uses the right code to describe the object, most people aren't skilled enough in the language of drawing to sketch its shape.

The Ethical Dimension of Creativity

Earlier we noted that Kenneth Burke's description of humans as symbol-using/symbol-*mis*using animals highlights the ethical component of creativity. Our capacity as symbol users enables us to reshape the world as we see fit. Unfortunately, we frequently misuse our creative power to injure others and ourselves and to harm the environment. For this reason, ethical considerations must play an important role in the creative process. The term ethics refers to judgments about whether human behavior is right or wrong.[31] For example, is it right to:

- develop a public relations strategy for a company that manufactures products which are harmful to human health?
- create an advertising campaign that is sexist or racist?
- write new legislation which benefits the rich at the expense of the poor?
- design a new toy that endangers the safety of children?
- label a new product as "environmentally friendly" when it's not?

We may disagree about which course of action is right in such cases. Yet, each of us has a responsibility to make informed ethical choices. In this final section of the chapter we'll examine some widely accepted principles that can guide our ethical decision making.

> The product of creative achievement is always some form of power, ranging in extent from the power to support or destroy whole civilizations to the power to make a single listener laugh. . . . Power always has ethical implications, and those who produce it are to some extent accountable for the uses that are made of it.
>
> Robert Grudin

Ethical Guidelines

Incorporating ethical standards or principles into our decision making processes can significantly improve the quality of our ethical choices. Communication ethicists Clifford Christians, Kim Rotzoll and Mark Fackler identify these widely used principles which have played a significant role in ethical decision making in Western society:[32]

Aristotle's Golden Mean. Ancient Greek philosopher and rhetorician Aristotle argued that the best ethical choice is generally the one that takes the middle course between two vices or evils.[33] In contemporary society this principle is frequently applied to the manufacture and sale of harmful substances. Legislatures and government agencies permit the production and sale of cigarettes, beer and other products which threaten human health but put controls on how they are advertised, sold and used. In so doing, they hope to avoid the evils of prohibition on the one hand and the dangers of unlimited product use on the other. A number of colleges and universities apply the Golden Mean to the controversy generated by the use of animals in experiments conducted on campus. Administrators and faculty don't want to prohibit experiments using animals because such a moratorium might prolong human suffering. At the same time, they want to avoid needless cruelty to animals. In an attempt to resolve this ethical dilemma, they appoint supervisory panels which carefully monitor the number and type of animal experiments.

Kant's Categorical Imperative.   German philosopher Immanuel Kant argued that decision makers ought to do what is morally right no matter what the consequences.[34] The word "categorical" means "without exception." To apply this standard, we need to ask if we would want everyone to make the same decision we did. For example, if we're tempted to make up statistics to build a more compelling case for a charitable cause, we need to ask ourselves what would happen if every speaker used deceit to raise money. A climate of suspicion and hostility might be created which would bankrupt many worthy organizations. Our duty, then, is to present accurate information even though misleading statistics might convince a particular audience to give more money. Based on this reasoning, such behaviors as cheating, lying and murder are always wrong.

Application of the Categorical Imperative may mean that we decide not to create or disseminate certain products or ideas. If we're uncomfortable with allowing every couple to conceive a child outside the womb, for instance, then we might prohibit the use of in-vitro fertilization (see the Creative Dilemma on page 24).

Utilitarianism. In contrast to the Categorical Imperative, utilitarianism is based on the premise that ethical choices should be based on their consequences. The best decisions are those that 1) generate the most benefits as compared to their disadvantages, and 2) benefit the largest number of people.[35] Simply put, utilitarianism is attempting to do the greatest good for the greatest number of people. Rising health care costs have prompted the state of Oregon to apply the Principle of Utility to medical treatment decisions. In order to provide the greatest number of medical benefits to the largest group of needy citizens, the state will decide whether or not to pay for treatment based on the severity of the condition, how well the illness responds to treatment, and the amount of money available.

Creators who apply the Principle of Utility must balance potential benefits against potential costs. This evaluation sometimes leads decision makers to take different courses of action on the same issue. Consider the question of whether or not to announce national election results before the polls close. Exit polls allow networks to predict the results of national elections before some voters have cast their ballots on the West Coast. In 1980, for instance, President Carter conceded defeat at 6:45 P.M. Pacific Standard Time. Although the public benefits from this free flow of information, some observers complain that announcing the winner in a landslide election damages the integrity of the electoral process and decreases voter turnout in Western states. In weighing the benefits and costs of projecting results, Canadians have decided to ban predictions until polls are closed in all time zones. Americans, on the other hand, still allow news organizations to broadcast the name of the projected winner.

Rawls' Veil of Ignorance. According to contemporary ethicist John Rawls, fairness or justice ought to be the primary consideration when making ethical choices.[36] Rawls suggests stepping behind a "veil of ignorance" when situations are inequal, such as when one party in a dispute is rich and influential and the other is poor and powerless. Behind this veil, wealth, education, gender and race disappear, and both parties negotiate on an equal basis. The least advantaged party usually benefits when social class differences are excluded from the decision-making process. Our judicial system is one example of an institution that should treat all disputants fairly. Every citizen ought to receive equal treatment under the law. Unfortunately, economic and racial considerations influence the selection of juries, the determination of guilt and innocence, the length of sentences, and nearly every other aspect of the judicial process.

Fairness is an important consideration in creative problem solving. Creators need to ask themselves if they are favoring the needs of the rich over the needs of the poor. Should political consultants help the wealthiest or the worthiest candidates, for example? Should advertising firms only work for corporate clients or donate a portion of their services to nonprofit groups and social

Creative Dilemma: Baby M and the Ethics Gap

Discussion of the ethical implications of creative ideas often lags behind the development of new products and procedures. This "ethics gap" is greatest in the field of biomedical technology. No sooner do we begin to grapple with the ethics of one biomedical advance than another appears on the scene. As a result, we have yet to reach an ethical consensus about the use of support systems to extend human life, animal to human transplants, DNA fingerprinting, fetal research and other new biomedical ideas. Developments in reproductive technology are particularly controversial. Until recently, children could only be conceived through sexual intercourse. Now there are a number of reproduction techniques, including artificial insemination and in-vitro fertilization. In artificial insemination, sperm from a donor is injected by syringe to increase the chances of conception. In-vitro fertilization is a procedure by which eggs are removed from a woman's ovaries, fertilized, and then reimplanted to a uterus.

The Baby M court case in 1987 focused national attention on the ethical implications of the new birth technologies. For a fee of $10,000, Mary Beth Whitehead agreed to be artificially inseminated with sperm taken from William Stern and to turn the child over to Stern (a biochemist) and his wife Elizabeth (a pediatrician) after giving birth. When "Baby M" was born, however, Whitehead sued to retain custody of the child. New Jersey judge Harvey Sorkow ruled in favor of the Sterns, not because Whitehead had violated her contract, but because the interests of the child would be better served by granting the Sterns custody. An appeals court later amended the judge's decision to allow Whitehead visitation rights.

The ruling in the Baby M case drew criticism from many different groups. Many ethicists were troubled by the fact that surrogacy encourages women to "rent" their wombs. Feminists argued that surrogacy exploits women for the benefit of men and the male dominated medical establishment. Others noted that since only the wealthy can afford to pay for the procedure, surrogacy favors the rich over the poor. They pointed out that Judge Sorkow awarded custody to the Sterns in part because they were of higher social standing than Whitehead and her husband, a sanitation worker. The Roman Catholic Church and some orthodox Jews spoke out against surrogacy on the grounds that the technique separates love from procreation. In the years following the Baby M decision, legislatures in thirteen states voted to outlaw commercial surrogate contracts.

Despite this strong opposition, couples are still employing surrogate mothers. In one recent case, for example, a mother acted as a surrogate for her daughter who was born without a uterus. In another, the "natural" parents and surrogate mother were granted joint custody of a child. Proponents of surrogate parenthood and other reproductive technologies argue that banning such procedures takes away the right of infertile couples to have children. They sympathize with those who want to have children but can't. To the supporters of surrogacy, birth technologies are the only hope for the one-out-of-six married couples in America who experience infertility problems.

The issues raised by surrogate parenting are far from resolved. Yet, even as we consider these ethical questions, new reproductive techniques are being developed. In a few years we may be able to choose the genetic traits of our children or create children who are the exact genetic replicas of ourselves. If we don't start thinking about these developments now, the ethics gap will grow still larger.

Discussion Questions

1. Do you agree that there is an "ethics gap" because creative ideas are being developed faster than we can evaluate them carefully? If so, what can we do to close this gap?

2. Apply each of the ethical principles discussed in this chapter to the discussion of surrogate parenthood. What conclusion do you reach about the rightness or wrongness of surrogacy based on each principle? Do some principles lead you to support surrogate parenthood while others lead you to the opposite conclusion?

3. Which ethical principles can be applied to emerging technologies like choosing the genetic traits of children or creating genetic replicas of ourselves?

Sources:

Blank, R. (1985, October). Making babies: The state of the art. *The Futurist*, pp. 13–17.

Blank, R. (1984). *Redefining human life: Reproductive technologies and social policy*. Boulder, CO: Westview.

Eaves, M. H. (1992, October). *Surrogate motherhood and in vitro fertilization: An ethical dilemma in the reproductive rights area*. Paper presented at the Speech Communication Convention, Chicago, IL.

Kantrowitz, B., McKillop, P., & Brailsford, K. (1987, April 13). After the Baby M case. *Newsweek*, pp. 22–23.

Lacayo, R. (1987, April 13). In the best interests of a child. *Time*, p. 71.

Nash, J. M. (1991, August 19). All in the family. *Time*, p. 58.

Rosenblatt, R. (1987, April 6). Baby M.—emotions for sale. *Time*, p. 88.

Rowland, R. (1987). Technology and motherhood: Reproductive choice reconsidered. *Journal of Women in Culture and Society, 12*, 512–528.

Stewart, L. P. (1992, October). *Silencing the "surrogate" mother: Ethical issues in the rhetorical construction of birth mother*. Paper presented at the Speech Communication Convention, Chicago, IL.

Tifft, S. (1990, November 5). It's all in the (parental) genes. *Time*, p. 77.

agencies? Should drug manufacturers maximize their profits or reduce their prices to make it easier for AIDS patients and others to receive treatment?

Judeo-Christian Persons as Ends. The belief that the supreme end of humans is to love God and other people is at the heart of the Judeo-Christian tradition and other faiths.[37] According to this principle, God is love and humans are made in the image of God. We have a responsibility to love others no matter who they are and no matter what their relationship to us. Mother Teresa and her fellow nuns in India provide a vivid demonstration of unconditional love in action. This religious order ministers to the needs of every stranger who comes for help.

Creative communicators who attempt to live by the Judeo-Christian ethic must determine if their creations work to the benefit of others. This is not always easy to do. For instance, committed religious people disagree about the legitimacy of war. Some create weapons and serve in the armed forces on the grounds that defending their families and neighbors is an act of love. Others oppose the development of weapons systems and the military because they believe that war violates the injunction to love others as we love ourselves.

The quality of our ethical decisions will improve as we learn to use ethical standards to guide our judgments in problematic situations. To demonstrate how these five ethical principles can be applied to one series of creative discoveries, review the Creative Dilemma on page 24.

Summing Up

The study of creativity is more important than ever before. As the pace of change accelerates, so does the need for creative ideas and creative problem solvers. In this chapter we introduced the topic of creativity from a communication perspective. Kenneth Burke's definition of humans as symbol users suggests that 1) symbolic ability is the basis for creative ability, 2) creativity is a distinctly human characteristic, 3) symbols, while the foundation for creativity, also limit our creative capacity, 4) creativity is a response to the negative—the difference between what is and what ought to be, and 5) creativity involves ethical choices.

Most definitions of creativity have three elements in common—originality (novelty), relevance and lateral (divergent) thinking. Creative ideas combine existing elements into new configurations which are relevant to solving problems or meeting needs. These new combinations or associations are the result of divergent thinking that takes a variety of perspectives and proposes a variety of solutions. From a communication perspective, creativity is human (symbolic) communication which generates new and relevant combinations or associations of existing elements (materials, words, ideas, facts, sounds, movements, colors, lines, mathematical notations, procedures, etc.) through lateral (divergent) thinking.

There are a number of conceptual blocks or barriers which keep us from reaching our potential as creative problem solvers. Perceptual blocks obscure our vision both of the problem itself and of the information we need to solve the problem. Emotional blocks are negative thoughts and feelings which derail the creative process. Cultural roadblocks are unproductive attitudes and values acquired from society at large. Environmental blocks result from poor working conditions or social climates that discourage creative thinking. Intellectual blocks come from choosing the wrong thinking strategies and inadequate or inaccurate information. Expressive blocks interfere with the transmission of ideas.

We ended the chapter with a discussion of the ethical dimension of creativity. The term ethics refers to judgments about whether human behavior is right or wrong. Ethical principles or standards can act as guidelines which help us choose between alternative courses of action during the creative process. Five widely used ethical principles include: 1) Aristotle's Golden Mean, 2) Kant's Categorical Imperative, 3) Utilitarianism, 4) Rawls' Veil of Ignorance, and 5) Judeo-Christian Persons as Ends.

Application Exercises

1. Make a creativity log. While taking this course, record your creative ideas and when and how you generated them. Near the end of the quarter or semester, analyze your creative output. Did your rate of creative ideas increase? When were you most creative? Least creative? What conditions encouraged your creative thinking? What concepts discussed in this text or in class were most useful? Write up your conclusions.

2. Conduct an animal creativity debate. Do you agree with the authors that creativity is limited to humans only? Form a group with those who take the same position as you. Prepare to debate with those who take the opposing view. Your instructor will set the ground rules.

3. Take ten minutes and make your own "bug list," a list of minor irritations in your life that you would like to see eliminated. Next form a group and compare lists. How many items are shared in common by group members? Could any of these irritations spur significant new ideas?

4. Develop your own definition of creativity. Consider the following questions as you formulate your definition statement:

   a. Is there a difference between originality and creativity?

   b. Does a creative idea have to be relevant or useful? Who makes this determination?

   c. How does creative thinking differ from other forms of thought?

5. Which creative roadblock is the biggest barrier to your creative thinking? Outline a strategy for overcoming this conceptual block.

6. Create your own ethical case study for class discussion. Describe the situation carefully. What ethical issues does this case raise? How can they be resolved based on ethical principles discussed in the chapter?

Endnotes

[1] For more information on the relationship between creativity and change, see: Adams, J. L. (1986). *The care and feeding of ideas*. Reading, MA: Addison-Wesley, Ch. 1.

[2] Peters, T. (1991). *Speed is life: Go fast or go broke*. Schaumburg, IL: Video Publishing House.

[3] Cohen, A. R., & Bradford, D. L. (1990). *Influence without authority*. New York: John Wiley & Sons, Ch. 1.

[4] Maney, K. (1991, July 12). Consumers face flood of products. *USA Today*, pp. 1b–2b.

[5] Burke, K. G. (1966). *Language as symbolic action*. Berkeley: University of California Press, Ch. 1.

[6] Burke, p. 5.

[7] Burke, Ch. 3.

[8] Pearce, W. Barnett (1989). *Communication and the human condition*. Carbondale, Il: Southern Illinois University Press, pp. 56–57. Philosophers use the label

"counterfactual conditionals" to refer to messages about what could have happened if some event that did not take place had happened.

9 Tompkins, P. K. (1982). *Communication as action: An introduction to rhetoric and communication.* Belmont, CA: Wadsworth, p. 14.

10 Welsh, G. (1979). *Creativity and intelligence: A personality approach.* Chapel Hill, NC: Institute for Research in Social Science, p. 4.

11 Pearce, p. 52.

12 Ortony, A. (1979). Metaphor: A multidimensional problem. In A. Ortony (Ed.), *Metaphor and thought* (pp. 1–16). Cambridge: Cambridge University Press.

13 Adams, J. L. (1986). *Conceptual blockbusting* (3rd ed.). Reading, MA: Addison-Wesley, pp. 112–113.

14 Ackoff, R. L., & Vergara, E. (1988). Creativity in problem solving and planning. In R. L. Kuhn (Ed.), *Handbook for creative and innovative managers* (pp. 77–89). New York: McGraw-Hill.

15 For summaries of various orientations or emphases in studies of creativity see:

Welsh, G. S. (1973). Perspectives in the study of creativity. *Journal of Creative Behavior, 7,* 231–246.

Mooney, R. L. (1963). A conceptual model for integrating four approaches to the identification of creative talent. In C. H. Taylor & F. Barron (Eds.), *Scientific creativity: Its recognition and development* (pp. 331–340). New York: John Wiley & Sons.

16 Barron, F. (1965). The psychology of creativity. In T. M. Newcomb (Ed.), *New directions in psychology II* (pp. 3–134). New York: Holt, Rinehart and Winston, p. 3.

17 Koestler, A. (1964). *The act of creation.* New York: Dell Publishing, p. 120.

18 Arieti, S. (1976). *Creativity: The magic synthesis.* New York: Basic Books, p. 4.

19 Weick, K. (1979). *The social psychology of organizing.* Reading, MA: Addison-Wesley, p. 252.

20 Parnes, S. J. (1975). "Aha!" In I. A. Taylor & J. W. Getzels (Eds.), *Perspectives on creativity* (pp. 224–248). Chicago: Aldine.

21 Mednick, S. A. (1962). The associative basis of the creative process. *Psychological Review, 69,* p. 221.

22 MacKinnon, D. W. (1962). The nature and nurture of creative talent. *American Psychologist, 17,* p. 485.

23 (1964, November 23). The glass revolution. *Newsweek,* p. 87.

24 deBono, E. (1967). *New think: The use of lateral thinking in the generation of new ideas.* New York: Basic Books, p. 4.

25 deBono, pp. 16–17.

26 Paul, R. (1991, August). *Teaching students intellectual standards they can use to reason persuasively, master content and discipline their minds.* Keynote address delivered at the Eleventh Annual International Conference on Critical Thinking and Educational Reform, Roehnert Park, CA.

For more information on critical thinking, see:

Paul, R. (1989). *Critical thinking: What every person needs to survive in a rapidly changing world.* Santa Rosa, CA: Foundation for Critical Thinking.

27 Maslow, A. H. (1972). A holistic approach to creativity. In C. H. Taylor (Ed.), *Climate for creativity* (pp. 287–293). New York: John Wiley & Sons, p. 293.

28 For more information on "creative courage," see:

May, R. (1975). *The courage to create.* New York: W. W. Norton & Company.

[29] Adams.

For other descriptions of creative blocks, see:

von Oech, R. (1983). *A whack on the side of the head.* New York: Warner Books.

Simberg, A. L. (1978). Obstacles to creative thinking. In G. A. Davis & J. A. Scott, *Training creative thinking* (pp. 119–142). Huntington, NY: Robert E. Krieger Publishing.

[30] Adams, p. 71.

[31] Johannesen, R. L. (1990). *Ethics in human communication* (3rd ed.). Prospect Heights, IL: Waveland, p. 1.

[32] Christians, C. G., Rotzoll, K. B., & Fackler, M. (1990). *Media ethics* (3rd ed.). New York: Longman.

[33] McKeon, R. (Ed.) (1947). *Introduction to Aristotle.* New York: Modern Library.

[34] Kant, I. (1964). *Groundwork of the metaphysics of morals* (H. J. Ryan, Trans.). New York: Harper & Row.

[35] See, for example:

Bentham, J. (1948). *An introduction to the principles of morals and legislation.* New York: Hafner Publishing.

Gorovitz, S. (Ed.) (1971). *Utilitarianism: Text and critical essays.* Indianapolis, IN: Bobbs-Merrill.

[36] Rawls, J. (1971). *A theory of justice.* Cambridge: Harvard University Press.

[37] See, for example:

Brunner, E. (1947). *The divine imperative* (O. Wyon, Trans.). Philadelphia: Westminister Press.

Outka, G. (1972). *Agape: An ethical analysis.* New Haven: Yale University Press.

Quotations

Fulghum, R. (1991). *Uh-Oh. Reflections from both sides of the refrigerator door.* New York: Villard.

Welsh, G. S. (1975). *Creativity and intelligence: A personality approach.* Chapel Hill, NC: Institute for Research in Social Science.

Grudin, R. (1990). *The grace of great things.* New York: Ticknor & Fields.

2 | Theoretical Approaches to Creativity

> How stupid not to have thought of that!
>
> Thomas Huxley upon hearing of
> Darwin's theory of natural selection

PREVIEW

- ► Cognitive Approaches
    Psychometric Studies
    Creativity as Ordinary Problem Solving
- ► Person-Centered Approaches
    The Creative Personality
    Historiometric Surveys
    Case Studies: The Creative Person at Work
- ► Motivational Approaches
    Problem Finding as Creative Motivation
    Creativity and Mental Health
    The Intrinsic Motivation Hypothesis
- ► Summing Up
- ► Application Exercises

Mystery lovers know that detectives solve "who-done-its" by determining what happened at the scene of the crime and by identifying possible suspects and their motives. Like detectives, theorists and researchers interested in creativity focus on what, who and why. They want to know what makes up creative thinking, who is creative and why individuals engage in creative activity. The answers to these questions help take the mystery out of creative problem solving. In this chapter, we survey important theories of creativity which focus on cognitive processes, creative persons, and creative motivation.

Cognitive Approaches

Psychometric Studies

Psychologist J. P. Guilford is often considered the father of modern creativity research. At the 1950 convention of the American Psychological Association, Guilford (the group's outgoing president) chided his colleagues for neglecting the study of creativity and offered several hypotheses about the abilities or factors that make up creative thinking.[1] In the years that followed, he created a number of paper and pencil tests known as psychometric instruments to measure these factors. Other investigators followed Guilford's lead, and the number of books and journal articles devoted to creativity increased dramatically.

Guilford focused primarily on the divergent nature of creative thought. He was critical of traditional intelligence tests because they largely ignored divergent thinking processes essential to creative problem solving. He developed an expanded model of human intelligence, called the Structure of Intellect, which incorporated both divergent and convergent thinking abilities.[2] According to Guilford, important divergent thinking factors include fluency, flexibility, originality and elaboration.[3]

Fluency.   Fluency breaks into three subfactors. Ideational fluency refers to the number or quantity of ideas produced by problem solvers when they are asked to name all the possible consequences of an action or event, or to list all the possible uses for bricks (Brick Uses Test) and other objects. Associational fluency consists of completing relationships. Tests of this subfactor require examinees to think of terms that mean the opposite of a word such as "good."

Expressional fluency describes the generation of meaningful discourse. In one expressional fluency measure, subjects are provided with the initial letters of four words (i.e. "W____ c____ e____ n____.") and must write as many sentences as possible using these letters (i.e. "We can eat nuts." "Weary cats evade nothing.").

Flexibility. Flexibility is either spontaneous or adaptive. When taking the Brick Uses Test, inflexible problem solvers limit their responses to a few categories (use the brick as a weight or to build something). Flexible test takers naturally or spontaneously generate ideas that fall into many different classifications (use the brick in a science experiment, as a measuring stick, for a portable chair, as a weapon or piece of art). Adaptive flexibility implies a change of some kind during the problem solving process. Adaptive problem solvers either change the way they interpret the task itself, take a different approach, or adjust their possible solutions. The Plot Titles test measures this flexibility subfactor. In this exercise, participants are told a short story and then must come up with different titles for the piece.

Originality. Originality is another name for unique or unusual responses. Originality scores are determined by asking observers to rate the novelty of ideas or by noting how frequently answers show up in a test group. Infrequent responses earn the highest marks.

Elaboration. Elaboration refers to the number of implications drawn by problem solvers when they're faced with a dilemma. To determine this ability, researchers provide test takers with the basic outline of a plan and ask them to spell out the steps they need to follow in order to execute the plan. The more details they add, the higher their elaboration scores.

One of the researchers who answered Guilford's call for more creativity research was educational psychologist E. Paul Torrance. Torrance modified many of Guilford's creativity measures to make them more suitable for elementary age children and added tests of his own. He then used the Minnesota (or Torrance) Tests of Creative Thinking to study creativity in the classroom. Here are some of the measures that appear in the Minnesota Test Battery:[4]

- Product Improvement. Ex: think of ways to change a toy dog so that children would have more fun playing with it.
- Product Utilization. Ex: list ways to use a toy dog as something other than a plaything.

- Circles. Ex: draw objects which have a circle as the main part.
- Ask and Guess. Ex: after viewing a picture, develop a list of questions about items in the picture and generate a list of guesses about the causes of the action portrayed in the picture. Create a list of possible consequences that might result from the action shown in the picture.
- Figure completion. Ex: complete a drawing of a house, tree or person.
- Story completion. Ex: write a story about a topic such as "The Dog That Doesn't Bark" and "The Doctor Who Became a Carpenter."

Using the Minnesota tests and other measures, Torrance and his fellow researchers examined a number of factors that impact the fluency, flexibility, originality and elaboration scores of pupils. Some of their experiments measured the effects of creativity skills training. Others focused on the relationship between creativity test results and teacher behaviors, peer evaluation and other environmental influences. Torrance reached two fundamental conclusions based on decades of research conducted first at the University of Minnesota and later at the University of Georgia: 1) students can learn creative thinking skills, and 2) the classroom environment can either foster or suppress creativity. His suggestions for nurturing creativity in the classroom are found in table 2.1.

At the same time that Guilford and Torrance were measuring a variety of creative thinking abilities, other psychometric researchers focused their attention on the associative basis of creativity. They emphasized that creative products are the result of combining or associating elements. A leading advocate of this associational approach to creativity was Sarnoff Mednick.[5] Mednick suggested that creative responses are governed by levels of association called **associative hierarchies**. Conventional, stereotyped responses—the answers that come to mind first—are strongest and take the highest position in the associative structure. Unique associations, which are weaker and occupy a lower level in the hierarchy, emerge later.

Low and high creative individuals possess contrasting associative hierarchies. When given a stimulus word, low creatives immediately produce lots of conventional responses but quickly run out of ideas. As a consequence, they fail to generate unique associates. The response curve for creative people is flatter. Because their associative hierarchies contain fewer stereotyped connections,

---

Table 2.1 How to Reward Creativity in the Classroom

1. Treat questions with respect.

   Finding answers to questions is one of the greatest rewards for curiosity. Don't be shocked by embarrassing questions but teach and encourage inquiry skills. (We'll take a closer look at the important role of questions in chapter 4.)

2. Respect imaginative, unusual ideas.

   Presenting an unusual idea is risky because it is likely to be greeted with scorn. Reduce the risk by treating imaginative contributions with respect and by encouraging class members to do the same.

3. Show students that their ideas have value.

   Encourage them to write down their ideas and to display their creative work.

4. Give opportunities for practice or experimentation without evaluation.

   External evaluation is threatening and cuts off idea generation. A practice period which allows for experimentation and exploration helps overcome this anxiety.

5. Encourage self-initiated learning.

   Almost all children start life as self-starters who take the initiative in learning about the world around them. To keep this spirit of curiosity alive, avoid highly prescribed curricula and do not supervise pupils too closely.

6. Link evaluations with causes and consequences.

   When evaluating ideas, don't merely react ("This is good or bad") but explain why based on the likely causes and consequences ("I like this because. . . ."; "This could be made better by. . . .").

Sources:
Torrance, E. P. (1961). Give the "devil" his due. *Gifted Child Quarterly, 5*, 115–118.
Torrance, E. P. (1965) *Rewarding creative behavior.* Englewood Cliffs, NJ: Prentice-Hall.

---

creative individuals provide fewer initial responses but produce a greater number of uncommon associations over time.

Mednick developed the Remote Associates Test (RAT) to measure associative ability. The RAT consists of sets of three common words that are only remotely connected. Examinees have forty minutes to find the link between each set of terms. Sample RAT items include:

1. rat   blue   cottage
2. cookies   sixteen   heart
3. wheel   electric   high

(Answers: cheese, sweet, chair or wire).

Unfortunately, the Remote Associates Test measures divergent thinking by asking for convergent answers.[6] To overcome this shortcoming, Michael Wallach and Nathan Kogan created a divergent alternative to the RAT which includes five instruments, three verbal and two visual.[7] The verbal tests ask for instances ("Name all the round things you can think of"), alternative uses ("Tell me all the different ways you could use a newspaper"), and similarities ("Tell me all the ways that a cat and a carrot are alike"). The visual assessment instruments present participants with a series of designs or lines and ask for interpretations. Selected items from the design portion of the test are reproduced below.

Figure 2.1 Visual Associates Test

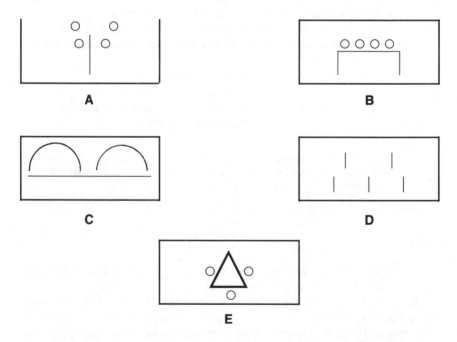

A   B

C   D

E

Source: Wallach, M. A., & Kogan, N. (1965). *Modes of thinking in young children: A study of the creativity-intelligence distinction.* Reprinted by permission of Holt, Rinehart and Winston, Inc.

Obvious answers include: A) flower, B) table with objects on top, C) igloos, D) raindrops, E) three people sitting around a table. Creative responses would be: A) a lollipop bursting into pieces, B) foot and toes, C) two haystacks on a flying carpet, D) five worms hanging, and E) three mice eating a piece of cheese.

Wallach and Kogan described their tests as "games" in order to create a permissive, relaxed atmosphere and imposed no time limits on test takers. They found that elementary students who scored high on their associates test did not necessarily excel on traditional aptitude and intelligence measures.[8]

Psychometric approaches to creativity are much less popular today than they were in the 1950s, 60s and 70s.[9] Skeptics note serious methodological flaws in many psychometric studies, including small test samples, statistical errors, and variations in how different experimenters administer the same instruments. Improvements in creativity scores attributed to training might be caused by other factors instead. Of even greater concern is the fact that psychometric test results have little if any relationship to creative performance in real life. Individuals who score high on creativity instruments aren't necessarily more productive as students, writers, scientists, engineers or artists.

Although their research findings have been called into question, early psychometric researchers played a key role in the history of creativity research. They were the first group of scholars to study creativity in a systematic way using scientific measurement techniques. Their efforts focused academic attention on creative problem solving and helped define creativity as a divergent process.

Creativity as Ordinary Problem Solving

Cognitive scientists treat creativity as a form of ordinary problem solving. The leading proponents of this approach are Herbert Simon and John Hayes of Carnegie Mellon University.[10] Simon, Hayes and other cognitive scientists compare problem solving to a search. Complex problems are harder to solve because there are more possible pathways for problem solvers to follow. The number of possible moves in a chess game, for example, is equivalent to the number 10 raised to the 120th power, a sum greater than the total number of molecules in the universe!

Problem solvers use a number of strategies to simplify their search for solutions. They call on their past experiences with similar problems, look for patterns, employ problem-solving guidelines and so forth. Process-tracing studies, which ask problem solvers to record their thoughts out loud as they work, reveal that solutions evolve through a series of intermediate steps. Creators generally look for the most obvious solution first. When this answer proves inadequate, they move to the next possible solution and then the next. The final solution emerges after a series of attempts to overcome the shortcomings of earlier answers.[11] See if you follow this procedure when searching for a creative solution by solving the problem posed in the Creative Dilemma.

Creative Dilemma: The Candle Problem

The candle problem described below has been used in problem-solving experiments for over 50 years. Read the problem description carefully and work until you come up with a suitable answer. The solution is found on page 40.

Imagine that you've been given a candle, a book of matches and a box of tacks. Your task is to attach the candle to a wooden door so that there will be light for reading. The candle must also burn properly. Using only these objects, how would you attach the candle to the door?

To back up their contention that there is nothing extraordinary about creative thinking, cognitive scientists have developed computer programs which simulate human thinking by playing chess, composing music and proving mathematical theorems through reading and manipulating symbols. Simon sums up the cognitivists' "nothing special" view of creativity this way:

> No sparks of genius need to be postulated to account for human invention, discovery, or creation. These acts are acts of the human brain, the same brain that helps us dress in the morning, arrive at our office, and go though our daily chores—however uncreative most of these activities may be. The same processes that people use to think and to solve problems can explain the thinking and problem solving that is creative.[12]

While cognitive scientists argue that creative thinking processes are not unusual, they do acknowledge that creative products are new and different. Novel products are most likely to emerge when problem solvers are well prepared, work diligently for long periods of time, tolerate ambiguity and take calculated risks. Let's examine each of these factors in more detail.

Extensive preparation. All of the techniques for simplifying problem searches that we described earlier (drawing on past experience, looking for patterns, applying rules) are founded on prior knowledge. Extensive preparation increases the probability of finding creative solutions. Prominent creators typically spend ten years or more in intensive effort before they reach world class status. Mozart wrote his first music at age four, but his outstanding works did not come until his late teens and early twenties. Picasso painted as a child but achieved notoriety only after he became an adult. Simon and Hayes estimate that during this decade of preparation, experts familiarize themselves with some fifty thousand pieces or chunks of information. Their knowledge of the familiar enables them to capitalize on "lucky breaks." For example, Alexander Fleming noticed that mold stopped the growth of bacteria in a petri dish in his laboratory. He realized that this was an unusual event because he was familiar with the normal appearance of the bacteria. His informed observation led to the development of penicillin.

Extended Effort. Taking the knowledge they've accumulated through extensive preparation, successful problem solvers make a persistent effort to solve creative dilemmas. Consider the case of Princeton professor Andrew Wiles. It took him seven years to solve Fermat's Last Theorem, one of the most famous problems in mathematics. Simon and other cognitivists discount those moments of inspiration that play such a prominent role in stories of creative discoveries. What appear as sudden insights, they argue, are really the products of extensive preparation combined with extended effort.

Tolerance of Ambiguity. Creative problems are often ill-defined (see chapter 5). Creators must tolerate the ambiguity or "messiness" associated with such vague dilemmas, resisting the temptation to settle for quick, easy solutions.

Calculated Risk Taking. Creativity is always risky because it takes problem solvers down new paths. However, productive thinkers are anything but reckless when it comes to taking chances. They take calculated risks instead, applying their superior knowledge to those situations where it is most likely to have the greatest effect.

> Thinking is information processing that involves reading symbols, writing symbols, assembling symbols in relational symbol structures, storing symbols, comparing symbols for identity or difference, and branching on the outcome of the comparison.
>
> Herbert Simon

Solution: The Candle Problem

According to Robert Weisberg of Temple University, most people assigned this problem first consider nailing the candle to the door or gluing it with melted wax. Those who realize that these solutions won't work (the tacks may split the candle and a candle attached by wax won't burn properly) then go on to think of other variations based on attaching. Eventually the successful problem solvers think of building a platform of tacks to hold the candle up and then move to the most creative solution of all—nail the empty tack box to the door and use it as a platform.

Weisberg uses the candle problem to illustrate how problem solutions evolve. Everyone starts at the same place (creative thinkers have no special insights), but productive problem solvers learn from their mistakes. When they discover that one solution is deficient, they move on to another and still another. Creativity is not the product of creative leaps but is, instead, the result of a series of intermediate steps.

Discussion Questions

1. Did you solve the problem in the manner outlined above? What was your initial solution? Second? Third?
2. Do all creative solutions evolve over a series of intermediate steps or do they sometimes result from creative leaps of thought?
3. Is it possible that there may be a better, more creative solution to the candle problem that hasn't yet been discovered? Why or why not?

Source: Weisberg, R. (1986). *Creativity, genius and other myths.* New York: W. H. Freeman and Company.

Cognitive scientists have done much to dispel the myths of creativity we described in the first chapter. By treating creative thinking as an ordinary, symbolic process, they highlight the fact that everyone has the ability to generate creative ideas. Their emphasis on preparation and persistent effort is a strong reminder that creativity is hard work. Yet, the scope of their theory is limited. While cognitivists stress that preparation and persistence are critical factors in creative thinking, they say little about what motivates problem solvers to tackle difficult and often thankless tasks. In order to develop a comprehensive understanding of creativity, we need to combine cognitive explanations with those that describe the creative individual and account for creative motivation. With this in mind, we turn next to theories that focus on the person involved in the creative process.

Person-Centered Approaches

Person-centered theories are based on the premise that creative people share common characteristics that set them apart from their contemporaries. Researchers looking for these characteristics hope to build a composite image or profile of the creative individual. Some investigators study personality traits as they search for clues as to the nature of the creative person. Others conduct statistical analysis of archival data; others examine case studies. In this section of the chapter we'll survey all three of these methods, beginning with attempts to identify the creative personality.

The Creative Personality

Personality studies generally center around standards or criteria which are used to separate highly creative people from other individuals employed in the same professions. In some of these criterion group studies, only outstanding individuals are tested and/or observed. In other projects, both high creatives and low creatives are assessed to see if their personalities differ in significant ways.

The most extensive series of criterion group studies was carried out at the Institute for Personality Assessment and Research (IPAR) at the University of California-Berkeley.[13] From 1950 to 1975, Donald MacKinnon, Frank Barron, Richard Crutchfield and their colleagues collected data on artists, writers, students, architects, scientists and mathematicians using a combination of creativity tests and personality measures. Three instruments, in particular, played an important role in IPAR studies:

> *Gough Adjective Check List.* The Adjective Check List asks examinees to circle the items that best describe themselves from a list of three hundred adjectives. Harrison Gough and other institute researchers found that a subscale of thirty items differentiated between more and less creative subjects. Eighteen items were positively related to creativity: capable, clever, confident, egotistical, humorous, individualistic, informal, insightful, intelligent, wide interests, inventive, original, reflective, resourceful, self-confident, sexy, snobbish, and unconventional. Twelve items were negatively related to creativity: affected, cautious, commonplace, conservative, conventional, dissatisfied, honest, narrow interests, mannerly, sincere, submissive, and suspicious.[14]

The Barron-Welsh Art Scale. The Barron-Welsh Art Scale consists of sixty-five drawings which range from simple and symmetrical to complex and asymmetrical. High creatives prefer more complicated, asymmetrical lines and figures. Preference for complexity is positively correlated with originality, independence of judgment and broader interests.[15]

Crutchfield Conformity/Independence of Judgment Test. In the original Crutchfield conformity tests, experimental subjects were pressured into going along with majority opinion. Yielders (those who gave in and responded with the wrong answers to math problems and other questions) were more anxious and passive, struggled with feelings of inferiority, and held conventional attitudes. Those who resisted group pressure had stronger egos and were more receptive to new ideas. Later, researchers developed a questionnaire to measure independence of judgment. Independent thinkers answer false to such statements as "I prefer team games" and "youth need strict discipline," and true to such statements as "some of my friends think that my ideas are impractical, if not a bit wild" and "science should have as much to say about moral values as religion does."[16]

Donald MacKinnon's study of creative architects is the most widely cited example of criterion group research. In this study, editors of architectural journals and professors of architecture named the most creative architects in the United States who were invited to the UC-Berkeley campus for a "living-in assessment."[17] During their stay, the highly creative architects interacted socially, participated in tests and interviews, and were evaluated by center staff. Test instruments were mailed to two comparison samples. The first sample consisted of individuals who had worked two years or more with the high creatives. The second sample was made up of architects who had not been associated with members of the group invited to the Berkeley campus.

The highly creative architects (all males) described themselves as inventive, independent, individualistic, enthusiastic, determined and industrious. They were also more intuitive, open to emotions and self-aware. The less creative architects who had not been associated with members of the assessment group were more likely to describe themselves in ways that emphasized their good character, rationality and concern for others. MacKinnon argued that these results established that highly creative architects have a unique set of personality traits. However, critics later pointed out that the personality scores of the individuals who had worked with the highly creative architects were nearly identical to those of the high creatives themselves. This indicates that there is no one set of characteristics that sets highly creative architects apart.[18]

MacKinnon's failure to isolate common traits among creative architects is typical of the findings of personality trait studies. Traits researchers have yet to generate a comprehensive, widely accepted personality profile of the creative individual. Most agree that creative people are hard working, independent individuals who are more comfortable with complexity and ambiguity. Beyond this point, however, opinions diverge. As you can see by examining the lists of creative characteristics in table 2.2, traits that appear on one list don't appear on others and various inventories contain conflicting elements. Morris Stein, for example, claims that creative individuals are motivated by the need for order, while Marie Dellas and Eugene Gaier argue that they tolerate disorder. Even items on the same list appear to conflict with one another, as in the case of Stein who describes creative people as dominant but reserved, and unstable but adjusted. Identification of traits also leaves the question of causality unanswered: Do certain personality traits encourage creativity or do people develop these traits in response to creative success? Highly creative people may have strong egos and resist group pressures because their past efforts have been rewarded.

Frank Barron (one of the chief investigators at the Institute for Personality Assessment and Research mentioned earlier) now seems to argue that we should pay less attention to the creative personality and more attention to the self. According to Barron, the self incorporates our personal philosophy, career choices, ability to use and transform symbols, and thinking skills. He suggests that it is the meaning we build for our lives through our symbols, not our personality traits, that will ultimately determine how creative we are:

> Creative people come in all shapes and sizes, all colors and ages, and all sorts of personality types. There are introverts and extroverts, manics and depressives and manic-depressives, schizothymes and hysterics, sociopaths and good citizens—in brief, a wide variety of temperaments among people who are especially creative. It is not, in my judgment, the personality type that makes the difference, but the self. To the self I ascribe motivation and style, the choice of meaning, and *the making of meaning*, in work, career, life course.[19]

Table 2.2 Personality Traits of Creative People

Dellas and Gaier
  relative absence of repression and self-defensiveness
  tolerance of complexity and disorder
  openness to internal and external stimuli
  wide interests
  openness to emotions and feelings, aesthetic sensitivity and awareness
    of self
  strong ego
  intuitiveness—recognition of potential, search for deeper meanings
  independence in attitudes and social behavior
  strong sense of identity and self-acceptance

Amabile
  high discipline in work-related matters
  ability to delay gratification
  perseverance in the face of frustration
  independence of judgment
  tolerance for ambiguity
  a high degree of autonomy
  absence of sex-role stereotyping
  internal locus of control
  risk taker
  self-initiated, task-oriented striving for excellence

Stein
  high achiever
  motivated by a need for order
  curious
  self-assertive, dominant, aggressive, self-sufficient, takes initiative
  rejects repression
  less inhibited, formal and conventional
  persistent, capacity for work, self-discipline, thorough
  independent and autonomous
  constructively critical, less contented, dissatisfied
  widely informed, wide ranging interests, versatile
  open to feelings and emotions
  aesthetic in judgment and value orientation
  low in economic values

freer expression of feminine interests, lack of masculine
  aggressiveness
little interest in interpersonal relationships, introverted, reserved
emotionally unstable while adjusted to society and work
sees self as creative
intuitive and empathetic
less critical of self
makes a greater impact on others

Sources:

Dellas, M. & Gaier, E. L. (1970). Identification of creativity: The individual. *Psychological Bulletin, 73*, 55–73, p. 69.

Amabile, T. M. (1983). *The social psychology of creativity*. New York: Springer-Verlag.

Stein, M. I. (1974). *Stimulating creativity, Vol. 1: Individual procedures*. New York: Academic Press.

Historiometric Surveys

Historiometrics is the study of historical (archival) data using quantitative or statistical analysis. Historiometric investigators interested in creativity isolate highly creative populations in historical records and then look for factors that contribute to the success of these groups. The goal of historiometric experts is to develop a set of universal laws or generalizations that explain and predict creative behavior no matter when or where it occurs. Dean Keith Simonton, the leading historiometric authority, identifies a number of variables associated with creative people throughout history.[20]

Productivity. Those who produce the most ideas have the greatest creative impact. In many disciplines, 10 percent of the members generate half of the total published work. Of the 250 composers of classical music, for instance, 16 account for about 50 percent of the repertoire of musical pieces. Quantity can lead to quality, although being prolific also increases the likelihood of failure. Even such creative giants as Isaac Newton and Albert Einstein made significant mistakes. Newton spent 25 years looking for magic elixirs, and Einstein rejected quantum mechanics, one of the foundations of modern physics. Because major poets "write a lot," W. H. Auden once noted, "the chances are that, in the course of his [her] lifetime, the major poet will write more bad poems than the minor."[21]

Age.   Creative productivity generally peaks in an individual's late 30s or early 40s and then declines gradually. However, age curves differ significantly between disciplines (mathematicians and lyric poets peak earlier than geologists, for example) and the decline in production is so gradual that some creators in their 60s and 70s will be more active than they were in their 20s. A number of creators experience a secondary peak as they near the end of life.[22]

Family Background.   High achievers are more likely to have a) lost one or more parents, b) been firstborn children, and c) grown up in a stimulating home environment where parents provided lots of books and magazine subscriptions and encouraged hobbies. Simonton speculates that the death of parents disrupts typical socialization patterns and produces people who see the world in a less conventional manner. Firstborn children tend to get more stimulation which promotes their intellectual development. An invigorating home environment encourages reading and introduces creators to many different interests.

Role Models.   Eminent creators often model their efforts after those of earlier achievers. Role models can be "paragons" (eminent creators like Michelangelo or Marie Curie who are admired at a distance) or mentors who act as counselors and guides. According to one study, over half of the Nobel Laureates in science served as apprentices or protegés to previous laureates. However, there are dangers in emulating either a paragon or a mentor. Following someone too closely encourages conformity rather than originality.

Formal Education.   Creators need to master the basics of their fields, but too much training in traditional methods can stifle original thinking. For this reason, the relationship between creativity and education is curvilinear. Creativity rises with level of education up to a point (Simonton suggests the junior or senior year of college) but then declines with further schooling.

Marginality.   Those on the margins of a culture or profession frequently combine ideas and fields of study previously treated as separate from each other. As a consequence, immigrants and those who change careers are often the most innovative.

Cumulative Advantage.   In creativity as in economics, the "rich get richer and the poor get poorer." Those who experience early success receive recognition and advancement that encourages them to achieve yet more. For instance, scientists who publish books and articles at the beginning of their careers generally land jobs at prestigious universities which provide them with high-quality laboratories, research assistants and release time for their work. Those who fail to publish early on may end up in teaching universities which are less supportive of research. They generally publish less and less over time. Sociologist Robert Merton calls the cumulative advantage that accrues to early producers the "Matthew Effect" after a passage in the book of Matthew in the Bible. This passage states: "For everyone who has will be given more . . . Whoever does not have, even what he [she] has will be taken from him [her]."[23]

Zeitgeist ("Spirit of the Times"). Individual creativity is highest during times of political and cultural change brought about by such events as civil disturbances and the breakup of empires. The stress of war and anarchy, however, generally discourages creative activity.

Although historiometricians often treat their findings as if they were established facts, conclusions drawn from historiometric analysis are tentative at best. A major problem of the historiometric approach is its reliance on secondary sources like biographical dictionaries and encyclopedias. The amount of space given a famous person in an encyclopedia or dictionary (a commonly used indicator of how productive a person has been) may depend more on the interests of the compiler than on the creativity of the individual.[24] In addition, these sources equate prominence with creativity, even though someone may be popular but not creative or be creative but not popular. Consider the experience of seventh-century Dutch inventor Cornelius Drebbel. Drebbel designed microscopes and telescopes, invented refrigeration and incubation methods, produced and tested the first working submarine and torpedoes, and proposed the first large scale solar heating project. Instead of being honored, he spent the last days of his life as a pub owner and was largely forgotten after his death.[25]

Despite these concerns, some of the variables identified by historiometricians can have an impact on our creative efforts. First, quality is a function of quantity. If we want high quality solutions, we need to generate lots of ideas and recognize that many of them will be unsuccessful. Second, role models play an important role in creative development. Our chances of creative success improve substantially if we can find mentors or sponsors who will assign us to important projects and provide information and counsel.[26]

Third, early victories often snowball, leading to greater success and recognition as careers continue. The Matthew Effect is a powerful argument both for seeking mentors and other assistance early in life and for providing help to others as they begin their careers.

> If I have seen farther it is by standing on the shoulders of giants.
>   Isaac Newton

Case Studies: The Creative Person at Work

Personality and historiometric researchers look for patterns in groups of creators while paying relatively little attention to individual lives. Experts who utilize case studies, on the other hand, focus on particular creators. They are often most interested in the way in which creative communicators accomplish their work—how creators approach and organize creative tasks, handle delays, develop their ideas and so on. The analysis of individual cases then forms the basis for generalizations about creative activity.

The Evolving Systems approach to creative work is an excellent model of how individual observations can lay the foundation for theory development.[27] Howard Gruber, along with his doctoral students and colleagues like Doris Wallace and Sarah Davis, analyzed detailed descriptions of the lives of Charles Darwin, writers Dorothy Richardson and Anais Nin, physicist Robert Burns Woodward and others. Gruber concluded that highly creative people are engaged in clusters of purposeful, related projects and activities called **networks of enterprise**. These networks of enterprise make up the life-long tasks of creative individuals, shaping their self-concepts and directing their time and energies. When one project or path is blocked, the creator shifts to another project in the enterprise. Successfully completing a line of work opens up new avenues of discovery.

Evolving Systems theory gets its name from Gruber's observation that the creative person at work is a system made up of three subsystems: the creator's knowledge base, ultimate purpose, and affect or emotional state. All three subsystems constantly change and interact in the mind of the individual as the following example illustrates:

> Let us suppose that a creative person at work is baffled by a task, discouraged, and inclined to put it aside. Fortunately, his [her] activity level does not go to zero, because other enterprises are liberated and activated by the very process of stopping work on

one project. Fortunately, too, his [her] discouragement and motivational reorganization does not destroy all the knowledge and skill he [she] has acquired relating to the project in question; when his [her] mood shifts or a new opening for further progress on the fallow project presents itself, he [she] does not begin at zero, but takes up more or less where he [she] left off.[28]

Evolving Systems theorists emphasize the difficulty and duration of creative labor. Because it is so demanding, creative work must be broken into small tasks. Creative ideas evolve through a series of small steps over the course of months and years. Creative individuals must maintain a sense of direction in the face of the inevitable delays associated with achieving their subgoals. Developing an "initial sketch" or rough draft is one way to keep the ultimate goal in mind. Darwin kept a set of notebooks which outlined the major themes of his life's research. Piaget identified his important lines of study through a poem and novel written before he began his work as a psychologist.

Much of the attraction of the case study approach lies in the fact that it "fleshes out" the study of creativity. Most of us are fascinated by the achievements of prominent creators. Their work habits should serve as a model for us as we tackle creative tasks. We, too, need to develop networks of enterprise, sketch out our goals and plans, and break major projects into subtasks. (For additional strategies based on the habits of highly creative individuals, see the Creative Profile on page 50.)

Unfortunately, Evolving Systems theorists and other case study researchers are forced to rely on data which is often incomplete or inaccurate. Some emininent creators like Sigmund Freud and Henry James destroyed material to keep it from biographers. Others left behind misleading information. English poet and literary critic Samuel Taylor Coleridge claimed that the poem *Kubla Khan* came to him unedited in a drug-induced dream and that the appearance of a visitor prevented him from recording the entire poem after he awoke. Since Coleridge's account, however, another edited version of the piece has been found. The poet apparently lied about his source of inspiration to generate public interest in a poem that he never finished.[29]

Perhaps the most serious deficiency of the case study method is one shared by the personality trait and historiometric approaches as well. All three person-centered approaches are based on the notion that creative individuals are different from the rest of the population. Granted, some people are obviously more productive than others, and we can gain important insights by studying their characteristics and work habits. However, in reality we all engage in creative thinking.

Creative Profile: MacArthur Fellows

The MacArthur Award is one of the country's most unusual honors. You can't apply for a MacArthur grant (approximately 120 scouts across the country nominate some 300 individuals a year), and you don't know if you're going to get one because the nomination and selection process is secret. However, if you are named a MacArthur fellow, you can spend the money—from $150,000 to $375,000 distributed over five years—any way you want.

Administered by a foundation established by billionaire insurance salesman and real estate mogul John D. MacArthur, this unique program encourages creative breakthroughs by freeing highly creative people from financial pressures. MacArthur's son John put it this way: "Like the Medicis, we'll fund Michelangelo. If even one of them produces a great work of art, it will have been worth the risk." Recipients range in age from 18 to 82 and work in many different fields, including science, film making, writing, education, community activism, conservation and the fine arts.

Freelance journalist Denise Shekerjian wondered if MacArthur fellows share common characteristics that would provide a clearer picture of "how creative work gets done." She interviewed 40 MacArthur award winners and asked them a series of questions about what got them interested in a particular area, how they approached their labor, when they knew a project was complete, and how they dealt with discouragement and failure. Despite their diversity of talents and interests, the MacArthur fellows interviewed by Shekerjian often took similar approaches to creative problem solving. We can apply many of their tactics to our own creative projects. Strategies used by the MacArthur Fellows include:

- Find your talent and stick with it. Identify your strengths and be committed to developing them over the long term. This stick-to-itiveness was demonstrated by art historian Henry Kraus. By visiting the museums of Paris over many years, he came up with new interpretations of paintings which had already been viewed by millions of people.
- Stay loose. Tolerate ambiguity and break out of your normal, narrow perspective by accumulating information from many different sources. Social scientist and MacArthur fellow Robert Axelrod routinely scans a number of different magazines while poet Joseph Brodsky listens to classical music to learn about composition.
- Set up the conditions that make creative insight more likely for you. Some MacArthur fellows prefer quiet, uncluttered places while others thrive in crowded, hectic situations. Because creators step outside the cultural mainstream, the social environment can become hostile. Reduce this hostility by developing interpersonal communication skills which include the ability to express ideas clearly and tactfully. Also,

keep the audience in mind. If people can use your product or idea in many different ways, they're more likely to embrace it.
* Seek the greater good. Many of the fellows in Shekerjian's sample work for the public good by promoting conservation, helping inner-city kids, reducing population growth and so on. This focus on vision and values encourages them to create even in the face of opposition and failure. "Limit yourself to your own private world" Shekerjian notes, "and you've limited your creativity by worrying about how to protect what you've got and how to get what you're missing. Get yourself out of the way in pursuit of some greater good, in response to a strong pull of mission, and you've liberated the mind."
* Try a shift in scenery. MacArthur fellows travel frequently, broadening both their geographical and creative perspectives. Traveling overseas brings exposure to new cultures with different ways of seeing the world and its problems.
* Encourage luck. Louis Pasteur once noted that "chance favors the prepared mind." MacArthur recipients seem to have more than their share of fortunate "accidents" because they're ready to respond when they come. They encourage luck by paying attention to small details, following their curiosity, and maintaining a relaxed, playful attitude.
* View any creative product as a work in progress. Moving on is much easier if any given project is seen as the foundation for the next creative effort.
* Build resiliency. Cope with failure by working on a number of projects, building a network of friends, leaving a project to return to it later, and accepting failure as a learning opportunity.

Discussion Questions
1. Does freeing people from financial pressures encourage creativity?
2. Would the MacArthur program be more successful if it required recipients to account for how they spend their grant monies?
3. Which of the eight strategies do you find most useful? Why?
4. What similarities do you note between the tactics used by the MacArthur fellows and those described by Evolving Systems theorists and cognitive scientists?

Source: Shekerjian, D. (1990). *Uncommon genius: How great ideas are born.* New York: Penguin Books.
For additional information on the MacArthur fellows program, see:
Matthews, A. (1992, June 7). The MacArthur truffle hunt. *New York Times*, p. 25+

Motivational Approaches

Motivational theorists try to identify the reasons behind creative labor. These investigators have been particularly interested in 1) determining if creators solve existing problems or discover new ones, 2) clarifying the relationship between creativity and mental health, and 3) discovering if creative behavior is the product of internal or external forces.

Problem Finding as Creative Motivation

In chapter 1 we noted that creativity is often motivated by imperfections and suggested that actively seeking problems to solve is one way to spark creative thinking. The notion that creators identify new problems instead of solving existing ones is the basis of what Norman Mackworth and Jacob Getzels call the problem finding approach to creativity.[30] They note that posing and solving novel problems can generate significant change. More humane treatment of gifted and talented children is one example of the revolutionary impact of problem finding. At one time, gifted children were seen as "queer kids" who were immature and underdeveloped. Parents and teachers believed that these bright students would be failures later in life unless their premature intellectual development was tightly controlled ("early ripe," they believed, "early rot"). Attitudes changed when one researcher posed the problem as: "What is giftedness and how does it relate to achievement later in life?" Answering this new question uncovered the fact that gifted children often achieve more as adults and encouraged teachers to help children develop their talents.[31]

The creative act, according to Getzels, begins with the recognition that an ill-defined conflict or gap exists. Motivated by the desire to resolve the tension generated by this conflict, the creator puts the problem into a form that can be dealt with through symbolic means. Solving the problem then moves the creator to a new and different state of emotional and cognitive balance. A songwriter, for example, may harbor a vague resentment against a domineering parent. She may relieve this tension by writing a song about a child escaping an oppressive home situation.

Getzels and his colleague Mihaly Csikszentmihalyi studied the work habits of students at the Chicago Art Institute.[32] They equipped studios with a variety of objects and asked juniors and seniors to create paintings based on these items. The highest rated paintings were drawn by artists with a "discovery orientation." These painters spent more time playing with the objects in the room before they started drawing. They were also more willing to reformulate the problem as they painted, taking longer to complete the final structure of their creations. A follow-up study conducted seven years later found that the discovery-oriented students were the most successful commercial artists. Getzels and Csikszentmihalyi conclude that "the character of the process at the time of posing the problem is related systematically to the quality of the creative product."[33]

Two important implications can be drawn from the problem finding approach to creativity. First, our creative success depends on our skill at sensing problems. The more sensitive we are to imperfections or gaps, the more likely it is we'll generate significant new ideas. Second, formulating the problem is often the key to solving the problem. A problem should never be taken as a given but should be carefully explored and defined. We'll have more to say about the important role of problem exploration and definition when we examine creative group problem solving and creative writing in the second half of this text.

Creativity and Mental Health

For centuries observers of highly creative people have speculated that creativity is somehow linked to or motivated by mental illness. In 360 B.C., for example, Aristotle declared that "those who have become eminent in philosophy, politics, poetry, and the arts have all had tendencies toward melancholia."[34] Biographers and historians have compiled a long list of eminent creators who apparently suffered from some form of mental disturbance. This list includes those diagnosed as schizophrenic (Mendelssohn, Kant, Ezra Pound, Descartes, Newton, Pascal), delusional (Beethoven, Schumann), and depressed (Rousseau, Emerson, Hemingway, Kafka).[35]

Despite anecdotal evidence that suggests that creativity is generated by mental illness, most scholars who study the question believe that there is no causal connection between the two. For every notable historical figure who suffered from depression or delusions, many more did not. In his book *Creativity and Madness*, Milton Rothenberg offers impressive evidence that mental dysfunction interferes with the creative process.[36] After interviewing winners of the Nobel and Pulitzer prizes, conducting psychological experiments, analyzing literary manuscripts, and interviewing the surviving families of highly creative individuals, Rothenberg concludes that the creative achievements of psychotic people occur in spite of, not because of, their emotional and mental problems. To create, mentally ill individuals must shift temporarily to healthy, creative thought processes that Rothenberg labels as **janusian**. Janus, the Roman god of doorways and beginnings, is often pictured as having several faces that simultaneously look in opposite directions. Janusian thinkers integrate elements previously considered to be contradictions or opposites. Novelist John Hersey's book *Too Far to Walk* is based on the idea that love and hate are the same. Playwright Arthur Miller wrote the play *Incident at Vichy* in an attempt to capture both the physical beauty of Germany and the evil of Hitler.

According to Rothenberg, two factors probably account for the popular perception that creators must be at least a little mad. One, both creative thinkers and psychotic thinkers generate unusual products. Two, since the ideas of creators often put them in conflict with society, observers may look for behaviors that reinforce negative stereotypes of creative communicators.

At the other end of the spectrum from those who suggest that pathology motivates creativity are those who contend that creative thinking is a byproduct of a person's overall mental health. Humanistic psychologists, guided by the writings of Abraham Maslow and Carl Rogers, believe that creativity is part of self-actualization—the natural human drive which pushes us to reach our fullest potential.[37] They argue that we are born with the drive to explore and develop but that this motivation is often subverted or buried as we leave childhood. However, the desire to become a "fully functional person" can be released under the proper conditions. These conditions include acceptance of the unconditional worth of individuals, absence of external evaluation, empathetic understanding by others, and complete freedom to express ideas in symbolic form. Self-actualized, constructive creators are marked by playfulness, openness to experience, internal motivation, and integration—the absence of significant inner conflicts. They live in a state of creativeness that allows them to "emit" creative ideas in the same way that uranium emits radioactivity.[38]

The Intrinsic Motivation Hypothesis

Americans often link productivity to such external rewards as pay and status. Provide enough incentives, they reason, and people will work harder and produce a better product. In her intrinsic motivation hypothesis, social psychologist Teresa Amabile challenges the belief that external rewards increase creative productivity. She argues that we're most creative when we're motivated by the challenge and enjoyment of the task itself.[39] Our performance drops when external constraints like time pressures, financial rewards and evaluation are imposed on us. In these situations we attribute our effort to outside forces and our motivation to create diminishes. In addition, when we're engaged in extrinsically motivated behavior we're so focused on achieving the goal that we ignore important cues in the environment that could help us come up with a more creative solution.

To test her hypothesis that internal motivation promotes creative behavior while external factors detract, Amabile and her colleagues conducted a series of consensual assessment experiments. In these projects, participants ranging from elementary students to Stanford undergraduates created paper collages, stories and other products which were then given creativity ratings by panels of judges. Results from these studies, along with findings from other motivational investigations, indicate that:

- external rewards (opportunity to play with a desired object, money, etc.) lower creative performance whether offered before or after a task;
- evaluation or the expectation that one's performance will be evaluated by outsiders lowers creativity;
- being given a choice about whether or not to participate in an activity and how to accomplish the task increases creativity;
- the detrimental effects of external constraints can be reduced by emphasizing internal motivational factors (the value of the project, the pleasure of the work) before attempting a task;
- some individuals (those who are extremely motivated by the task and those who can ignore outside influences) are more resistant to the negative effects of external constraints.

The intrinsic motivation hypothesis seems to provide the best explanation for the behavior of creative communicators who (as the cognitivist scientists point out) must persevere over long periods of time in the face of strong opposition. Clearly such individuals are driven by internal forces that are more powerful than external barriers. Like them, we can sustain our creative momentum if we willingly choose to create, find satisfaction in the task and believe in what we're doing.

By contrasting the impact of internal and external motivational elements, Amabile directs attention to social and environmental factors that are ignored by many other theorists. Her theoretical framework (which we'll examine in more detail in chapter 3) has already proven its value by serving as the foundation for a productive research program. However, questions can be raised about the generalizability of her findings. How students and others respond in short experimental tasks may not reflect what actually happens in real life laboratories, offices, courtrooms and studios. In chapter 6, for example, we'll see how the proper mix of internal and external rewards can increase creative productivity in organizational settings. Instead of disregarding external motivational factors as Amabile suggests, we should acknowledge that both internal and external forces play a role in sparking creative behavior.

Summing Up

In this chapter we surveyed theories which focus on the what, who and why of creativity. We began by examining cognitive theories which identify the mental processes involved in creative thought. Psychometric researchers use paper and pencil tests to measure the special components or factors that underlie creative thinking. These divergent thinking abilities include fluency, flexibility, originality, elaboration, and association. Other cognitive theorists treat creativity as a form of ordinary problem solving. When searching for solutions, creators and other problem solvers pass through a series of intermediate steps. Solutions are tested and discarded until the final answer emerges. Creative products are most likely to emerge when problem solvers are well prepared, work hard for long periods of time, tolerate the ambiguity associated with ill-defined problems, and take calculated risks.

Next we looked at person-centered approaches which are based on the premise that creative individuals share common characteristics. Personality researchers isolate groups of highly creative people and then collect data using creativity tests and personality measures. To date, they have yet to agree on a comprehensive set of traits common to all creative individuals. Historiometric investigators identify highly creative populations in historical records, look for factors that contribute to the success of these groups, and then develop generalizations that explain and predict creative behavior. Important variables associated with creative people include: productivity, age, family background, the presence of role models, an optimal level of formal education, being on the margins of a culture or profession, the cumulative advantage that accrues from early success, and zeitgeist or spirit of the times. Case study experts study the lives of individual creators to determine how they accomplish their work. The Evolving Systems theory, which is based on the case study method, suggests that highly creative people spend their lives engaged in clusters of related projects and activities called networks of enterprise. When one project fails or is blocked, the creator (whose thinking is shaped by her/his knowledge base, ultimate purpose and affect or emotional state) shifts to another.

We concluded with a look at motivational theories which try to explain why people engage in creative behavior. Those who view creativity as problem finding argue that creators identify new problems instead of solving existing dilemmas. Creative success depends on sensing potential problems and then carefully exploring and defining them. Other observers speculate that creativity is caused by mental illness. Most experts, however, believe that there is no causal connection between the two. Humanistic psychologists treat creativity as a byproduct of mental health. They believe that creativity is part of the natural drive for self-actualization which can be released under the proper conditions. The intrinsic motivation hypothesis suggests that our creative productivity is highest when we are motivated by the challenge and enjoyment of the task itself. External constraints like time pressures, financial rewards and evaluation detract from creative performance.

Application Exercises

1. As a group project, use the Brick Uses test to generate fluency, flexibility and originality scores for class members. Pay particularly close attention to your coding scheme. How will you determine flexibility and originality scores?

2. Make a list of the personality characteristics of creative people. Then form a small group and generate a composite list. To make the group's list, a characteristic must be accepted by all the members of the group. Keep a second list of the characteristics that were nominated but not accepted. As part of your report, name those characteristics that were rejected by the group. Explain why these factors failed to make the master list.

3. Divide into debate teams and argue for or against each of the assertions listed below. Your instructor will determine the debate format.
   a) Creativity is the product of ordinary thought processes.
   b) Creativity is a sign of mental health.
   c) Creative communicators are problem finders rather than problem solvers.

d) External factors (rewards, time limitations, evaluation) always detract from creative performance.

e) Too much education can make a person less creative.

4. Write an 8–10 page research paper on one of the theories presented in this chapter or on another theory of your choice. Present a brief summary of your findings to the rest of the class.

5. As an extension of your creativity log started in chapter 1, identify significant goals that could direct your networks of enterprise in the years to come. Develop an initial sketch that outlines possible ideas and projects.

Endnotes

[1] Guilford, J. P. (1950). Creativity. *The American Psychologist, 5,* 444–454.

[2] Guilford, J. P. (1967). *The nature of human intelligence.* New York: McGraw Hill.; Guilford, J. P. (1977). *Way beyond IQ.* Buffalo, NY: Bearly Limited.

[3] Guilford, J. P. (1967). Factors that aid and hinder creativity. In J. C. Gowan, G. D. Demos & E. Paul Torrance (Eds.), *Creativity: Its educational implications* (pp. 106–123). New York: John Wiley & Sons.

[4] Torrance, E. P. (1962). *Guiding creative talent.* Englewood Cliffs, NJ: Prentice-Hall; Torrance, E. P. (1965), *Rewarding creative behavior.* Englewood Cliffs, NJ: Prentice-Hall.

[5] Mednick, S. A. (1962). The associative basis of the creative process. *Psychological Review, 69,* 320–332.

[6] For a critique of the Remote Associates Test, see:

Buros, O. K. (Ed.) (1972). *The seventh mental measurement yearbook.* Highland Park, NJ: Gryphon Press.

Buros, O. K. (Ed.) (1978). *The eight mental measurement yearbook.* Highland Park, NJ: Gryphon Press.

[7] Wallach, M. A., & Kogan, N. (1965). *Modes of thinking in young children.* Westport, CT: Greenwood Press.

[8] Wallach & Kogan.

[9] See:

Mansfield, R. S., Busse, T. V., & Krepelka, E. J. (1978). The effectiveness of creativity training. *Review of Educational Research, 48,* 517–538.

Brown, R. P. (1989). Creativity: What are we to measure? In J. A. Glover, R. R. Ronning & C. R. Reynolds (Eds.), *Handbook of creativity* (pp. 3–31). New York: Plenum Press.

Wallach, M. A. (1985). Creativity testing and giftedness. In F. D. Horowitz & M. O'Brien (Eds.), *The gifted and talented* (pp. 99–123). Washington, DC: American Psychological Association.

[10] Simon, H. A. (1979). *Models of thought.* New Haven, CT: Yale University Press; Simon, H. A. (1967). Understanding creativity. In J. C. Gowan, G. D. Demos & E. Paul Torrance (Eds.), *Creativity: Its educational implications* (pp. 43–53). New York: John Wiley & Sons.; Hayes, J. R. (1989). Cognitive processes in creativity.

In J. A. Glover, R. R. Ronning & C. R. Reynolds (Eds.), *Handbook of Creativity* (pp. 35–145). New York: Plenum Press.

[11] Weisberg, R. W. (1986). *Creativity: Genius and other myths*. New York: W. H. Freeman and Company.

[12] Simon, H. A. (1988). Understanding creativity and creative management. In R. L. Kuhn (Ed.), *Handbook for creative and innovative management* (pp. 11–24). New York: McGraw Hill, p. 13.

[13] See, for example:

Barron, F. (1968). *Creativity and personal freedom*. New York: D. Van Nostrand Company.

MacKinnon, D. W. (1978). *In search of human effectiveness*. Buffalo, NY: Creative Education Foundation.

[14] Gough, H. G. (1979). A creative personality scale for the adjective check list. *Journal of Personality and Social Psychology, 37*, 1398–1405.

[15] Barron, F. (1965). The psychology of creativity. In T. M. Newcomb (Ed.), *New directions in psychology II* (pp. 3–134). New York: Holt, Rinehart & Winston.

[16] Crutchfield, R. S. (1962). Conformity and creative thinking. In H. E. Gruber, G. Terrell & M. Wertheimer (Eds.), *Contemporary approaches to creative thinking* (pp. 120–140). New York: Atherton Press.

[17] MacKinnon, D. W. (1962). The nature and nurture of creative talent. *American Psychologist, 17*, 484–495.

[18] Gardner, H. (1988). Creativity: An interdisciplinary perspective. *Creativity Research Journal, 1*, 8–26.

[18] Barron, F. (1988). Putting creativity to work. In R. J. Sternberg (Ed.), *The nature of creativity* (pp. 76–98). New York: Cambridge University Press, p. 94.

[20] Simonton, D. K. (1984). *Genius, creativity, and leadership*. Cambridge, MA: Harvard University Press.; Simonton, D. K. (1988). Creativity, leadership, and chance. In R. J. Sternberg (Ed.), *The nature of creativity* (pp. 386–426). Cambridge, England: Cambridge University Press.

[21] Simonton, Creativity, leadership and chance, p. 411.

[22] Simonton, D. K. (1991, Spring). Creative productivity throughout the adult years. *Generations*, pp. 13–16.

[23] Merton, R. K. (1968). The Matthew effect in science. *Science, 159*, 56–63.

[24] Stein, M. I. (1974). *Stimulating creativity, Vol. 1: Individual procedures*. New York: Academic Press, Ch. III.

[25] Grudin, R. (1990). *The grace of great things*. New York: Ticknor & Fields, Ch. 13.

[26] For a more in-depth discussion of the functions of mentors, see:

Hackman, M. Z., & Johnson, C. E. (1991). *Leadership: A communication perspective*. Prospect Heights, IL: Waveland, Ch. 7.

[27] Gruber, H. E. (1988). Inching our way up Mount Olympus: The evolving-systems approach to creative thinking. In R. J. Sternberg (Ed.), *The nature of creativity* (pp. 243–270). Cambridge, England: Cambridge University Press.; Wallace, D. B., & Gruber, H. E. (Eds.), (1989). *Creative people at work*. New York: Oxford University Press.; Gruber, H. E. (1988). The evolving systems approach to creative work. *Creativity Research Journal, 1*, 27–51.

[28] Gruber, Inching our way up Mount Olympus, p. 266.

[29] Weisberg.

[30] Mackworth, N. H. (1965). Originality. *American Psychologist, 20*, 51–66.; Getzels, J. W. (1975). Problem-finding and the inventiveness of solutions. *Journal of Creative Behavior, 9*, 12–18.

[31] Getzels, J. W. (1973, November 21). Problem finding. The 343rd Convocation Address, the University of Chicago. *The University of Chicago Record, 9*, 281–283.

[32] Getzels, J. W., & Czikzentmihalyi, M. (1976). *The creative vision.* New York: John Wiley and Sons.; Czikszentmihalyi, M., & Getzels, J. W. (1976). Discovery-oriented behavior and the originality of creative products. *Journal of Personality and Social Psychology, 19,* 47–52.

[33] Getzels, J. W. & Czikzentmihalyi, The creative vision, p. 137.

[34] Prentky, R. (1989). Creativity and psychopathology: Gamboling at the seat of madness. In J. A. Glover, R. R. Ronning & C. R. Reynolds (Eds.), *Handbook of creativity* (pp. 243–269). New York: Plenum Press, p. 244.

[35] Prentky.

[36] Rothenberg, A. (1990). *Creativity and madness.* Baltimore, MD: Johns Hopkins Press. Examples of Janusian thinking are provided by Rothenberg as well.

[37] Maslow, A. (1959). *Creativity in self-actualizing people.* In H. H. Anderson (Ed.), Creativity and its cultivation (pp. 83–94). New York: Harper & Row.; Rogers, C. R. (1971). Toward a theory of creativity. In R. Holsinger, C. Jordan, & L. Levenson (Eds.), *The creative encounter* (pp. 2–12). Glenview, IL; Scott Foresman.

[38] Maslow.

[39] Summaries of this theory are found in:

Amabile, T. M. (1983). The social psychology of creativity: A componential conceptualization. *Journal of Personality and Social Psychology, 45,* 357–376.

Hennessey, B. A., & Amabile, T. M. (1988). The conditions of creativity. In R. J. Sternberg (Ed.), *The nature of creativity* (pp. 11–38). Cambridge: Cambridge University Press.

Quotations

Gruber, H. E. (1988). Inching our way up Mount Olympus: The evolving-systems approach to creative thinking. In R. J. Sternberg (Ed.), *The nature of creativity* (pp. 243–270). Cambridge, England: Cambridge University Press.

Simon, H. A. (1988). Understanding creativity and creative management. In R. L. Kuhn (Ed.), *Handbook for creative and innovative managers* (pp. 11–24). New York: McGraw Hill.

3 | The Creative Process

The real magic of discovery lies not in seeking new landscapes but in having new eyes.

Marcel Proust

The techniques individuals use to generate and develop creative ideas vary considerably. Some people report experiencing bursts of creative insight, while others must labor methodically to clarify and refine their ideas. Diane English, the producer of the successful situation comedy "Murphy Brown," noted the idea for the program came to her as a "vision" while driving on the Ventura Freeway.[1] Compare this to the painstaking process undertaken by Robert Boyle who developed Boyle's Law in the seventeenth century. Boyle's Law focuses on the way in which the volume of a gas changes with pressure. In order to explain this relationship, Robert Boyle conducted countless experiments where he isolated each particular gas from background variables, such as changes in temperature.[2] Boyle's Law was not developed in a flash of inspiration; rather, it was developed through the slow simmer of determined investigation.

Whether an idea is developed in a split-second vision or through a decade of deliberation, explaining "how" creativity works is no simple matter. Over the years, several models of the creative process have been proposed. These models do not represent foolproof prescriptions for developing creative ideas. Instead, these models of the creative process offer insight into techniques by which creative ideas may be generated. They can serve as valuable tools for initiating creative thinking. You may find it useful to modify, mix and match components of the models discussed in this chapter to develop your own model for generating creative ideas.

Models of the Creative Process

The Wallas Stage Model

One of the earliest and most widely cited models of creativity was developed by Graham Wallas in 1926.[3] Wallas suggested the creative process consisted of four stages: preparation, incubation, illumination, and verification. All four stages may not be evident in every creative act. Some stages may be skipped entirely or may occur so quickly as to be hardly noticeable. At other times, it may be difficult to clearly define where one stage ends and another begins.

1. *Preparation.* The preparation stage involves clarifying and defining the problem, collecting data, looking for patterns and relationships, and considering solutions. This may take a matter of moments or may last for years. Preparing to solve one of the

creative problems in this book may take just a few minutes of reflection, while a graduate student seeking solutions to a creative research problem may spend years learning theory, studying related problems and collecting data. As Thomas Edison pointed out, "genius is 1 percent inspiration and 99 percent perspiration."

2. *Incubation.* Here the problem is put on the back burner. You have probably noticed that when you work on a complex project such as writing a research paper, remodeling a room or designing a computer program you take frequent breaks. These breaks allow you to refresh yourself physically and also afford the opportunity to let your ideas incubate. This incubation takes place beneath the surface, as the problem moves from the conscious mind to the unconscious mind. While you hike, sleep, drink a cup of coffee or just stare out the window, your unconscious mind continues to wrestle with the problem. In one high tech organization, research and development engineers took juggling breaks, during which they juggled various objects (balls, cups, blocks, but fortunately not chainsaws to the best of our knowledge) as a means to relax and to clear their minds. Seymour Cray, the founder of Cray Computers, engaged in an even more extreme form of incubation. For many years Cray divided his time between building the fastest, most powerful computer in the world and digging a tunnel beneath his house. As Cray explained, "When I get stumped, and I'm not making progress, I quit. I go and work in the tunnel. It takes me an hour or so to dig four inches." For Cray, digging his tunnel is more than a simple diversion. Says a Cray executive, "The real work happens when Seymour is in his tunnel."[4]

3. *Illumination.* In this stage an idea, solution or new relationship emerges. This illumination generally presents itself as a sudden insight—known as the "Aha!" experience. Edwin Land, the inventor of the Polaroid Land Camera, described the insight of the illumination stage as "the sudden cessation of stupidity."[5] This stage of the creative process is perhaps the most well known. However, we must realize that preparation and incubation are precursors to illumination. Few ideas really emerge out of the blue. Most sudden insights are more likely the result of previous research and reflection. Consider the following examples:

> While in the bathtub, the ancient Greek scientist Archimedes realized the principle that "a body immersed in liquid loses as much in weight as the weight of the fluid it displaces." Afterwards he celebrated his discovery by running naked through the streets, shouting "Eureka!" ("I have found it."). The problem of displacement first plagued Archimedes when he was asked by his king to determine whether

a gift of a crown was solid gold or not. Under threat of death if he was unable to determine the authenticity of the crown, Archimedes tried to relax himself in the bath. Only at this point, after significant preparation and incubation, did Archimedes experience his sudden illumination.[6]

The formula for the molecular structure of benzene came to German chemist Friedrich August Kekule during a dream. At the time of his discovery, all known chemical structures were composed of linear chains of atoms. Like other chemists, he had tried in vain to fit the six carbon atoms and six hydrogen atoms of benzene into a chain that satisfied the rules of chemistry. One night, after a good meal and a couple of glasses of brandy, he settled down to relax by an open fire. Half-asleep, he watched the flames twisting and curling upon themselves. To Kekule, the flames looked like snakes circling around to bite their own tails. He woke up with a start. Flames do not go around in circles, but carbon atoms in the benzene molecule could. Benzene, he suddenly realized, was a closed chain, a ring structure. Painstaking preparation fueled by incubation (and two glasses of brandy) finally led to illumination.[7]

4. **Verification.** In this last stage, the creator fully develops her or his idea. Verification, like the preparation stage, generally involves ongoing effort to test the ideas, solutions and relationships generated. Although illumination is a sudden, often joyful experience, verification is frequently sustained and painful.[8] Verification can include writing poetry and novels, testing mathematical theorems, or producing a work of art. In this stage the "Aha!" is turned into reality.

Creative Profile: The Dreams of Robert Louis Stevenson

From early in life, author Robert Louis Stevenson experienced intense nightmares. His dreams were often so vivid and frightening Stevenson would awaken with "a flying heart, a freezing scalp, cold sweats, and speechless fear." As a child, only his father was able to pacify him after one of his horrified awakenings. As a student at Edinburgh College in Scotland, Stevenson's dreams became so disturbing that he sought treatment from a doctor. The unknown treatment helped to minimize the physical reactions Stevenson experienced, but did nothing to reduce the frequency of his dreams.

As an adult, Stevenson began to harness his dreams as an outlet for his creativity. His dreams appeared to him in a peculiar shade of brown so he coined the phrase "Brownies" to refer to the characters in his dreams. Observing the nightly performances of his Brownies afforded Stevenson a front row seat to an assortment of entertaining tales. The

Brownies provided inspiration for a number of Stevenson's works, the most famous of which was *The Strange Case of Dr. Jekyll and Mr. Hyde*.

Stevenson tried for days without success to write a story about the dual nature of the human experience. After a particularly grueling day of wrestling with the plot without success, the story of Dr. Jekyll and Mr. Hyde came to him in a dream. The dream was intense enough to cause him to scream so loudly and with such horror that his wife Fanny woke him. "I was dreaming a fine bogey tale," he informed his wife, and at daybreak he began writing. Within three days he had completed a thirty thousand word manuscript. Upon completion, he triumphantly read the manuscript aloud to his wife. Fanny was disappointed. She believed that he had missed the point with his story. The story was too literal and sensational when it should have been presented as an allegory. After reflection Stevenson agreed with his wife and threw the entire manuscript into the fireplace. For three more days he worked feverishly rewriting the tale as an allegory. When he was finished, he read the story to his wife who overwhelmingly approved. For six weeks more he polished the manuscript and then sent the final draft to a publisher.

Discussion Questions

1. What role do you believe Stevenson's dreams played in his creative endeavors? What other activities might serve the same function?

2. Have you ever had an idea come to you in a dream? Did you take action on the idea? What happened?

3. Stevenson completed the first draft of his manuscript for *The Strange Case of Dr. Jekyll and Mr. Hyde* in only three days and his second draft in a mere three days more. Do you believe such intensity of effort increases creativity? What work patterns are most conducive to creativity for you?

Sources:

Bell, I. (1993). *Dreams of exile*. New York: Henry Holt and Company.
Hennesy, J.P. (1975). *Robert Louis Stevenson*. New York: Simon and Schuster.
Madigan, C.O., & Elwood, A. (1983). *Brainstorms and thunderbolts*. New York: Macmillan, pp. 85–86.

Osborn's Creative Problem-Solving Process

Advertising executive Alex Osborn, the pioneer of the brainstorming technique described in detail in chapter 5, suggests the creative problem-solving process ideally includes three procedures: fact-finding, idea-finding, and solution-finding.[9]

1. **Fact-finding.** The fact-finding procedure involves defining the problem under investigation and preparing for problem

resolution. This is accomplished by gathering and analyzing pertinent data. Defining the problem is an important first step in the creative process. According to Albert Einstein, "The formulation of a problem is far more essential than its solution, which may be merely a matter of mathematical or experimental skill."[10] Creative dilemmas are almost always resolved as a result of careful research and meticulous definition of the problem.

> I'd rather know some of the questions than all of the answers.
> James Thurber

2. *Idea-finding.* The idea-finding procedure involves developing tentative ideas. Osborn suggests using *idea-spurring* questions to assist in uncovering new associations among ideas. Ideas are rearranged, combined, modified and expanded to create possible solutions to a problem. Rearrangement of ideas usually offers an incredible number of alternatives. For instance, a baseball or softball manager can shuffle the team's batting order 362,880 times by merely rearranging his or her 9 starting players.[11] Consider how a common household item such as a hammer could be modified by the following idea-spurring questions on Osborn's list:

Put to other uses? New ways to use as is? Other uses if modified?

Adapt? What else is like this? What other idea does this suggest? Does past offer parallel? What could I copy? Whom could I emulate?

Modify? New twist? Change meaning, color, motion, sound, odor, form, shape? Other changes?

Magnify? What to add? More time? Greater frequency? Stronger? Higher? Longer? Thicker? Extra value? Plus ingredient? Duplicate? Multiply? Exaggerate?

Minify? What to subtract? Smaller? Condensed? Miniature? Lower? Shorter? Lighter? Omit? Streamline? Split up? Understate?

Substitute? What else instead? Other ingredient? Other material? Other process? Other power? Other place? Other approach? Other tone?

Rearrange? Interchange components? Other pattern? Other layout? Other sequence? Transpose cause and effect?

Reverse? Transpose positive and negative? How about opposites? Turn it backward? Turn it upside down?

Combine? How about a blend, an alloy, an assortment, an ensemble? Combine units? Combine purposes? Combine ideas?[12]

Idea-spurring questions can be used to generate creative ideas by identifying previously unimagined connections. Perhaps your modifications to the common hammer were as preposterous—at first glance—as the ideas of George de Mestral and Eero Saarinen.[13] de Mestral developed a new type of fastener after a mountain hike in his native France left him and his dog covered with burrs. Anyone else might have cursed the pesky burrs, but de Mestral wondered why they clung with such tenacity. Examining the burrs under his microscope, de Mestral saw hundreds of tiny hooks. As a fastener the burr was without equal and, unlike a zipper, the burr could not catch or jam. Asking the question—can this pattern of tiny hooks be manufactured to create a fastening device?—de Mestral set out to develop the burr-inspired fastener for the commercial market. Some ten years later a product inspired by a walk in the mountains, Velcro, revolutionized the fastening industry.

An even more unlikely connection was made by architect Saarinen. Commissioned in 1956 to design a terminal for TWA at what is now New York's Kennedy Airport, Saarinen was struggling to develop a structure adequately expressing the excitement and movement of travel. Unhappy with his previous designs, Saarinen found a connection in the most unlikely of places—a grapefruit. One morning, as his wife watched, Saarinen turned the curved shell of his breakfast grapefruit over and began carving arches into it. He carried the grapefruit off to work with him and used it as the model for the final design of the TWA roof—four intersecting barrel vaults forming an umbrella over the passenger area. The final structure, completed in 1964, was described in architectural magazines as reminiscent of a "bird in flight." Unknown to Saarinen's admirers was the fact that the TWA terminal was inspired by an unlikely connection between a grapefruit and the terminal roof. See what kinds of creative connections you can make by working through the Creative Dilemma on page 68.

3. **Solution-finding.** The solution-finding procedure calls for evaluation and adoption. Evaluation involves examining the tentative solutions suggested in the idea-finding procedure. Adoption calls for deciding on and implementing the final solution.

When evaluating ideas, Osborn suggests using a check-list to detail the criteria most important to decision making. For example, if the creative problem involves developing a method for building circuit boards more quickly, the check-list might include items such as:

Is the method simple enough?

Is the method feasible?

Is the method safe?

What will the impact be on quality?

Is there going to be a reduction in costs?

Will implementing the method improve working conditions?

Will new equipment be needed?

The answers to check-list questions such as these enable creative problem solvers to select the best solution for implementation.

Although the fact-finding, idea-finding and solution-finding procedures are generally most effective when undertaken in sequence,

---

Creative Dilemma: Using Idea-Spurring Questions

Alex Osborn suggests using idea-spurring questions to assist in uncovering new associations among ideas. Use the list of idea-spurring questions on page 66 to answer the following:

- How could the aircrafts used by commercial airlines be improved? How could the services offered by the airlines be improved?

- What improvements could be made to the household television? What new stations or programs could be offered?

- How could university housing be improved? What changes in policy would make living on a university campus more desirable?

- How could clothing be improved? What changes would help clothes to look better? Be more comfortable? Last longer?

- What could be done to improve the telephone? What new services might phone companies offer?

- What could be done to improve library services. How could libraries be more attentive to the needs of patrons? How could access to books be improved?

- How could shopping for groceries be made more convenient? More enjoyable?

- What could be done to improve highway travel? How could highway travel be made safer? More efficient? More enjoyable?

Discussion Questions

1. How practical were the answers you generated? Is it always important to be practical when trying to be creative?

2. What advantages/disadvantages do you see in using idea-spurring questions?

3. Identify how the idea-spurring question technique could be applied to a creative problem you are involved with at school, at work, or at home.

every one of these procedures calls for deliberate effort and creative imagination. According to Osborn, by searching for facts, ideas and solutions, creative imagination can be fully involved in the problem-solving process.

deBono's Lateral Thinking Approach

As noted in chapter 1, lateral thinking is one of the defining characteristics of the creative process. Edward deBono, one of the most prolific writers and lecturers in the area of creativity, suggests a model of the creative process dependent on lateral thinking.[14] Lateral thinking allows an individual to break from traditional, or vertical, patterns of thinking. According to deBono, lateral thinking is quite distinct from vertical thinking. In vertical thinking an individual relies on sequential patterns of thought in which correct answers are required at each stage. In lateral thinking one may have to be wrong at some stage in order to achieve a correct solution.

> Slaying sacred cows makes great steaks.
>
> Dick Nicolosi

Lateral thinking is not a substitute for vertical thinking. Both processes are required for creative problem solving. Lateral thinking enhances the effectiveness of vertical thinking.

In table 3.1, deBono identifies ten critical differences between lateral thinking and vertical thinking.[15] By looking at these differences we gain a clearer understanding of vertical and lateral thought processes.

Vertical thinking is selective; lateral thinking is generative. Being correct is what matters most in vertical thinking. When an incorrect pathway is selected in vertical thinking one typically moves on to another pathway. The goal in vertical thinking is to find the "right" solution. In lateral thinking, richness matters more than being correct. One continues generating ideas after both failures and successes. Lateral thinking involves producing ideas for the sake of idea generation, not for the sake of uncovering the one "right" answer.

Vertical thinking moves only if there is a direction in which to move; lateral thinking moves in order to generate a direction. With vertical thinking one moves in a clearly defined direction towards the solution of a problem. The vertical thinker knows what he or she is looking for and attempts to move systematically to that end.

Table 3.1   Vertical versus Lateral Thinking

Vertical Thinking	*Lateral Thinking*
Is selective	Is generative
Moves in a clearly defined direction	Moves for the sake of moving
Is analytical	Is provocative
Is sequential	Can be non-sequential
Relies on correct answers at every step	Does not have to be correct at every step
Views wrong solutions as negative and tries to avoid them	Does not exclude options even if they have been wrong in the past
Excludes the irrelevant	Welcomes chance intrusions
Uses fixed categories, classifications, and labels	Uses variable categories, classifications, and labels
Moves in the most obvious direction	Often moves in the least obvious direction
Is a finite process	Is a probabilistic process

With lateral thinking one moves for the sake of moving. The lateral thinker may not be moving toward something, but rather, may be moving away from something. Lateral thinkers may not know what they are looking for until they find it.

Vertical thinking is analytical; lateral thinking is provocative. Vertival thinking involves the analysis of ideas, problems and situations. Lateral thinking challenges existing assumptions. The vertical thinker may view a spilled cup of coffee as a problem which needs to be solved. The vertical thinker would identify the most efficient technique for cleaning up the spilled coffee, focusing on factors such as the temperature of the coffee, the absorbency of available materials for soaking up the spill, and the distance to the nearest sink or garbage can. The lateral thinker might restructure the "problem" as an opportunity to attract and capture troublesome houseflies.

Vertical thinking is sequential; lateral thinking can make leaps. Vertical thinking involves moving forward one step at a time. The vertical thinker begins at the beginning, and each step arises directly from the preceding step. With lateral thinking the steps do not have to be sequential. The lateral thinker can jump ahead to a new point and fill in the gaps later. The lateral thinker may visualize a process at its completion or anywhere in time before figuring out how to get started.

With vertical thinking one has to be correct at every step; with lateral thinking one does not have to be correct at every step. The very essence of vertical thinking is that one must be accurate at each step. Vertical thought processes, such as finding the solution to a mathematical equation, require that the problem solver is correct at each step in the problem solving process. In lateral thinking one does not have to be right at each step; only the final conclusion needs to be correct. Lateral thinking is somewhat similar to constructing a bridge. The components of the bridge individually do not have to be self-supporting; only the completed bridge must be self-supporting.

With vertical thinking one blocks off certain pathways; with lateral thinking there are no blocks. Vertical thinkers view wrong solutions as negative and work to avoid them. Vertical thinkers block off pathways leading to wrong solutions by saying things like, "We've tried that before and it didn't work so we need to come up with something else." However, there are times when it may be necessary to be wrong in order to be right at the end. Lateral thinkers do not exclude options which have produced poor results in the past. They impose no blocks based on past experience.

With vertical thinking one concentrates on viable options and excludes what is irrelevant; with lateral thinking one welcomes chance intrusions. Vertical thinking is selection by exclusion. The vertical thinker works within a frame of reference and discards that which is not relevant. The lateral thinker welcomes outside influences and their provocative action. Robert Louis Stevenson's most famous book, *Treasure Island*, originated from Stevenson's attempt to amuse his thirteen-year-old stepson on a rainy autumn afternoon. To occupy the boy, Stevenson created a game played in an imaginary island locale that Stevenson painted in watercolor. As Stevenson and the boy played the game, the idea for *Treasure Island* became so intense that Stevenson paused to write down a list of chapter headings.[16] Stevenson did not set out that day to outline a book; rather he welcomed the intrusion of a rainy afternoon and the attempt to amuse an idle thirteen-year-old. (For more about Robert Louis Stevenson see the Creative Profile, page 64).

With vertical thinking categories, classifications and labels are fixed; with lateral thinking they are not. Vertical thinking depends heavily on the rigidity of definitions. Items placed in a particular category or class, or given a particular label must remain constant for vertical thinking to operate. A vertical thought process such as solving a math problem would not be possible if certain mathematical principles were not constant. Categories, classifications and labels may change with lateral thinking. This alteration allows the lateral thinker to look at problems in new ways.

Vertical thinking follows the most likely paths; lateral thinking explores the least likely. In vertical thinking one progresses along the path in the most obvious direction. Lateral thinking, on the other hand, can be deliberately perverse. Using lateral thinking, one tries to look at the least obvious approaches rather than the most likely approaches.

Vertical thinking is a finite process; lateral thinking is a probabilistic process. With vertical thinking one expects to come up with an answer, but with lateral thinking there may not be an answer at all. Vertical thinking promises at least a minimum solution. Lateral thinking, while increasing the chances of restructuring existing patterns and generating a maximum solution, offers no guarantees.

deBono suggests a number of techniques for using lateral thinking to generate creative ideas. The most developed of deBono's techniques is the Six Thinking Hats Method.[17]

The Six Thinking Hats Method. In the Six Thinking Hats Method each of six fundamental modes of thinking behavior is assigned an imaginary hat of a different color. At any moment a thinker may choose to put on one of the hats or may be asked to put on or take off a hat by someone else. Each hat involves problem solvers in a mental role play. In this way thinking can be switched at will from one mode to another. The color of each hat is related to its function.

White Hat. White is neutral and objective. The White Hat represents information thinking. This type of thinking is like that of a computer—unbiased and factual. The White Hat thinker strives to be as neutral and objective as possible in her or his presentation of information.

Red Hat. Red suggests anger, rage and emotion. The Red Hat represents intuitive and emotional thinking. The Red Hat legitimizes emotions as an important aspect of problem solving. When a thinker is using the Red Hat, there should never be any attempt to justify feelings or to provide a logical basis for emotion.

Black Hat. Black is gloomy and negative. The Black Hat represents cautionary and logically negative thinking. Black Hat thinking is specifically concerned with negative assessment. The Black Hat thinker points out what is wrong, incorrect and in error.

Yellow Hat. Yellow is sunny and positive. The Yellow Hat represents logically positive thinking. Yellow Hat thinking is positive and constructive and focuses on positive ideas ranging from the logical and practical at one end to dreams, hopes and vision at the other end. When generating new ideas, the Yellow Hat should always be worn before the Black Hat.

Green Hat. Green relates to grass, vegetation and abundant fertile growth. The Green Hat represents creative, generative thinking. The search for alternatives is a fundamental aspect of Green Hat thinking. Lateral thinking strategies are always used when wearing the Green Hat.

Blue Hat. Blue is cool; it is also the color of the sky, which is above everything else. The Blue Hat represents controlled and organized thinking. The Blue Hat thinker defines the subject, sets the focus and shapes questions. Blue Hat thinking is used for summaries, overviews and conclusions.

According to deBono, when thinking is clear and simple, it is more enjoyable and more effective. The Six Thinking Hats Method simplifies creative thinking by allowing a creative problem solver to deal with one aspect of the thought process at a time. The technique is used purposefully as an individual consciously switches from one thinking hat to another.

Creators may feel awkward using the Six Thinking Hats at first. However, as they become more familiar with each of the thinking hats, problem solvers may find this an easy-to-use approach for looking at ideas from different perspectives.

A group of students, for example, might find the Six Thinking Hats Method useful in preparing a classroom presentation. Some group members may want to impress the instructor by presenting lots of research and statistics; other group members may feel it is most important to entertain the audience and to evoke an emotional response. By switching hats, group members can insure that their presentation incorporates both goals. The Six Thinking Hats Method can help group members to avoid decisions which lack creative inspiration while guarding against excessively negative or overly emotional deliberations. When the discussion becomes too logical, negative or emotional, for example, group members simply request that an individual switch thinking hats. The framework of the six thinking hats has been adopted by many major corporations, including IBM, DuPont and Prudential Insurance.[18]

Amabile's Componential Model of Creativity

Brandeis University psychology professor Teresa Amabile and her colleagues believe that creativity is best explained in terms of the relationship among personal characteristics, cognitive abilities and the social environment. Amabile's model of the creative process consists of the three components noted in figure 3.1: domain-relevant skills, creativity-relevant skills and task motivation.[19]

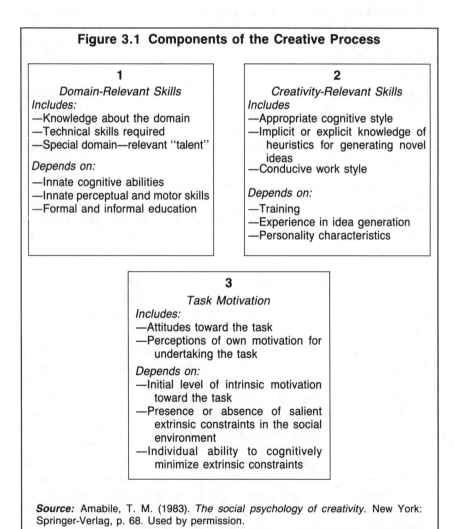

Figure 3.1 Components of the Creative Process

1
Domain-Relevant Skills
Includes:
—Knowledge about the domain
—Technical skills required
—Special domain—relevant "talent"

Depends on:
—Innate cognitive abilities
—Innate perceptual and motor skills
—Formal and informal education

2
Creativity-Relevant Skills
Includes
—Appropriate cognitive style
—Implicit or explicit knowledge of heuristics for generating novel ideas
—Conducive work style

Depends on:
—Training
—Experience in idea generation
—Personality characteristics

3
Task Motivation
Includes:
—Attitudes toward the task
—Perceptions of own motivation for undertaking the task

Depends on:
—Initial level of intrinsic motivation toward the task
—Presence or absence of salient extrinsic constraints in the social environment
—Individual ability to cognitively minimize extrinsic constraints

Source: Amabile, T. M. (1983). *The social psychology of creativity.* New York: Springer-Verlag, p. 68. Used by permission.

Domain-relevant skills are the basic building blocks of creativity. These skills reflect an individual's level of expertise and skill as related to the creative area, or domain, under investigation. Domain-relevant skills include both basic intelligence and technical skills (often referred to as "talent"). Some aspects of these skills are innate, but domain-relevant skills can be developed through education and life experience. Research suggests, for instance, that highly creative scientists seek more information and read a greater number of articles in professional journals than their less creative counterparts.[20] The more developed an individual's domain-relevants skills, the more able that individual will be to produce new ideas. For example, an experienced carpenter would be more likely to create a new woodworking technique than would an individual who had worked infrequently as a carpenter. A high level of domain-relevant skills may contribute to feelings of comfort which, in turn, enable an individual to think and act at her or his creative peak. Hockey superstar Wayne Gretzky attributes his enormous success to picturing and skating to where the puck will be and not to where it is.[21]

Creativity-relevant skills are the "something extra" in creative performance. These skills include cognitive and personal styles conducive to generating novel and useful ideas across domains. Creativity-relevant skills include independence and non-conformity, perseverance, an orientation toward risk-taking, a tolerance for ambiguity, the ability to break cognitive sets by moving readily from one problem-solving strategy to another, the use of "wide" categories in which relationships among diverse bits of information are made apparent, and the use of heuristics, or sets of rules, for generating novel ideas. To some extent, creativity-relevant skills may be innate, but these skills, like domain-relevant skills, can be enhanced through training and experience.

Task motivation refers to one's self-motivation for engaging in a particular task. Task motivation, as we learned earlier, may be primarily intrinsic or primarily extrinsic. Intrinsic motivation is the motivation to engage in an activity for its own sake—because the activity itself is involving, interesting, satisfying or personally challenging. Extrinsic motivation is motivation to engage in an activity in order to achieve some external goal or reward. Although both motivations frequently coexist, one is usually dominant. Task motivation depends on two things: the individual's basic like or dislike for the task and the presence or absence of strong motivational cues in the social environment.

According to Amabile the most creative individual will demonstrate a high level of domain-relevant skills; a high level of creativity-relevant skills; and will be intrinsically motivated to perform the task (see chapter 2). That is, the individual is knowledgeable and technically skilled, cognitively sophisticated and internally motivated to undertake the creative task.

Amabile, like Wallas and Osborn before her, views the creative process as occurring in stages. The first stage is the *problem presentation* stage. Here, an individual is presented with a problem to be solved. Task motivation plays a central role in the problem presentation stage. The intrinsically motivated problem solver will be more creative and more likely to formulate the problem than the extrinsically motivated problem solver.

The second stage in the creative process is the *preparation* stage. In this stage, the problem solver compiles necessary information and resources. Domain-relevant skills figure prominently in the preparation stage. Those with strong domain-relevant skills move more efficiently through the preparation stage than those who need further development of domain-relevant skills.

The third stage of the creative process is *idea generation*. Success in this stage depends primarily on creativity-relevant skills and task motivation. The ideas generated are more likely to be creative if the individual has a high level of creative thinking skill and if motivation is intrinsic rather than extrinsic.

The fourth, and final, stage in the creative process is *validation* of the ideas generated. In this stage, domain-relevant skills are most important as they provide a grounding for determining the appropriateness of the ideas generated. If problem solvers do not have sufficient skills and motivation to move effectively through each of the four stages of the creative process, one of the following outcomes is likely:

- a reasonable solution will not be generated
- a technically correct but mundane solution will be generated
- a bizarre, unworkable solution will be generated

Von Oech's Four Roles of the Creative Process

Creativity consultant Roger Von Oech suggests that creative thinkers need to adopt a different creative thinking role during each stage of the creative process.[22] Von Oech identifies four main roles; each embodies a different type of thinking. The roles are: the explorer, the artist, the judge and the warrior.

The Explorer. The explorer is a role for searching, looking and probing. When adopting the role of the explorer it is particularly useful to seek new directions, to pay attention to unusual patterns, and to venture off the beaten path. Playing the explorer involves taking risks. To be an explorer, a problem solver must avoid: getting stuck in the routines of day-to-day interactions, the fear of failure and over-specialization. To perform effectively as the explorer, a problem solver must be flexible, courageous and open-minded.

The Artist. The artist turns resources into ideas. When playing the role of the artist, a problem solver takes materials collected in the explorer role and transforms the data into original ideas. The artist role is designed to stimulate action and change. A problem solver playing this role should experiment with a variety of approaches and techniques. As an artist the creative thinker can change contexts, look for connections, seek comparisons, break existing rules and search for outrageous adaptations.

The Judge. The judge evaluates the merits of the ideas generated by the artist. When adopting the role of the judge, a problem solver decides what to do with an idea—implement it, modify it or discard it completely. As judge, a problem solver critically weighs the evidence and ultimately makes a decision.

The Warrior. When a problem solver carries an idea into action, she or he plays the role of the warrior. A problem solver as warrior develops a strategy, commits to achieving objectives, and implements a plan of action. The greatest deterrent to the warrior is self-doubt. In the words of Henry Ford, ''Whether you can or you can't, you're right.''[23]

According to Von Oech, the four roles of the explorer, the artist, the judge and the warrior allow for the generation and implementation of new ideas. Depending upon the role a problem solver plays, any given situation can be approached in a variety of ways which produces differing results. On a camping trip, for example, the explorer will want to do things like look for wild flowers and go hiking. The artist will make up stories about the stars or design a natural shelter to sleep under. The judge will be concerned about the weather and any dangerous animals. The warrior will be prepared to handle any situation which arises.

The four roles are not always used in the linear progression from explorer-to-artist-to-judge-to-warrior. Usually there is some shifting between roles during the creative process. Common shifts include the judge returning an idea to the artist for further development, the artist asking the explorer to generate additional data, and the warrior asking the judge to provide more detailed evaluation of an idea before implementation. In general, however, Von Oech suggests that problem solvers play the explorer role in the early stages of the creative process, the artist and judge roles in middle stages of the creative process, and the warrior role toward the end of the creative cycle.

Creativity and the Brain

Regardless which model of the creative process a problem solver chooses to follow, creativity is, first and foremost, a cognitive process. Understanding the capabilities and potential of the human brain can help to foster creative thinking.

Left Brain/Right Brain

In 1836 a French physician named Marc Dax first advanced the idea that each side of the human brain might perform different functions.[24] Dax had treated many patients who suffered brain damage caused by blows to the head. Curiously enough, those who had been struck on the left side of the brain often experienced permanent loss of speech while those hit on the right side exhibited no such problems. Dax's observations went unnoticed until a young French surgeon named Paul Broca began to research brain physiology in the late 1800s. Broca noted that the frontal area of the left side of the brain seemed to be most closely associated with speech.[25] This portion of the brain is known today as Broca's Area.

Beginning in the 1950s, a group of researchers at the California Institute of Technology began piecing together the complex connections between the left and the right brain. The research, led by Nobel Prize winner Roger Sperry, shed new light on the function of the left and right hemispheres of the brain. Sperry and his colleagues discovered that the connecting cable between the two hemispheres, known as the *corpus callosum*, acts primarily as a transmitter shuttling information back and forth between the left and right brain.[26] Each of the hemispheres operates asymmetrically with its own unique form of processing.

By studying patients who have had the connection between the left and right hemispheres severed as either a treatment for severe epilepsy or through some sort of accident, researchers have identified the differing functions of the left and right brain. The left brain (which controls the right side of the body) appears to deal mainly with language, reasoning, logical and rational thought, and linear processing. The right brain (which controls the left side of the body) appears to deal primarily with vision, intuition, visual and spatial thought, and holistic processing (see table 3.2).

Table 3.2
Left and Right Brain Processing

Left Brain	Right Brain
• Treats information serially, one piece at a time	• Treats information as a whole
• Logical, analytical thinking, calculation	• Visualization, intuitive ability
• Reading, speaking, reasoning, arithmetic	• Spatial ability, touch, musical ability, motor skills
• Center of language ability, writing	• Some language functions
• Objective, concrete thought	• Subjective, abstract thought
• Directed behavior	• Free, impulsive behavior
• Rational	• Sensuous, emotional

The impact of the left brain/right brain dichotomy on creativity has been a matter of speculation for some time. Early research suggested creativity was primarily a right brain function. Contemporary research, however, dismisses the notion that the right hemisphere *alone* is responsible for creative thought.[27] Most researchers now believe that creative functions exist in both halves of the brain. They suggest that the hemispheres work in a complementary fashion. The left hemisphere is good at detailed processing, the use of language and fine analysis. The right hemisphere is proficient in larger, broader processing, with better interpretation of vague, novel material.[28]

Robert Williams and John Stockmyer apply left brain/right brain functioning to the Wallas Stage Model discussed earlier in this chapter.[29] Williams and Stockmyer agree that both sides of the brain are involved in the creative process. During the preparation stage, the left brain acquires knowledge. In the incubation stage, the right brain begins to identify patterns while the left brain relaxes. The right brain translates the answer derived to the left brain in the illumination stage, and in the verification stage, the left brain tries out and evaluates possible solutions. Albert Einstein's development of the theory of relativity provides an example of how coordination of left and right brain functions can lead to creative insight. Einstein's work on the theory of relativity came together while he was lying on a hill one summer day. Looking at the sky with his eyes half-closed, the sun dappled through his eyelashes and fragmented into tiny sunbeams. Einstein visualized himself as a passenger holding a mirror as he rode on one of the rays of light. He determined that his image would never reach the mirror because both he and the glass would move at the speed of light. In contrast, a stationary observer could catch Einstein's reflection in a mirror as the scientist passed by. Following up on this right brain visualization, Einstein spent a decade using the left brain functions of calculation and reasoning to develop his theory.[30]

Mind Maps

The mind map, developed by creativity consultant Tony Buzan, is a method for organizing and storing information which utilizes both left and right brain processing.[31] Mind maps offer an alternative to the traditional, linear outline format. Mind maps allow individuals to organize material in a graphic form so that information and relationships can be viewed in a visual holistic pattern. This involvement of the right brain in information processing allows for greater fluidity and flexibility of thought.

The basic idea of the mind map is to imitate mental patterning in a visual representation or diagram. As such, the structure of each mind map differs from person to person. The basic format of the mind map, however, is uniform. As noted in the example in figure 3.2, the main point appears in the center of the mind map. Related ideas or concepts branch outward from the center with more important ideas nearer the center and less important ideas at the edge. Links are indicated among ideas through the use of lines, arrows and other geometric shapes. The structure of the mind map makes it easy to add, delete or restructure information without difficulty. Diagrams, color and other visual effects can be used to enhance the mind map. After an initial draft of a mind map is completed, it may be useful to reassemble the map into a more polished final product. This permits the creative process to go beyond the first idea or pattern and allows an individual to break initial mind sets.

Buzan offers the following suggestions for creating mind maps:

- Words should be printed in capitals. This will make it easier to read the mind map.
- A single word or short phrase should be used to identify ideas or concepts.
- The designer should be open and free when creating the mind map. Don't censor where information should be placed or evaluate order or organization. If something appears not to fit, it can be moved after the initial mind map has been completed.

The mind map can be used to take notes on textbooks or lectures, to review and remember information, to organize a speech or paper, to plan for the future, or to solve problems.

Figure 3.2

Mind Map of this Chapter

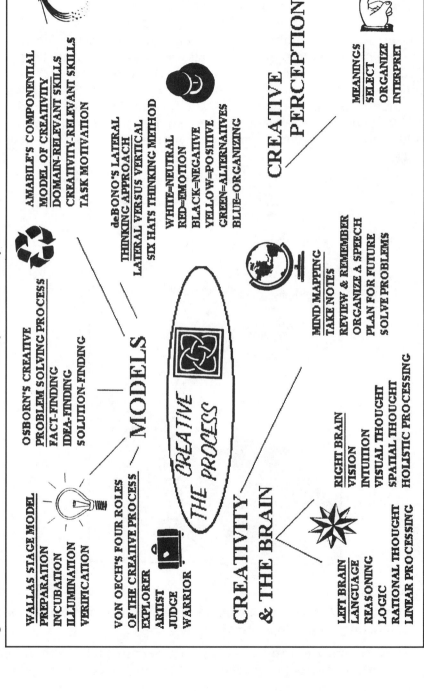

CREATIVE
THE PROCESS

MODELS

WALLAS STAGE MODEL
PREPARATION
INCUBATION
ILLUMINATION
VERIFICATION

OSBORN'S CREATIVE
PROBLEM SOLVING PROCESS
FACT-FINDING
IDEA-FINDING
SOLUTION-FINDING

VON OECH'S FOUR ROLES
OF THE CREATIVE PROCESS
EXPLORER
ARTIST
JUDGE
WARRIOR

AMABILE'S COMPONENTIAL
MODEL OF CREATIVITY
DOMAIN-RELEVANT SKILLS
CREATIVITY-RELEVANT SKILLS
TASK MOTIVATION

deBONO'S LATERAL
THINKING APPROACH
LATERAL VERSUS VERTICAL
SIX HATS THINKING METHOD
WHITE=NEUTRAL
RED=EMOTION
BLACK=NEGATIVE
YELLOW=POSITIVE
GREEN=ALTERNATIVES
BLUE=ORGANIZING

CREATIVE PERCEPTION

MEANINGS
SELECT
ORGANIZE
INTERPRET

MIND MAPPING
TAKE NOTES
REVIEW & REMEMBER
ORGANIZE A SPEECH
PLAN FOR FUTURE
SOLVE PROBLEMS

CREATIVITY & THE BRAIN

LEFT BRAIN
LANGUAGE
REASONING
LOGIC
RATIONAL THOUGHT
LINEAR PROCESSING

RIGHT BRAIN
VISION
INTUITION
VISUAL THOUGHT
SPATIAL THOUGHT
HOLISTIC PROCESSING

Creative Perception

One of the greatest inhibitors of the creative process is the tendency
to view the world in the way we believe it should operate. People
usually see what they expect to see. The process of creation,
however, often requires that we see things differently. Seeing from
a different perspective can be difficult. Look at the picture in figure
3.3. What do you see? Some may see a young woman looking away;
others may see an old woman with a large nose. Can you see them
both?

Figure 3.3

Our perceptions, or the meanings we attach to our experiences,
are generated through a three-step process.[32]

Selection. We are exposed to far more sensory stimuli than we
can possibly acknowledge. The first task in the perception

process is to select what to pay attention to and what to ignore. Factors such as the intensity of the input, repetition, familiarity and internal motivation influence our awareness. For example, if a train passes near your home every night at midnight, you will be less likely to attend to the noise of the train than you would to unexpected noises heard at the same hour.

Organization. Once we have selected information from the environment, we must arrange it in some meaningful way. You can see how the principle of organization works by looking at figure 3.4. What do you see? You can organize this picture by selecting either white or black for the background and foreground. If you create an organizational pattern in which white is in the foreground and black in the background, you will see a vase. If you reverse the organizational pattern you will see two faces. Neither image is correct nor incorrect, but the prominence of each image depends on how you organize and decode sensory input.

Figure 3.4

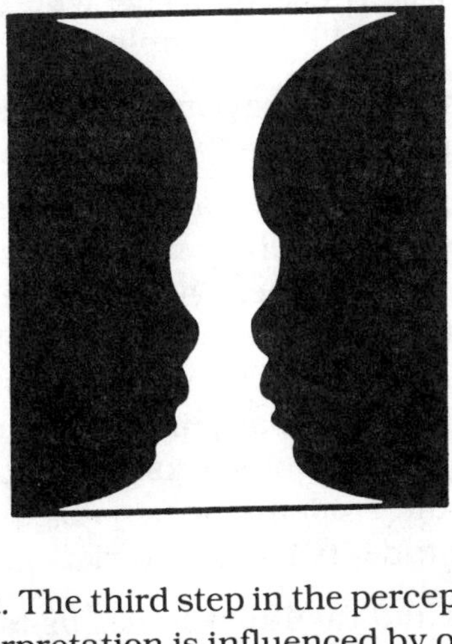

Interpretation. The third step in the perception process is interpretation. Interpretation is influenced by our past experiences, expectations, beliefs, values, knowledge, emotional states and so on. Exposure to the same sensory stimuli, therefore, does not necessarily result in the same interpretation.

Intelligence is the ability to see many points of view without going completely bonkers.

Douglas Adams

The ability to make observations from multiple perspectives is critical to thinking creatively. Creative problem solvers select multiple inputs, use a variety of organizational patterns, and generate a broad range of interpretations.

Roger Von Oech suggests playing "the fool" as a method for overcoming rigid perceptions.[33] During the Middle Ages and the Renaissance, the fool's job was to poke fun at proposals that came before the king. Through the use of humor, the fool challenged the perceptions of the king and his advisors, helping to prevent poor decisions. Playing the fool today can have the same impact. According to Von Oech:

> The fool stimulates our creative juices. Foolish ideas can jolt the mind in the same way that a splash of cold water wakes up a sleeping man. Thus, the fool forces us to think—even for just an instant—about what we think is real. Whatever assumptions we hold about the nature of things must suddenly be suspended, and the field of view greatly widened.

To practice playing the fool, try a game called "The Fools and the Rules." Take a widely accepted rule where you learn, work or live and then debunk it.[34] For example:

Rule: "Students should be penalized when they don't turn in their papers on time."

Fool: "If students turned in papers late, instructors would face less stress because they would have fewer assignments to grade at one time. They might even do a better job of grading. With more time to complete their work, students will learn more and turn in higher quality papers. Besides, many professors don't start grading papers until days or weeks after the papers are due, so why should students be penalized? Maybe we should *reward* students for late work."

Playing The Fools and the Rules forces us to consider radically different points of view and generates a variety of ideas. At the very least, challenging a rule can reveal if there is a solid foundation for having the rule in the first place. In addition to taking the role of the fool, we can broaden our perspectives and overcome rigid perceptions through travel, trying new things (foods, music, books, classes, etc.) and establishing relationships with people from diverse backgrounds.

Summing Up

In this chapter we looked at the creative process. We began by looking at models of the creative process. The Wallas Stage Model suggests that creative ideas move through four stages. The preparation stage involves clarifying and defining the problem, collecting data, looking for patterns and relationships, and considering solutions. The incubation stage provides an opportunity to put the problem on the back burner. In the illumination stage an idea, solution or new relationship emerges. In the final stage, verification, the idea is fully developed and tested.

Osborn's Creative Problem-Solving Process includes three procedures. Fact-finding involves defining the problem under investigation and preparing for problem resolution by gathering and analyzing pertinent data. Idea-finding involves developing tentative ideas using the idea-spurring question technique. Solution-finding involves the evaluation and adoption of ideas.

deBono's Lateral Thinking Approach allows an individual to break from traditional patterns of thinking. The Six Hats Thinking Method uses lateral thinking techniques to enable a problem solver to deal with one aspect of the thought process at a time. When using the Six Thinking Hats Method a problem solver wears one of the following imaginary hats: white hat (the neutral and objective hat); red hat (the emotion hat); black hat (the negative questioning hat); yellow hat (the positive questioning hat); green hat (the alternative seeking hat); blue hat (the organizing and summarizing hat).

Amabile's Componential Model of Creativity suggests the creative process is influenced by three primary components. Domain-relevant skills relate to an individual's level of expertise and skill in the creative area. Creativity-relevant skills include cognitive and personal styles that are conducive to generating novel and useful ideas. Task motivation refers to an individual's self-motivation for engaging in a particular task. The most creative individual demonstrates a high level of domain-relevant skills, a high level of creativity-relevant skills, and is intrinsically motivated to perform the creative task.

Von Oech's Four Roles of the Creative Process are the explorer, the artist, the judge and the warrior. According to Von Oech, creative thinkers need to adopt a different creative role during each stage of the creative process. The explorer searches and probes. The artist turns resources into ideas. The judge evaluates ideas. The warrior carries ideas into action.

Regardless which model of the creative process a problem solver chooses to follow, creativity is, first and foremost, a cognitive process. The human brain has two hemispheres. The left brain appears to deal mainly with language, reasoning, logical and rational thought, and linear processing. The right brain appears to deal primarily with vision, intuition, visual and spatial thought, and holistic processing. Both the left and right brain are important to the creative process. A creative technique that involves both hemispheres of the brain is the mind map. Mind maps allow individuals to organize material in a graphic manner so information and patterns can be viewed in a holistic form.

We concluded this chapter by looking at perception. Perceptions are the meanings attached to experiences and are generated through a three-step process. First, sensory stimuli are selected. Next, information selected is organized into meaningful patterns. Finally, sensory stimuli are interpreted based upon past experiences, expectations, beliefs, values, knowledge, emotional states and other personal factors. The ability to make observations from multiple perspectives is critical to creative thinking. One strategy for overcoming rigid perceptions is The Fools and the Rules strategy developed by Von Oech.

Application Exercises

1. Analyze how you solved a recent problem. Try to determine if your creative activities mirrored the stages identified by Wallas. Did you experience each stage? Which stage was most difficult for you? Were you more creative after periods of incubation? How can you increase your flow of creative ideas in the future? Report your findings.

2. Get into a group and discuss the advantages and disadvantages of lateral and vertical thinking. Identify the types of problems which would be best solved using each type of thought. Which type of thinking do group members rely on most?

3. Use lateral thinking techniques to try to solve the following problems:
   a) Look at the nine dots drawn on the next page. The problem is to connect all of them by using only four straight lines and never retracing a line or removing your pen or pencil from the paper as you draw.

b) In the following line of letters, cross out six letters so that the remaining letters, without altering their sequence, will spell a familiar English word.

B S I I C X L E Y T C T E L R S E

4. Try to persuade other members of a group to use the Six Thinking Hats Method to solve a problem. Discuss how using this method affected typical patterns of group interaction. Did the group come to a more creative resolution to the problem?

5. Use the mind map technique to take notes in class. Compare your mind map with those of others in the class. Do you find the mapping technique useful? Easier or more difficult than traditional notetaking?

6. Play The Fools and the Rules in a volunteer or work group. What new ideas are generated? Should any of the rules you fool with be discarded or changed? Which ones appear to be justified?

Solutions:

a)

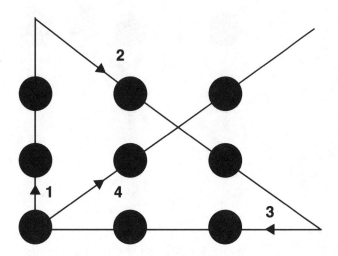

b) Remove S-I-X L-E-T-T-E-R-S to spell B-I-C-Y-C-L-E

Endnotes

[1] For a new TV show to go on, it's gotta have legs. (1993, October 25). *Colorado Springs Gazette Telegraph*, p. D3.

[2] Bohm, D., & Peat, F.D. (1987). *Science, order, and creativity*. New York: Bantam Books, p. 18.

[3] Wallas, G. (1926). *The art of thought*. New York: Harcourt.

[4] Russell, P., & Evans, R. (1992). *The creative manager*. San Francisco: Jossey-Bass, p. 52.

[5] Bransford, J. D., & Stein, B. S. (1984). *The ideal problem* solver. New York: W. H. Freeman, p. 103.

[6] Dacey, J. S. (1989). *Fundamentals of creative thinking*. New York: Lexington Books, p. 67.

Madigan, C. O., & Elwood, A. (1983). *Brainstorms and thunderbolts*. New York: Macmillan, pp. 2–4.

[7] Russell & Evans, pp. 58–59.

[8] Armbruster, B. B. (1989). Metacognition in creativity. In J. A. Glover, R. R. Ronning, & C. R. Reynolds (Eds.), *Handbook of creativity* (pp. 177–182). New York: Plenum Press.

[9] Osborn, A. F. (1963). *Applied imagination* (3rd ed.). New York: Charles Scribner's Sons.

[10] Osborn, pp. 86–87.

[11] Osborn, p. 273.

[12] Osborn, pp. 286–287.

[13] Madigan & Elwood, pp. 239–244.

[14] deBono, E. (1970) *Lateral thinking*. New York: Harper & Row, p. 9.

[15] deBono, *Lateral thinking*, pp. 39–45.

[16] Madigan & Elwood, pp. 30–31.

[17] deBono, E. (1985). *Six thinking hats*. Boston: Little, Brown, and Company.

deBono, E. (1992). *Serious creativity*. New York: HarperCollins.

[18] deBono, E. (1993). *Six action shoes*. New York: HarperBusiness, p. 3.

[19] Amabile, T. M. (1983). *The social psychology of creativity*. New York: Springer-Verlag.

Amabile, T. M., & Tighe, E. (1993). Questions of creativity. In J. Brockman (Ed.). *Creativity* (pp. 7–27). New York: Touchstone.

[20] See, for example:

Chambers, J. A. (1964). Relating personality and biographical factors to scientific creativity. *Psychological Monographs, 78*, 7.

Kasperson, C. (1978). An analysis of the relationship between information source and creativity in engineers and scientists. *Human Communication Research, 4*, 113–119.

[21] Geis, G. T. (1988). Making companies creative: An organizational psychology of creativity. In R. L. Kuhn (Ed.). *Handbook for creative and innovative managers* (pp. 25–34). New York: McGraw-Hill.

[22] Von Oech, R. (1986). *A kick in the seat of the pants*. New York: Harper & Row.

[23] Von Oech, p. 134.

[24] Springer, S. P., & Deutsch, G. (1985). *Left brain, right brain*. New York: W. H. Freeman.

[25] Critchley, M. (1970). *Aphasiology and other aspects of language*. London: Edward Arnold.

[26] See, for example:

Myers, R. E., & Sperry, R. W. (1958). Interhemispheric communication through the corpus callosum: Mnemonic carry-over between the hemispheres. *Archives of Neurology and Psychiatry, 80*, 298–303.

Sperry, R. W. (1968). Hemispheric disconnection and unity in conscious awareness. *American Psychologist, 23*, 723–733.

[27] See, for example:

Hines, T. (1991). The myth of right hemisphere creativity. *Journal of Creative Behavior, 25*, 223–227.

[28] Fabian, J. (1990). *Creative thinking and problem solving*. Chelsea, MI: Lewis.

[29] Wiliams, R. H., & Stockmyer, J. (1987). *Unleashing the right side of the brain*. Lexington, MA: Stephen Greene Press, pp. 18–21.

[30] Hunt, M. (1982). *The universe within: A new science explores the human mind*. New York: Simon and Schuster.

[31] Buzan, T. (1988). *Make the most of your mind*. London: Pan Books.

Buzan, T. (1983). *Use both sides of your brain*. New York: E. P. Dutton.

[32] Adler, R. B., & Towne, N. (1993). *Looking out, looking in* (7th ed.). Fort Worth: Holt, Rinehart and Winston.

[33] Von Oech, R. (1990). *A whack on the side of the head*. New York: Warner Books.

[34] Von Oech, *A whack on the side of the head*, pp. 114–116.

Quotations

Russell, P., & Evans, R. (1992). *The creative manager*. San Francisco, Jossey-Bass.

Von Oech, R. (1986). *A kick in the seat of the pants*. New York: Harper & Row.

Wujec, T. (1988). *Pumping ions*. Toronto: Doubleday.

4 | **Creativity and Language**

Symbolization is what makes human beings "human." How well we are able to perceive, attend, and express thoughts is dependent upon a variety of symbol systems like pictures, gestures, music, and marks. Any human psychology that does not study symbols is bankrupt.

Howard Gardner

PREVIEW

► Words and Thought
► Creative Word Tools
    Asking Provocative Questions
    Harnessing the Power of Metaphor
► Semantic Traps
► Alternative Intelligences/Alternative Languages
► Summing Up
► Application Exercises

In chapter 1 we defined creativity as a special form of human or symbolic communication. In this chapter we'll take a closer look at the relationship between symbols and creative thinking. We will examine how language shapes our thoughts, highlight some important word tools, identify semantic barriers to creativity, and describe other symbol systems that play an important role in creating.

Words and Thought

Discussions of the relationship between words and thought sometimes resemble the debate over the question: "What came first, the chicken or the egg?" On one side of the debate are those who contend that words come before thought. They note that it is impossible to develop concepts or to categorize items without using words to identify and organize these ideas and categories. On the other side are those who argue that thoughts come before words. We first must be able to think in abstract terms, they assert, before we need words to label the products of our thought processes.[1]

One way to resolve the word-thought debate is to take a third position—that language and cognition both play a critical role in the development of higher mental processes. To describe how words and thought interact to shape mental development, we'll rely on the insights of Russian psychologist Lev Vygotsky.[2] (See the Creative Profile on page 95 for more information on this influential social scientist.) Vygotsky, Alexander Luria and others believe that thinking and verbal abilities begin on separate tracks at birth. Following a period of preintellectual and prelinguistic development, these tracks meet at about age two when "thought becomes verbal and speech becomes rational."[3] The convergence of language and cognition marks the most important moment in human intellectual development. At this point a child no longer merely reacts to information acquired through the senses, but can begin to master his or her environment through the use of symbols. Even after words and thought come together, however, they are not identical. Not only can thoughts be expressed in more than one way, but sometimes we find ourselves at "a loss for words" when we want to communicate an idea.

Children initially acquire words and sentences in order to communicate with others and to solve problems. They use language to produce immediate effects like getting mom or dad to feed them or pick them up. In this social speech, words refer to specific objects in the immediate environment and their meaning is highly dependent on the context in which they are used. When children begin to analyze problems and plan actions on their own by talking to themselves, they then engage in egocentric or self-centered speech. By age seven such egocentric talk "goes underground" to become silent mental or inner speech. Words in inner speech stand in the place of or represent other things, which makes conceptualization possible. For example, in a child's social speech the word "cup" may refer to only one particular item in the family kitchen. In inner speech the same label represents a whole category of drinking utensils which appear in many different settings—in the kitchen or bath, at school and so on.

Once it develops, inner speech becomes the "principal mechanism of thought," coming into play whenever we "think about something, plan or solve problems in our mind, recall books read or conversations heard, read and write silently."[4] Vygotsky and his colleagues suggest that important clues to the structure of inner speech can be found by examining egocentric talk. In its earliest stages egocentric speech resembles social speech, consisting of full sentences complete with subjects, nouns and objects. As a child matures or when difficulties arise, egocentric speech becomes fragmented and disjointed as the following example illustrates:

> At first, their planning speech [when faced with a problem] has a completely expanded and overt character ("But the paper is slipping, what can I do so it doesn't slip? Where can I get a thumb tack? Maybe I should lick the paper and wet it so that it won't slip?"). Then this speech gradually undergoes a fundamental change. It becomes abbreviated and fragmentary. What remains, in an overt whispered form, are mere fragments of the former complete phrases ("but the paper . . . it's slipping . . . what can I do? . . . where can I get a tack? . . ."). Later this speech becomes even more abbreviated ("paper, tack, how can I?")[5]

Inner speech shares the short, fragmented character of the latter stages of egocentric talk.[6] Since we already know the subject or theme of the message when we talk to ourselves, we don't need to speak in full sentences but abbreviate messages. When the light turns green at a cross walk, for example, we substitute the message "Cross" for a longer message like "I should cross the street now." In the same way, we take shortcuts when reasoning to ourselves. Seldom do we think through every step of a problem; instead, we condense our thought processes into a few key words and use these terms to store our ideas in memory. Words in inner speech become "saturated" with meaning in that they have many more interpretations for us than can be expressed to others. Take the word "mother," for instance. You might use the word in external speech to identify the individual who will be visiting you next week. In inner speech the same term conjures up a vast number of meanings—nurturer, disciplinarian, friend, helper, etc.

The abbreviated structure of inner speech makes it ideal for storing and retrieving information, analyzing, generalizing, associating and performing other creative problem solving functions at high speeds. However, you face several translation tasks as you develop ideas generated by your inner speech and try to communicate them to others.[7] To begin, you must unfold or unpack concepts which are encapsulated in words or sentence fragments. Imagine that you've been asked to give a five-minute presentation in class. In searching for a topic for your speech, you may identify the words "stage fright." This internal message specifies a subject, but the idea must be developed before you can give your talk. Next you must translate your original abbreviated self-talk into a form that is understandable to others. Your presentation on stage fright will have to follow a logical sequence and be delivered in full sentences. If you're writing a paper on stage fright in addition to delivering a speech, you face a third and even more formidable translation task. You can't rely on inflection and other vocal cues when communicating in writing and won't receive any immediate feedback. You must also pay attention to grammar, punctuation and sentence structure. As a result, your written message will be longer and more complex than your spoken one. (For a discussion of creative written communication, see chapter 7.)

Creative Word Tools

Since language forms the basis for our higher mental processes, it's not surprising that words are our most important creative problem solving tools. Two essential word tools are questions and metaphors. If you know how to ask provocative questions and channel the power of metaphors, you'll be more likely to reach creative solutions.

Asking Provocative Questions

Questions serve many different functions during the creative process. They reveal gaps in current knowledge, challenge

Creative Profile: A Most Unlikely Genius

If the story of Lev Vygotsky's life were written as a script for a feature film, it probably would be rejected as too unrealistic even by Hollywood standards. However, in the case of the man who is now known as the Father of Soviet Psychology, truth is indeed stranger than fiction.

Lev Vygotsky was born into a middle class Jewish family in western Russia in 1896. Although he was an outstanding student in secondary school, quotas on the number of Jews who could earn university degrees almost prevented him from enrolling in college. Fortunately, his name was drawn by lot from a pool of applicants and he was admitted into Moscow University. There he demonstrated the broad range of interests that was to mark his entire life. A law major, he also took history and philosophy classes at an alternative university founded by students and faculty who opposed the tsar. In addition, he pursued an interest in the theater.

Vygotsky moved back to his hometown after earning his law degree and began teaching literature at a provincial school and at a teachers' college. During this time he contracted tuberculosis, the disease that would later end his life. In spite of his illness and constant food shortages brought on by the Communist Revolution and Russian civil wars, Vygotsky taught his first lectures in psychology, read widely in such areas as linguistics and philosophy, and completed work on a Ph.D. dissertation on the psychology of art.

1924 marked the beginning of the second period of Vygotsky's life. That year he delivered his first paper (without notes) at a psychology conference. Observers report that his speech had an "electrifying effect" on the audience. Lev was invited to become a research fellow at the Moscow Institute following his presentation. There he, Alexander Luria and others set out to develop a new psychology which would help solve the problems of the newly formed Soviet Union. As part of this effort, Vygotsky studied children who were hearing impaired and learning disabled. He lectured, researched and wrote between bouts of tuberculosis. By the time Lev died in 1934 (only ten years after he had started his full-time work in psychology), he had authored approximately 180 articles and books.

Since the 1970s, Vygotsky's ideas on language and thought, inner speech and the role that adults play in child development have become increasingly popular among communication scholars, educators, psychologists and others in the United states. Some larger universities offer classes based on his theories. Vygotsky's popularity in capitalist America is ironic given the fact he was an ardent Communist who often cited Marx, Engels and Hegel in his writings.

Some would argue that Vygotsky's creative success was due to his intellectual brilliance. Yet, while Vygotsky was clearly one of this century's brightest minds, there are three other factors that help account for his creative influence. First, he worked at a time of great social upheaval in Russia. Vygotsky helped fill the vacuum created when the new Communist regime rejected the past, including traditional ways of studying psychology. Second, Vygotsky worked at a frantic pace because he was committed to making the new Soviet state succeed and knew that his time on earth was short. His daughter reports, for example, that he sometimes began writing at 2:00 A.M. after his other duties were completed. Third, his diverse intellectual background allowed him to generate new insights that those who had only studied psychology were unable to offer. Vygotsky (who had no formal training in psychology) was able to take ideas from such fields as the comparative study of cultures, history, philosophy, and literary analysis and weave them into a new approach to psychological study.

Discussion Questions

1. How much was Lev Vygotsky a product of his times? Do you think he would have been as productive and influential had he been born in, say, contemporary America?

2. Would Vygotsky have emerged as the Father of Soviet Psychology if he had studied psychology as a university student? How important was broad academic training to his success? How important is it to ours?

3. In what ways does society encourage specialization and discourage the integration of academic disciplines, professions and ideas? What steps can be taken to reverse the pressures to specialize?

Sources:

Wertsch, J. V. (1985). *Vygotsky and the social formation of mind.* Cambridge: Harvard University Press.

Kozulin, A. (1986). Vygotsky in context. In L. Vygotsky (A. Kozulin, Trans.) *Thought and language* (pp. xi–lvi). Cambridge: MIT Press.

Wertsch, J. V. (1985). *Culture, communication and cognition: Vygotskian perspectives.* Cambridge: Cambridge University Press.

assumptions, spark the search for new ideas and additional information, foster different perspectives and so forth.[8] Our creative success rests on the quality of the questions we ask. Few of us, however, receive any formal training in question asking, perhaps because educators and others assume that we'll learn to formulate effective questions as part of the educational process. Sadly, the typical American classroom may be one of the worst places to sharpen our questioning skills. Of all questions asked by teachers and textbooks, 60–90 percent test knowledge and recall of subject matter. During classroom discussions, instructors only wait an average of 1–3 seconds for responses and often answer their own questions. Students generally take the role of passive learners, asking only a few questions designed to clarify what instructors have said.[9]

Learning how to classify questions is the key to improving the quality of the questions we pose.[10] Classification helps us differentiate between questions that test current knowledge and those that require higher levels of thought. Armed with this knowledge, we are more likely to formulate "provocative" questions that encourage divergent thinking.[11] The most popular question classification system is Bloom's Taxonomy of Educational Objectives.[12] The taxonomy, which was developed by a group of college examiners and named after one of its authors, is both a goal-setting tool and an assessment instrument. Teachers, administrators and students set learning goals using this system and then formulate questions and assignments to determine if they've reached their objectives. The higher the level on the taxonomy, the more complex the desired behavior and the more demanding the question or assignment. The six levels of Bloom's Taxonomy are:

1. *Knowledge*: recalling or recognizing information, including terminology, facts, rules or conventions, trends and sequences, classification, criteria, methodology, principles and theories.

2. *Comprehension*: understanding, grasping the meaning of information. Comprehension involves either a) translating a communication into another form (i.e. stating the problem in your own words), b) interpretation (identifying and understanding major ideas and their relationships), or c) extrapolation (making predictions and estimates, drawing implications, determining consequences).

3. *Application*: application or transfer of learning (skills, knowledge, generalizations, values, principles) to new situations.

4. *Analysis*: breaking down a communication into its parts, determining how the parts are related, identifying organizational principles.

5. *Synthesis*: putting elements together in a way that is new to the learner in the form of an original message, a new plan or a set of abstract relationships.

6. *Evaluation*: making judgments based on criteria and standards. Judgments can be based on internal evidence, like the logical accuracy and consistency of a message, or on such external criteria as how one message compares to other similar messages.

Even though synthesis is the only category in Bloom's Taxonomy that emphasizes originality, all six levels of behavior play an important role in creativity. Creative problem solvers must know and comprehend existing facts, apply old principles to new situations, analyze problems, develop unique products, and critically evaluate their creative efforts. Thanks to our classroom experiences, most of us know how to formulate knowledge and comprehension questions. We're not so skilled at writing queries which stimulate more complex thinking. For this reason, you may want to take a few minutes to sharpen your questioning skills by generating a list of application, analysis, synthesis and evaluation items based on material presented in this chapter. Start each question with descriptors taken from the appropriate category in table 4.1. A related exercise is found in Application Exercise 2, page 113.

Table 4.1

Learner Outcomes: Bloom's Taxonomy of Educational Objectives

Cognitive Domain Levels and Learner Outcomes

Knowledge	defines, repeats, lists, names, labels, asks, observes, memorizes, records, recalls, fills in, listens, identifies, matches, recites, selects, draws
Comprehensive	restates, describes, explains, tells, identifies, discusses, recognizes, reviews, expresses, locates, reports, estimates, distinguishes, paraphrases, documents, defends, generalizes
Application	changes, computes, demonstrates, shows, operates, uses, solves, sequences, tests, classifies, translates, employs, constructs, dramatizes, illustrates, draws, interprets, manipulates, writes
Analysis	dissects, distinguishes, differentiates, calculates, tests, contrasts, debates, solves, surveys, appraises, experiments, diagrams, inventories, relates, maps, categorizes, subdivides, defends
Synthesis	composes, proposes, formulates, sets up, assembles, constructs, manages, invents, produces, hypothesizes, plans, designs, creates, organizes, prepares, speculates
Evaluation	compares, concludes, contrasts, criticizes, justifies, supports, states, appraises, discriminates, summarizes, recommends, rates, decides, selects

---

Source: From Freiberg, H. J., & Driscoll, A., *Universal Teaching Strategies.* Copyright © 1992 by Allyn and Bacon. Reprinted by permission.

So far we've focused on writing provocative questions of our own. However, using prewritten or standardized questions can also make us more creative. Sets of questions aimed at boosting the flow of original ideas can be found in many popular books on creativity. One question checklist designed to improve existing products was developed by John E. Arnold of the Massachusetts Institute of Technology.[13] Arnold's Area-thinking Method focuses attention on four areas or features—functions (uses), performance, costs and sales.

- Can we increase the *function*? Can we make the product do more things?

- Can we get a *higher performance level*? Make the product last longer? More reliable? More accurate? Safer? More convenient to use? Easier to repair and maintain?

- Can we lower the *cost*? Eliminate excess parts? Substitute cheaper materials? Design to reduce hand labor or for complete automation?

- Can we increase the *saleability*? Improve the appearance of the product? Improve the package? Improve its point of sale?

The usefulness of prewritten or standardized questions extends beyond their application to immediate problems. For instance, even if an organization is successful, a questioning attitude can keep its members from overlooking potential problems and missing valuable opportunities. Creativity consultant Roger von Oech suggests that asking questions is one way to give ourselves a "kick in the seat of the pants" or a "whack on the side of the head" that can keep us from becoming complacent.[14] He recommends asking "What if?" to encourage anticipatory thinking which is essential to organizational survival. Simply start with "What if?" and then fill in the rest of the question with some situation that doesn't exist. Picture the impact the following changes would have on your college's faculty, facilities, registration procedures, and programs:

What if American students could earn their bachelors' degrees in three years instead of four?

What if the student body doubled in size? What if it shrunk by half?

What if all student loan programs were ended?

What if college educations were provided free of charge?

What if students could earn their degrees without leaving home?

Although many of the ideas generated by "what-iffing" will be impractical, von Oech suggests that these fanciful ideas can be stepping stones to more useful ones. Earning a degree at home might not be feasible in the foreseeable future. Yet, by asking this what-if question, your school might decide to use television, computers and other technologies to help students take more courses off campus.

Harnessing the Power of Metaphor

Metaphors are creative verbal expressions which connect two elements (objects, emotions, experiences, situations) normally considered to be different from each other. Most people under-estimate the importance of metaphors, treating them as just another form of flowery speech. In actuality, metaphors are powerful language tools which help us interpret or make sense of the world, shape our actions, and enable us to share our insights with others.[15]

The metaphors we adopt shape or frame our perspectives on situations and problems. Their interpretive power is particularly apparent when we're faced with novel events. Take the first year of college, for example. Understanding and surviving the freshman experience is much easier if we link it to an athletic contest, the family or some other familiar context. One group of researchers surveyed university and small college students and found that common metaphors for the freshman year describe:

- being in a new environment ("a breath of fresh air," "a new chapter");
- having a higher or lower status (a "right or privilege," "back to square one");
- feeling in control or powerless (the "opening ceremony for the learning process," being "a child at the bottom of a hill trying to make it to the top");
- being engaged with others or disengaged ("feel like part of something big," "being the new kid on the block");
- feeling satisfied or dissatisfied ("an interesting window for the world," "a big slumber party where you don't know anyone and have to share a bathroom").[16]

By guiding our perspectives of both new and familiar situations, metaphors control our actions. They act as self-fulfilling prophecies because they highlight the similarities between two experiences and we then behave in ways that bring these similarities to pass.[17] Consider the case of the quiet freshman woman who thinks that she is the "new kid on the block." She believes that other residents on her floor (like unfriendly neighborhood children) are deliberately excluding her when they don't invite her to go with them on social outings. She then withdraws further, making it even less likely that she'll be invited along the next time her dorm neighbors go out.

In addition to directing thoughts and actions, metaphors play a critical role in the communication process. They are the best devices to use when describing abstract concepts and expressing emotions.[18] To illustrate this point, pause a moment and write a short description of love using only literal language. Your definition probably sounds like a dictionary entry ("Love is a high degree of physical, social, and emotional attraction between two human beings. . . .") and may not capture what love means to you. Compare your literal definition of love with the metaphorical definition provided in the song "The Rose" which compares love to a river, a razor that cuts the soul, a hunger, and finally, a seed that flowers as a rose in the spring.[19]

Much of the communicative force of metaphors comes from the fact that they link the functions of the verbal/analytical left brain and the intuitive right brain (see chapter 3). Metaphors blend both reason and imagination, logic and images. As a consequence, they frequently have a strong, lasting impact on listeners. Over a quarter of a century has passed since Martin Luther King delivered his "I Have a Dream" speech. Yet, we're still stirred by this message of social justice based on King's metaphoric dream for America. Educational researchers report that combining verbal facts with visual images through metaphor increases information retention and encourages students to explore concepts on their own.[20]

> It is as though the ability to comprehend experience through metaphor were a sense, like seeing or touching or hearing, with metaphors providing the only ways to perceive and experience much of the world. Metaphor is as much a part of our functioning as our sense of touch, and as precious.
>
> George Lakoff and Mark Johnson

Just because metaphors are powerful tools does not mean that they always promote creative thinking. The self-fulfilling prophecy of the lonely freshman is one example. If you can't come up with a creative solution, it may be that you are viewing the problem through the wrong metaphor. Treating conflict as a form of war, for instance, often escalates disputes rather than resolving them. Like opposing armies, parties guided by this metaphor attack each other while defending their positions. In the end they create a hostile environment that makes it almost impossible to find a mutually satisfying solution.

The challenge is to channel the power of metaphors for productive ends. Harnessing this power requires that we recognize current metaphors while building effective metaphors of our own. Paying close attention to descriptions of problems and situations is the easiest way to identify prevailing metaphors. Speakers may make direct connections ("argument is war") or reflect metaphors through their verbs and adjectives ("he *shot down* my arguments," "your claims are *indefensible*").[21] Once identified, unproductive metaphors can either be modified or discarded in favor of more useful images. The notion that conflict is war, for example, can be replaced with a more collaborative metaphor (i.e. conflict is a dance) which encourages parties to listen to each other and to work together.[22]

Rhetorician Wayne Booth offers five suggestions for judging the effectiveness of metaphors as communication instruments. These guidelines can be used when evaluating existing metaphors or the ones that we generate. Good metaphors, according to Booth, are active (lively, forceful), concise (convey a great deal of information in a few words), appropriate to the task at hand (neither too grand or trivial), suitable for the audience, and build or sustain the credibility of the speaker.[23] Nature can serve as a rich source of inspiration if you're searching for the appropriate image. Some of history's most important creative discoveries have been based on metaphors drawn from the natural world. Darwin compared evolution to a branching tree and, as we saw in chapter 3, Kekule noticed similarities between atoms and snakes while Einstein explained relativity using the image of riding on a beam of light.

Semantic Traps

As we've seen, verbal symbols make abstract or conceptual thinking possible and serve as our most important problem-solving tools. Yet, words can also block the creative process. To explain this apparent contradiction, we'll rely on the insights of general semanticists, language specialists who use the metaphor of maps and territories to model the relationship between words and reality.[24] General semanticists believe that words help us picture reality in much the same way that maps serve as guides to territories. Both territory maps and word maps are abstract or incomplete because they leave out details. In addition, both are self-reflexive. We can make a map of a map of a map and use language to talk about language, think about our thinking and so on.

Semantic barriers to creativity spring up whenever communicators lose sight of the relationship between words and reality. Fortunately, there are some steps we can take to avoid these traps. Seven common symbolic blocks and some corrective strategies are described below.

1. *Fact/Inference/Judgment Confusion.* The first semantic barrier is confusing facts (which can be tested or verified against reality) with inferences (predictions based on current facts) and statements of judgment (opinions or conclusions).[25] Noting that "new home sales are down" is a fact which can be verified by checking sales figures. Arguing that "the sales decline signals the start of a recession" is an inference. Concluding that "homes are too expensive" is a statement of judgment which is based on whatever the speaker defines as high prices.

Creativity would be impossible without inferences and judgments. Creators must make predictions about the future based on what they already know and evaluate the products of their efforts. However, confusing these statements with facts is dangerous because inferences and judgments always carry an element of risk. What a creator accepts as a fact could really be an inference or judgment that could be wrong. Here are some notable examples of "facts" which turned out to be misguided predictions and opinions:[26]

- "It's too early for a Polish Pope." (Pope John Paul II, two days before his selection to the Papacy)
- "Nothing has come along that can beat the horse and buggy." (Chauncey Depew, a businessman who decided not to invest in Henry Ford's automobile company)
- "Man won't fly for a thousand years." (Wilbur Wright speaking to his brother Orville after one of their flying experiments failed)
- "I cannot imagine any condition which could cause this ship to flounder. I cannot conceive of any vital disaster happening to this vessel. Modern shipbuilding has gone beyond that." (E. J. Smith, Captain of the Titanic)
- "That is the biggest fool thing we have ever done. . . . The bomb will never go off, and I speak as an expert in explosives." (Admiral William D. Leahy speaking to President Truman on atomic weapons)

- "Can't act. Can't sing. Slightly bald. Can dance a little." (Studio talent scout's comments after Fred Astaire's first screen test)
- "Rock 'n' roll is phony and false, and sung, written and played for the most part by cretinous goons." (Frank Sinatra, 1977)

Correctives: Learn to distinguish between facts and nonfactual statements. State inferences and judgments tentatively, introducing them with such phrases as "in my opinion," "it could be" or "I think."[27] Working in a group is an excellent way to guard against faulty inferences and judgments. Groups generally make superior decisions because members challenge each others' assumptions.

2. ***Polarization.*** Language encourages us to describe the world in either/or terms or opposites. To illustrate how we tend to talk in extremes, take the following test. Write down the word that is the opposite of each of the following terms: "rich," "happy," "hot," "smart," "tall." Now record the word that represents a position between these two extremes. Chances are, identifying the intermediate word was more difficult than coming up with the opposite term.

Polarized language encourages rigid rather than divergent thinking. Evidence of how polarization undermines creativity can be found in the political arena. The nation is divided into conservatives or liberals, prochoicers or prolifers, environmentalists or timber interests, hawks or doves. As long as political interest groups think in opposites, they're not likely to work together to find creative solutions to such problems as health care reform, reducing the national debt, abortion, forest protection, or downsizing the military.

Correctives: The key to correcting either/or thinking is to focus on probabilities or degrees rather than on exclusive categories. Use quantifying terms ("most," "generally," "seldom," "average," "fairly," "medium") and remember that it is possible to be neither a conservative nor a liberal; neither an environmentalist nor a timber supporter.[28]

3. ***Allness attitudes.*** Few of us appreciate know-it-alls, those individuals who claim to be the ultimate authority on every topic. Yet, we often sound like know-it-alls ourselves when we make such assertions as "price is *always* more important than quality" or "you *never* do your share of the housework." Allness statements provoke defensive reactions ("What do you mean, I never do my share of the housework!") and signal that we're not open to new ideas.

Correctives: Recognizing the limitations of our knowledge is the most important corrective to allness attitudes. Statements that include the words "absolutely," "never," "all," "entirely" and "every" suggest that we harbor allness beliefs on certain issues. General semanticists tack on the phrase "et cetera" (etc.) at the end of sentences to remind themselves that no statement captures everything about a subject and that there is always much more to learn.

4. **Indiscrimination.** The process of classifying or abstracting is based on identifying what members of a category (plants, animals, students, instructors, rappers, athletes, farmers) have in common. Focusing on similarities blinds speakers to the fact that, more often than not, there are important differences among items with the same label. For instance, survival in the wild can depend on distinguishing between organisms within the same classification. Hikers and campers must be able to tell the difference between species of "snakes" (poisonous or nonpoisonous) and types of "fungi" (edible mushrooms or deadly toadstools).

> Once we begin to look for differences instead of similarities, it is practically impossible . . . not to get new ideas. For the habit of asking "How do these things differ?" or "How might this be different?" is one of the basic techniques of originality or creativeness.
>
> Wendell Johnson

Indiscrimination can make communicators less sensitive to the need for creative ideas. Consider the case of university administrators who oversee campus counseling services. They're not likely to develop new counseling programs if they believe that all students have similar problems which are being addressed by existing services. Motivation for starting new programs comes from recognizing that different students (minorities, parents of small children, victims of sexual abuse, drug users) have different needs.

Indiscrimination also cuts creators off from the resources they need for creative problem solving. Some supervisors, for example, believe that all blue collar workers are the same. According to these managers, production workers are only interested in earning their paychecks by doing as little work as possible. Because they believe that assembly line workers don't care about quality or cutting expenses, they don't ask these employees (the people who know the most about building the product) for their ideas.

Correctives: Remember that no two things—animals, trees, Republicans, Democrats, librarians or professors—are identical. Try indexing to keep from forgetting this principle. Make a mental note that members of a category are **not** identical to one another ("Cat$_1$ is not Cat$_2$"; "Communication Major$_3$ is not Communication Major$_4$").

5. ***Static Evaluation.*** Change is a fact of life. Cartographers recognize the inevitability of change by continually updating their atlases, state maps, globes and other guides. Regrettably, communicators are not as faithful in updating their word maps. Symbols for colleges, countries, people, cities, teams and organizations are static even though the realities they represent are dynamic. Compare who you are now to who you were five years ago. Although you probably have the same name or label today as you did back then, you're probably a very different person.

Forgetting that reality is dynamic tempts us to rest on past achievements instead of putting our energies into generating creative solutions. If we don't think we need to change or can change, we won't take steps to overcome our weaknesses as individuals (see the Creative Dilemma on page 108) or as organizations (see chapter 6).

Correctives: Dating statements is a reminder that people, objects and organizations are always changing. Roommate$_{1993}$ is not Roommate$_{1994}$ and College$_{1985}$ is not the same as College$_{1995}$. Be cautious about using forms of the verb "to be" that suggest that people or situations can't be altered. Instead, employ operational terms which focus on behaviors or situational elements that can be modified. Claiming that your boss "is insensitive," for example, implies that she will remain the same no matter what you do. Stating that "she made me angry because she forgot to give me credit for helping on the project" identifies an offensive behavior that you can bring to her attention in order to improve your working relationship.

6. ***Bypassing.*** This semantic barrier to creativity is based on the faulty assumption that words have the same meanings for everyone. When communicators fall into this trap, they talk past one another.[29] One form of bypassing is using different words to refer to the same thing, such as when colleges use different course titles for the same course content. Variation in course names can force some transfer students into retaking courses they have taken before. A second form of bypassing is using the same word to mean two different things. The following incident illustrates how this type of bypassing can have disastrous consequences:

A motorist was driving on the Merritt Parkway outside New York City when his engine stalled. He quickly determined that his battery was dead and managed to stop another driver who consented to push his car to get it started.

"My car has an automatic transmission," he explained, "so you'll have to get up to 30 to 35 miles per hour to get me started."

The second motorist nodded and walked back to the car. The first motorist climbed into his own car and waited for the Good Samaritan to pull up behind him. He waited—and waited. Finally, he turned around to see what was wrong.

There was the Good Samaritan—coming at his car at 30 to 35 miles per hour!

The damage to his car amounted to $2,400.[30]

Bypassing misleads speakers into believing that they are in agreement when they aren't or that they disagree when in fact they concur. Dating partners who end their romantic relationship with the statement "let's be friends" illustrate the problem of false agreement. These ex-lovers may believe that they agree on the new definition of their relationship. However, to one party being "friends" means keeping in touch on a regular basis. To the other, being "friends" means that he or she doesn't want to see the other person again! False disagreement can also generate conflicts. Parents may share the same philosophy of discipline but think they disagree about childrearing because they describe their parenting styles in different words ("strict" vs. "consistent").

Bypassing subverts collaborative problem solving. In order to work together effectively, relational partners and group members must develop a shared definition of problems and goals. If they mistakenly assume that they agree, they may not recognize that they have a problem to solve. If they wrongly assume that they disagree, they may waste time and energy generating a creative solution to a problem that doesn't exist.

Correctives: As a receiver, reduce the likelihood of bypassing by 1) asking questions to clarify the speaker's message, and 2) translating the message into your own words and checking with the source to see if your interpretation is correct. As a speaker, encourage feedback to make sure that the intended meaning has been received.

7. **Blindering.** Words can restrict our perspectives on problems much as blinders narrow the vision of horses. When our vision is restricted, we're less efficient as problem solvers. General semanticist and organizational expert William Haney uses the

Creative Dilemma: Semantic Transformation

Engaging in the wrong type of self-talk quickly shuts off creative thinking. For example, we often send ourselves the following message: "I am a failure."

This assertion reflects a low self-image and reduces our expectations of ourselves. Just thinking about being a failure lowers our self-esteem even further while draining away the energy we need to solve problems creatively.

Kenneth Johnson uses the statement "I am a failure" to illustrate how general semantics principles can radically change the way in which we perceive ourselves and promote creativity. By changing our self-talk, we open the door for new behaviors which, in turn, lead to higher self-esteem. Follow these steps to transform this self-defeating message:

1. Identify the semantic traps reflected by the statement "I am a failure."
2. Rewrite this message to acknowledge that it reflects your reactions to yourself.
3. Now add a date to this statement to make it more manageable. When were you a failure? Yesterday? Last year?
4. Next, add a phrase to soften the extreme, either/or thinking found in this assertion. What's an intermediate step between success and failure?
5. Are you a failure in every respect? Transform this statement to eliminate its allness characteristics.
6. Operationalize your message by specifying exactly what it is you fail to do ("study for tests," "get along with roommates," "mix well at parties").
7. Compare your new statement with the original. (Turn to page 110 to see how Professor Johnson transformed this assertion.)

Discussion Questions

1. How does your final statement differ from the first? Why is it less damaging to your self-esteem?
2. How does your transformed statement facilitate creative problem solving and behavioral change?
3. Identify some other common statements that would benefit from this kind of transformation.

Source:

Johnson, K. (1990). Harnessing self-reflexiveness for creatical thinking. In K. G. Johnson (Ed.), *Thinking creatically* (pp. 1–17). Englewood, NJ: Institute of General Semantics.

See, also: Payne, B. (1986). Uncovering destructive self-criticism: A teaching technique. In M. Morain (Ed.), *Enriching professional skills through general semantics* (pp. 87–91). San Francisco, CA: International Society for General Semantics.

words "malaria" and "atom" to demonstrate how labels can slow creative progress. The term "malaria" comes from the Italian words *mala aria* ("bad air"). This name blinded researchers because it suggested that malaria was transmitted through the air rather than by the bite of mosquitos. The origins of the word "atom" also misled investigators. "How many bright and willing scientists," Haney wonders, "were inhibited from even dreaming of the possibility that the *atom* (from the Greek *indivisible*) could be split largely because its name said that it could *not* be divided?"[31]

Labels for problems not only impede creative thought, they also generate faulty solutions. Every year millions of Americans go on diets because they believe they have a "weight problem." However, what many really have is a "lifestyle problem." Diet plans alone are not enough. To lose pounds and keep them off, dieters must also change the way they live by exercising, getting adequate sleep and so on.

Correctives: Be aware that words, like television cameras, focus attention on some parts of reality while ignoring others. To get a new perspective on a problem, put a new label on it. Test your assumptions to make sure that you're not defining the problem too narrowly or eliminating possible solutions.

Alternative Intelligences/Alternative Languages

So far our focus in this chapter has been on the relationship between verbal language and creativity. However, the connection between symbols and creativity is not limited solely to words. Alternative symbol systems or languages also play important roles in the creative process. Dancers, sculptors, musicians, architects, artists, engineers and others create through nonsemantic codes or languages as well as through the spoken word. Over the past three decades, these alternative languages have attracted the attention of neuropsychologist Howard Gardner and fellow investigators at Harvard University's Project Zero. [The Project Zero team is made up of psychologists, educators, anthropologists and others who study human potential. The group got the name from its founder, philosopher Nelson Goodman, who initially received a grant to study artistic symbol systems in 1967. At the time there was very little known about these alternative languages. This led Goodman to christen his research effort "Project Zero."] Gardner and his colleagues reject the traditional notion that people have one overall

---

Sample Semantic Transformation

1. "I am a failure" is a highly abstract statement that implies that meaningful change is impossible. It reflects static evaluation, either/or thinking and an allness attitude.
2. "I consider myself a failure."
3. "Right now I consider myself a failure."
4. "Right now I consider myself, to some degree, a failure."
5. "Right now I consider myself, in some degree and in some respects, a failure."
6. "Right now I do not do _____ as well as I would like to."

---

level of intelligence which can be measured through IQ tests and SAT exams. They argue that we have multiple intelligences instead. Each intelligence is based on a unique set of skills or operations and is housed in a specific region of the brain. From this biological base, every intelligence takes form or is embedded in its own symbol system. Individuals rate higher in some intelligences than others, resulting in a "jagged" cognitive profile. A trial lawyer, for example, may have high levels of linguistic and logical intelligence but low amounts of musical or spatial ability.[32]

While being gifted in one or more intelligences makes creative achievement more likely, Gardner cautions that innate ability does not guarantee that an individual will be successful or creative. Many gifted individuals are unproductive because they don't develop a "working style" (persistence, careful planning, effort) that helps them build on their gifts. Others have intelligence and effective work habits but never generate original products.[33]

The seven human intelligences identified by the Project Zero team are described in table 4.1. The "end-states" column of the table provides examples of occupations or roles which rely heavily on the mature development of each type of intelligence. Many occupations, though, require that practitioners skillfully blend languages. For instance, surgeons must use both spatial and bodily-kinesic codes as they perform operations.[34]

Table 4.1
The Seven Intelligences

Intelligence	End-States	Core Components
Logical-mathematical	Scientist Mathematician	Sensitivity to, and capacity to discern, logical or numerical patterns; ability to handle long chains of reasoning.
Linguistic	Poet Journalist	Sensitivity to the sounds, rhythms, and meanings of words; sensitivity to the different functions of language.
Musical	Composer Violinist	Abilities to produce and appreciate rhythm, pitch, and timbre; appreciation of the forms of musical expressiveness.
Spatial	Navigator Sculptor	Capacities to perceive the visual-spatial world accurately and to perform transformations on one's initial perceptions.
Bodily-kinesthetic	Dancer Athlete	Abilities to control one's body movements and to handle objects skillfully.
Interpersonal	Therapist Salesman	Capacities to discern and respond appropriately to the moods, temperaments, motivations, and desires of other people.
Intrapersonal	Person with detailed, accurate self-knowledge	Access to one's own feelings and the ability to discriminate among them and draw upon them to guide behavior; knowledge of one's own strengths, weaknesses, desires, and intelligences.

Source: Gardner, H., & Hatch, T. (1989, November). Multiple intelligences go to school. *Educational Researcher*, p. 6. Used by permission.

Summing Up

In this chapter we explored the relationship between symbols and creativity. Language and cognition combine to lay the foundation for conceptualization and reasoning. Children first acquire words and sentences for social purposes—to communicate with others. Next they engage in egocentric, self-centered speech in order to plan and to solve problems on their own. Later they replace egocentric speech with mental or inner speech which becomes the primary mechanism of thought. Inner speech is highly abbreviated, consisting of words or short phrases that condense thought processes and are saturated with meaning. Creative ideas generated by inner speech must first be unfolded or developed and then communicated in a form that is understandable to others.

Two language tools—questions and metaphors—play a particularly important role in creative problem solving. Classifying questions is the key to improving our questioning skills. Bloom's Taxonomy of Educational Objectives identifies six types of questions which should be generated during problem solving: knowledge, comprehension, application, analysis, synthesis and evaluation. In addition, sets of standardized or prewritten questions can be applied to specific problems or used to anticipate problems and opportunities. Metaphors (which connect two elements we normally think of as different) help us interpret the world around us, direct our actions and enable us to communicate abstract concepts and emotions to others. To harness their power, we must first identify and evaluate current metaphors and then develop new ones if needed. Effective metaphors are active, concise, appropriate to the task at hand, suitable for the audience, and build or sustain the credibility of the speaker.

Although words are the key to effective problem solving, they can also block the creative process. Common semantic barriers to creativity are: confusing inferences and judgments with facts; allness attitudes (believing that we can say or know everything about a topic); polarization (either/or thinking); indiscrimination (failure to distinguish between members of a category); static evaluation (forgetting that reality is constantly changing); bypassing (wrongly assuming that words mean the same thing to everyone); and blindering (when labels for problems delay solutions or lead to the wrong answers).

Nonsemantic symbolic codes or languages also play an important role in creativity. According to researchers at Harvard University's Project Zero, there are seven human intelligences—logical-mathematical, linguistic, musical, spatial, bodily-kinesthetic, inter-personal and intrapersonal—which take form in symbol systems. Each of these intelligences/languages is based on a unique set of skills or operations and is housed in a specific region of the brain.

Application Exercises

1. Observe a group of preschool or early elementary age children and note their use of social and egocentric speech. Compare your observations with those of Lev Vygotsky and his colleagues. Do your conclusions differ from theirs? Write up your findings.

2. Analyze an examination using Bloom's Taxonomy. Classify each of the questions on the test. How many fall into each category? Convert the knowledge and comprehension questions into higher order questions.

3. Use the What-if? question technique in a volunteer or work group. Keep track of the new ideas you generate. Are any of these ideas useful? Do they serve as stepping stones to other, more practical ideas? Do you identify any opportunities or problems that you hadn't noticed before?

4. Identify and evaluate the metaphors that students use to describe your college or university. How useful are these metaphors? How would you judge them based on the criteria given in the chapter? What alternative metaphors would you suggest in their place? Why?

5. Analyze a half-hour situation comedy. Which semantic barriers can you identify during the program? What role do these barriers play in plot development?

6. Think about a problem that you are currently trying to solve. Are there semantic barriers that may be keeping you from finding a creative solution? Name these traps and describe their effects. Develop a strategy for overcoming these barriers. Summarize your conclusions in a short paper.

7. Form a group and evaluate Project Zero's list of seven human intelligences/languages. Are there any intelligences that should be removed from the list? Others that should be added? Why? Report to the rest of the class.

Endnotes

1 For an excellent summary of the various theoretical approaches to cognition and language, see:

Byrnes, J. P., & Gelman, S. A. (1991). Perspectives on thought and language: Traditional and contemporary views. In S. S. Gelman & J. P. Byrnes (Eds.), *Perspectives on language and thought: Interrelations in development* (pp. 3–27). Cambridge, England: Cambridge University Press.

2 See:

Vygotsky, L. (1986). *Thought and language.* (A. Kozulin, Trans.). Cambridge, MA: MIT Press, p. 83.

Vygotsky, L. (1978). *Mind in society.* (M. Cole, V. John-Steiner, S. Scribner, & E. Souberman, Eds.). Cambridge, MA: Harvard University Press.

Luria, A. R. (1982). *Language and cognition.* (J. V. Wertsch, Ed.). New York: John Wiley & Sons.

Johnson, J. R. (1984). The role of inner speech in human communication. *Communication Education, 33,* 211–222.

Lee, B. (1985). Intellectual origins of Vygotsky's semiotic analysis. In J. Wertsch (Ed.), *Culture, communication and cognition: Vygotskian perspectives* (pp. 66–93). Cambridge: Cambridge University Press.

3 Vygotsky, *Thought and language,* p. 83

4 Sokolov, A. N. (1975). *Inner speech and thought.* (G. T. Onischenko, Trans.), pp. 1, 263–64.

5 Luria, p. 107.

6 Vygotsky, *Thought and language,* Ch. 7: Sokolov, Ch. 3.

7 Vygotsky, *Thought and language.*; Vygotsky, *Mind in society.*; Luria.

8 Torrance, E. P., & Myers, R. E. (1970). *Creative learning and teaching.* New York: Dodd, Mead & Company, Ch. 9.

9 See, for example:

Chaudhari, U. S. (1975). Questioning and creative thinking: A research perspective. *Journal of Creative Behavior, 9,* 30–34.

Rowe, M. (1974). Reflections on wait-time: Some methodological questions. *Journal of Research in Science Teaching, 11,* 263–279.

Rowe, M. (1974). Relation of wait-time and rewards to the development of language, logic, fate control: Part II rewards. *Journal of Research in Science Teaching, 11,* 291–308.

Pearson, J. C., & West, R. (1992). An initial investigation of the effects of gender on student questions in the classroom: Developing a descriptive base. *Communication Education, 40,* 22–32.

10 Sund, R. B., & Carin, A. (1978). *Creative questioning and sensitive listening techniques* (2nd ed.). Columbus, OH: Charles E. Merrill Publishing, Ch. 1.

11 Torrance & Myers, Ch. 9.

12 Bloom, B. S., Englehart, M. D., Furst, E. J., Hill, W. H., & Krathwohl, D. R. (1956). *Taxonomy of educational objectives I: Cognitive domain.* New York: David McKay Company.

13 Raudsepp, E., & Hough, G. P. (1977). *Creative growth games.* New York: Jove.

14 von Oech, R (1986). *A kick in the seat of the pants.* New York: Harper & Row; von Oech, R. (1990). *A whack on the side of the head.* New York: Warner Books.

15 Lakoff, G., & Johnson, M. (1980). *Metaphors we live by.* Chicago: University of Chicago Press.

16 Jorgensen-Earp, C., & Staton, A. (1993). Student metaphors for the college freshman experience. *Communication Education, 42,* 123–141.

17 Lakoff & Johnson.

[18] Ortony, A. (1975). Why metaphors are necessary and not just nice. *Journal of Educational Research, 25,* 45–53; Fainsilber, L., & Ortony, A. (1987). Metaphorical uses of language in the expression of emotions. *Metaphor and Symbolic Activity, 2,* 239–250.

[19] McBroom, A. (1977). *The rose.* Secaucus, NJ: Warner-Tamberline Publishing.

[20] Paivio, A. (1979). Psychological processes in the comprehension of metaphor. In A. Ortony (Ed.), *Metaphor and thought* (pp. 150–171). Cambridge: Cambridge University Press.; Sanders, D., & Sanders, J. (1984). *Teaching creativity through metaphor: An integrated brain approach.* New York, NY: Longman.

[21] Owen, W. F. (1985). Thematic metaphor in relational communication: A conceptual approach. *Western Journal of Speech Communication, 49,* 1–13.

[22] For further discussion of conflict metaphors, see:

Wilmot & Wilmot (1991). *Interpersonal Conflict* (3rd ed.). Dubuque, IA: Wm C. Brown.

[23] Booth, W. (1978). Metaphor as rhetoric: The problem of evaluation. In S. Sacks (Ed.), *On metaphor* (pp. 47–70). Chicago: University of Chicago Press.

[24] The General Semantics movement was founded by Alfred Korzybski, a Polish count who emigrated to the United States after World War II. Though never officially associated with any college or university, Count Korzybski held periodic seminars on General Semantics and attracted academic followers like professors Irving Lee, Wendell Johnson and S. I. Hayakawa. Brief summaries of the principles of general semantics can be found in:

Read, C. S. (1984). General semantics. In M. Morain (Ed.), *Bridging worlds through general semantics* (pp. 63–77). San Francisco: The International Society for General Semantics.

Murray, E. (1970). Developing formulations of general semantics. In L. Thayer (Ed.), *Communication: General Semantics perspectives* (pp. 33–41). New York: Spartan Books.

Budd, R. W. (1972). General semantics: An approach to human communication. In R. W. Budd & B. D. Ruben (Eds.), *Approaches to human communication* (pp. 97–119). Rochelle Park, NJ: Spartan Books.

[25] Hayakawa, S. I. (1990). *Language in thought and action* (5th ed.). San Diego: Harcourt Brace Jovanovich.

[26] Coffey, W. (1983). *303 of the world's worst predictions.* New York: Tribeca Communications.

[27] DeVito, J. (1990). *Messages: Building interpersonal communication skills.* New York: Harper & Row, Ch. 6.

[28] Haney, W. (1986). *Communication and interpersonal relations* (5th ed.). Homewood, IL: Irwin, Ch. 12.

[29] Haney, Ch. 9.

[30] Haney, p. 250.

[31] Haney, p. 294.

[32] Gardner, H. (1983). *Frames of mind.* New York: Basic Books.; Gardner, H. (1987). The theory of multiple intelligences. *Annals of Dyslexia, 37,* 19–35.

[33] Kirschenbaum, R. J. (1990, November/December). An interview with Howard Gardner. *Gifted Child Today,* pp. 26–32.

[34] Gardner, H., & Hatch, T. (1989, November). Multiple intelligences go to school. *Educational Researcher,* pp. 4–9.

Quotations

Buescher, T. M. (1985). Seeking the roots of talent: An interview with Howard Gardner. *Journal for the Education of the Gifted, 3,* p. 179–187.

Lakoff, G., & Johnson, M. (1980). *Metaphors we live by.* Chicago: University of Chicago Press.

Johnson, W. (1946). *People in quandaries.* New York: Harper & Brothers.

PART II

Creative Applications

5 | Creative Group Problem Solving

> The process of creating or innovating almost always involves more than an isolated person working alone.
>
> Thomas M. Scheidel

PREVIEW

► The Creative Group Process
  Elements of Small Groups
  Identifying the Right Type of Problem to Solve
  Emergent Problem Solving
► Prescriptive Approaches to Creative Group Problem Solving
  Problem Redefinition and Analysis Techniques
  Idea Generation Techniques
  Idea Evaluation and Selection Techniques
  Problem Solving Formats
► Characteristics of Highly Creative Groups
  Cooperative Orientation
  Concern for Excellence

119

During the past week you probably participated in a work team, class project group, committee or some other small group. Chances are, the group devoted at least part of its time to creative problem solving. Perhaps you had to find a way to work more efficiently, to complete a class assignment or to cut costs. Creative problem solving in a group requires the coordination of individual efforts. Group members must express themselves clearly, understand the perspectives of others, encourage everyone to participate, resolve their differences, and come up with a solution that incorporates the viewpoints of all the participants. The cooperative nature of group creativity puts an added burden on problem solvers because they must work effectively with others in order to be successful. As a result, many creative group problem solving sessions end in failure and frustration.

Our goal in this chapter is to help you increase the creative productivity of your group. To reach this objective, we'll examine the creative group process, survey creative problem-solving strategies, and describe important characteristics of highly creative groups. Your group's chances of success will be much greater if you understand these factors.

The Creative Group Process

Before we can understand how the creative group process works, we need to clarify just what a small group is. In common usage the word "group" is applied to any collection of individuals, whether it be ten people waiting for tables at a restaurant, an audience gathered for a concert, or all the students who attend a school. Our definition of a group is much more focused, however.

Elements of Small Groups

From a communication perspective, the following elements define small groups:[1]

A Common Purpose. Groups differ from collections of individuals because group members recognize that they are working together for a common purpose. Drawn together by a shared goal, members create their own sense of "groupness" or identity as a result of participation in the group. Group norms and roles are evidence of a shared group identity. Every group develops rules about how hard members must work, what types of humor are acceptable and other issues. In addition, members coordinate their actions by playing specialized roles. One participant may serve as the leader, another as a notekeeper, a third may mediate disputes and so on.

Interdependence. In a group, no one member can succeed unless everyone does his or her part. Your grade for a group project, for example, depends on how well other members carry out their assignments. You may do your part by gathering information, but if other members do a sloppy job of organizing and typing up the final paper, your grade will drop along with theirs.

Mutual Influence. Group members not only depend on one another, they influence each other by expressing their ideas, agreeing or disagreeing, listening and so on.

Communication. Communication is the most important element of any small group. In fact, "there is no group if there is no communication."[2] Group members use talk to complete the group's task, to build relationships with one another and to create the shared experiences that make each group unique. Group communication also includes such nonverbal behaviors as gestures, facial expressions and tone of voice. In order to process both verbal and nonverbal cues, group members must be close enough together to hear and to see one another clearly.

A Limited Size. Groups range in size from three to twenty people. The addition of a third person makes a group more stable than a dyad since a group can survive the loss of a member while a dyad cannot. Groups are also more complex than dyads because group members must manage several relationships, not just one. Twenty is generally considered to be the maximum size for a group because participants can't monitor the verbal and nonverbal communication of all the other members when the group grows beyond this number.

Identifying the Right Type of Problem to Solve

The creative group process begins with the selection of the right type of problem to solve. A problem exists whenever there is a perceived difference or gap between what is and what should be, between the initial and desired problem states.[3] Problem solving is aimed at closing the gap between current reality and the desired goal. A company that wants to sell more of its product must find a way to reduce the gap between its current performance and its sales objective. To increase sales, the firm may assign a group to develop new sales promotions.

Although task-oriented small groups typically spend most of their time dealing with problems like how to budget for next year, how to resolve complaints, whom to hire and what programs to offer, not all problems require creative solutions. Some problems, such as computing tax payments, reoccur frequently and can be solved by following the right series of steps. To figure out how much tax to pay, all the group needs to do is follow the formula on the tax form. Using creative problem solving techniques to solve *well-structured* problems like this one is a waste of time and effort since the group already has all the information it needs to come up with the solution.[4] Creative problem solving is most suited to developing answers to *ill-structured* problems which are more complex than well-structured ones. Information on how to solve an ill-structured problem must come out of the group's discussion and the solution is "custom made." Developing a new college governance structure or designing a plan for reducing theft in a dormitory are examples of ill-structured problems.

Many problems fall somewhere between well- and ill-structured. In these cases, a group must determine whether or not to rely on past procedures or to engage in creative problem solving. Consider the budgeting process, for instance. Developing a budget is a routine problem that occurs every year in organizations. Solving this problem is relatively easy if the group relies on this year's budget to make next year's projections. However, the group will need to engage in creative problem solving if it is dissatisfied with this year's budget and wants to develop new ways of allocating funds.

Making a distinction between well- and ill-structured problems can help clear up the confusion surrounding group decision making vs. group problem solving. Some small group texts use the terms "decision making" and "problem solving" interchangeably; others use one term or the other. We believe that there are important differences between decision making and problem solving. All decisions are attempts to solve problems but not all problems can be solved by decision making alone. When faced with a well-structured problem, the group generates a solution by deciding which procedures to follow. When faced with an ill-structured problem, the group must spend most of its time defining the problem, gathering information, generating ideas, developing solution criteria and so on. Deciding on the best option or solution is the final step in the process.

Emergent Problem Solving

As we indicated above, creative solutions to ill-structured problems emerge out of group deliberations. One description of how solutions emerge during group discussions was developed by B. Aubrey Fisher who studied groups that had no prior history or assigned leader. Fisher and his coworkers tracked how decision proposals (ideas about how to solve the problem) were transformed into solutions acceptable to the entire group. They recorded both what each member said about the proposal in the group (called a speech act) and how the next person responded. These statement/response pairings are called interacts. By studying series of interacts, Fisher discovered four group phases which make up the Decision Emergence Model.[5]

1. **Orientation Phase** When group members first get together they are not sure about their positions in the group and don't know how to handle the task. They want to get acquainted and figure out what the task requires. Communication during this initial phase can best be described as tentative and agreeable since members don't want to "rock the boat." Comments about the group's task are ambiguous and members rarely disagree with each other.

2. **Conflict Phase** In the conflict phase members express strong opinions about decision proposals. Communication is no longer tentative and agreeable. Instead, members debate ideas, provide evidence to support their positions and form coalitions.

3. **Emergence Phase** During this phase the group begins to commit itself to one solution. Conflict begins to die out and the coalitions formed in the conflict phase disband. Dissenters gradually drop their opposition to the solution.

4. **Reinforcement Phase** Group members achieve consensus on the solution during the reinforcement phase. In this stage,

interaction is largely positive. Comments which indicate support for the solution are followed by additional statements of agreement. Tension dissipates and members commit themselves to implementing the solution.

The Decision Emergence Model and other linear models view the group problem-solving process as one series of steps or stages. However, not everyone agrees that groups follow a single, orderly path as they solve problems. Thomas Scheidel and Laura Crowell, for example, argue that ideas develop through a spiral process rather than through a step-by-step progression.[6] According to Scheidel and Crowell, members respond to the introduction of an idea by evaluating and refining the proposal. The proposal becomes the foundation or anchor point for further ideas, a process called "reach-testing." Decision emergence resembles a spiral because the proposal expands as it moves through a series of anchor points on its way to final agreement.

Marshall Scott Poole suggests that groups follow different developmental paths depending on how they deal with three activity tracks or threads: 1) task process activities (how the group deals with the task), 2) relational character (the working relationships between group members), and 3) topical focus (what the group is talking about at a particular moment).[7] Groups proceed along these tracks at different rates and follow different patterns. "Breakpoints" are topic changes, delays, serious disagreements and other factors which mark the end of one phase of the group's development and the beginning of another. In a study of twenty-nine groups (including a medical teaching team, a city energy committee, a managerial team, student project groups and mock juries), Poole and fellow researcher Jonelle Roth found that groups followed three major paths when solving problems.[8] The most common path was complex cyclic. In this pattern, groups repeatedly focused on the problem, then on the solution, and then on the problem again. The second most frequent path was solution oriented. Groups on this path launched into a discussion of solutions without paying much attention to defining the problem. The third major path was a unitary sequence which resembles the linear, step-by-step pattern of the Decision Emergence Model. Poole and Roth conclude that groups apparently follow more than one sequence when developing solutions. Yet, they note that because some groups follow a linear path, both multiple and single sequence models can help explain the group process.

Although descriptions of the group process may vary, the concept of solution emergence has significant implications. First, timing is essential. If you offer a good proposal at the wrong moment—say when the group is just forming or is concentrating on relational issues—you may be ignored. Second, effective problem solving depends on the kind of communication that occurs between you and others in the group. The ultimate success of any group depends on how members interact verbally and nonverbally. Third, the creative group process is complex. Members must balance task and relational demands; the problem-solving process can break down at any point. Some groups forget to define the problem clearly while others fail to reach consensus on one solution. To prevent these problems, you may want to use a structured problem solving format. Prescriptive approaches to creative problem solving are the subject of the next section.

Prescriptive Approaches to Creative Group Problem Solving

Up to this point we've taken a descriptive approach to group creative problem solving. We've focused on how "natural" groups—groups without any special training or established agenda—tackle problems that demand creative solutions. As we've seen, these groups frequently make mistakes that derail the creative problem-solving process. Prescriptive approaches to creative problem solving consist of guidelines or directions which are designed to help groups avoid costly errors and to boost their productivity. These guidelines may prescribe the agenda (format) that groups should follow, the techniques they should use, the roles that the leader and other participants should play in the process, or a combination of these elements.[9] In general, groups are more effective if they use a systematic method of problem solving.[10] Prescriptive approaches supply groups with strategies they can use as they tackle difficult problems. Members of these groups are less likely to offer premature solutions or to fall back on old habits and assumptions which may block creative thinking.[11]

According to creative communication expert Arthur VanGundy, creative groups must accomplish three tasks in order to be successful.[12] The first task is to redefine and analyze the problem. Although groups frequently ignore this task, VanGundy argues that this is the most important step in the problem solving process because correctly understanding the problem often leads to the right solution. The following story illustrates this point:

A car travels down a deserted country road and blows a tire. Upon opening the car's trunk, the occupants discover that the jack is missing. This prompts them to pose their problem as: "In what ways might we obtain a jack?" One remembers a service station they passed a few miles back and they all decide to walk to it and borrow a jack. After they leave, another car, coming from the opposite direction, also blows a tire. When the occupants of this car open their trunk, they also discover that the jack is missing. This group defines their problem as: "In what ways might we raise the car?" One notices a barn nearby with a pulley for lifting hay bales to the loft. They push the car to the barn, raise the car with the pulley, and change the tire. As they drive off, the occupants of the first car are still walking to get a jack from the service station.[13]

The goal of the redefinition and analysis stage is to develop a new perspective on the problem. Redefining the problem forces the group to move beyond its original perceptions and forces it to use divergent thinking. Analysis breaks the problem into components which helps the group organize current information and discover new information. Group members may need to return to this task when new information becomes available later in the discussion.

> Discovery consists of looking at the same thing as everyone else and thinking something different.
>
> Albert Szent-Gyorgyi

The group's second task is to generate new ideas. Many people equate idea generation with creative problem solving and the majority of problem solving techniques are designed for this task. However, generating a number of divergent ideas is only one of the functions the group must perform.

The group's third task is to evaluate and select an idea(s) to implement from the list of options generated in the second stage. This task is best accomplished after the problem has been thoroughly analyzed and after the group has generated a variety of ideas. A group that reaches a consensus about what course of action to take is more likely to commit itself to implementing the idea.

Creative problem-solving techniques can be classified according to how they relate to the three group tasks described above. Some techniques assist in problem redefinition and analysis, others in idea generation, others in idea evaluation and selection. Problem solving formats are designed to help groups accomplish all three tasks. There are far too many creative problem solving techniques and formats to describe here (VanGundy identifies 110, for example). Instead, we will highlight a few widely used strategies.

Problem Redefinition and Analysis Techniques

5 Ws and H.   The Five Ws and H technique borrows the Who? What? Where? When? and Why? questions used by journalists when they gather information for stories and combines them with the question How?[14] The purpose of this technique is to help groups systematically gather data which can then be used to redefine the problem. Begin by stating the problem in the following way: In what ways might . . . ? (IWWM. . . ?). Then create separate lists of Who? What? Where? When? Why? and How? questions which relate to the problem. Next, respond to each question and use these responses to generate problem redefinitions. Write down all redefinitions and then select the redefinition that best reflects the problem your group is trying to solve. The 5 Ws and H technique works best when members withhold judgment while generating questions, responses and redefinitions and don't limit themselves by insisting that problem statements meet specific criteria.

To demonstrate this method, we'll use a group of college faculty, students and administrators faced with this problem: "In what ways might we reduce student plagiarism on term papers?" Here are some sample questions and responses that this group might generate:

Who are the students guilty of plagiarizing? Mainly undergraduate, not graduate students. Students in majors with the largest enrollments.

What is plagiarism? Using someone else's work without giving them credit.

Where is plagiarism the greatest problem? In majors with the largest enrollments where students feel unnoticed. In programs that are highly demanding.

When is plagiarism most likely to occur? When students don't know how to write term papers. When they feel that the professor won't find out. When they procrastinate or feel overwhelmed with their workloads.

Why do students plagiarize? Some students don't know what plagiarism is, others feel time pressures, others feel pressure to get a high grade.

How can plagiarism be stopped? By publicizing what

plagiarism is, by providing better training in writing term papers, by closer monitoring, by imposing stiffer penalties on violators.

These questions and responses might generate the following problem redefinitions:

IWWM we increase student understanding of what plagiarism is?

IWWM we reduce time pressures on students?

IWWM we better prepare students to write term papers?

IWWM we more closely monitor term papers to detect plagiarism?

IWWM we encourage professors to be tougher on plagiarizers?

One of these redefinitions could then be used as the problem statement which will determine the direction of the group. The plagiarism task force could focus on preventing plagiarism or on detecting plagiarism and punishing plagiarizers.

Organized Random Search.   All problem analysis techniques are designed to break down problems into subdivisions or parts. Perhaps the simplest such method is the Organized Random Search.[15] To use this strategy, examine the problem to determine if there are possible subdivisions or categories. Then write down the parts and use them as the starting points for developing ideas. Although the ideas you generate will still be random, at least your search will be somewhat organized. In the case of plagiarism on term papers, this problem could be divided into such subcategories as prevention, enforcement, student responsibilities and faculty responsibilities.

Idea Generation Techniques

Brainstorming.   Brainstorming is by far the most popular creative group problem solving technique. Alex Osborn developed brainstorming as a way to stimulate creativity at his advertising agency in the 1940s. Soon the ad agency was instructing its clients on how to brainstorm, and Osborn described the method in two editions of a best selling book.[16]

The goal of brainstorming is to stimulate as many ideas as possible based on the premise that greater quantity will lead to higher quality. In other words, the greater the number of ideas, the more likely it is that one or more of these ideas will be "good." The ideal brainstorming group, according to Osborn, is made up of five to ten members along with an assigned leader and assistant leader. Half of the group should consist of regular group members, half should be invited guests.

The leader begins the brainstorming session by describing the problem and reviewing the following basic rules:[17]

1. *Judicial judgment is ruled out.* Criticism of ideas must be withheld until later.

2. *"Free wheeling" is welcomed.* The wilder the idea, the better; it is easier to tame down than to think up.

3. *Quantity is wanted.* The greater the number of ideas, the higher the likelihood of winners.

4. *Combination and improvement are sought.* In addition to contributing ideas of their own, participants should suggest how ideas of others can be turned into better ideas or how two or more ideas can be combined into yet another idea.

During the next hour, group members produce ideas as fast as they can and these ideas are recorded on a flipchart, chalkboard or posterboard. If the discussion slows, the leader may "prime the pump" by introducing ideas, encouraging members to reach subgoals or asking Osborn's idea-spurring questions described in chapter 3.

Osborn claimed that the typical group could generate 100 ideas per hour, and the first researchers to test the technique reported that brainstorming groups produced more ideas and higher quality ideas than individuals.[18] Later investigators, however, found that individuals outperformed groups. To test individual vs. group productivity, these researchers compared nominal and real groups. Nominal groups are made up of individuals who work alone but whose scores are combined as if they had worked together. [One caution should be kept in mind when interpreting these findings. Researchers typically ignore many of the brainstorming guidelines prescribed by Osborn. Few experimental groups meet for as long as an hour or have assigned leaders and assistant leaders.] Nominal groups consistently generated a higher number of ideas than groups that brainstormed ideas together. Conduct your own comparison of nominal vs. real brainstorming groups by solving the problem described in the Creative Dilemma on page 130.

There are several possible reasons why real brainstorming groups are inferior to nominal groups.[19] Waiting for a turn to speak in a group may disrupt the thinking of group members and may block the production of ideas. Group members who fear negative

Creative Dilemma: Real vs. Nominal Groups

The following problems have been used in research studies which compare the brainstorming performance of real vs. nominal groups. Assign several individuals to solve one or more of these problems by themselves while a group works together on the same task. Then compare the total number of ideas generated by both groups.

- Develop a list of names for a brand new toothpaste.

- Imagine that at the end of this year everyone will have an extra thumb on each hand. This extra thumb will be built just as the present one is but located on the other side of the hand. It faces inward, so that it can press against the fingers, just as the regular thumb does now. Here is the question. What practical benefits or difficulties will arise when people start having this extra thumb?

- Each year a great many American tourists go to Europe to visit. Suppose that our country wanted to get many more Europeans to come to America during their vacations. What steps can you suggest that would entice more Europeans to come to this country to visit?

Discussion Questions

1. Which group generated the most ideas? Was there a significant difference in productivity?

2. What is the best explanation for the superior performance of nominal groups?

3. When should a group use brainstorming and when should it choose other techniques?

Sources:

Bouchard, T. J. (1972). Training, motivation, and personality as determinants of the effectiveness of brainstorming groups and individuals. *Journal of Applied Psychology, 56*, 324–331.

Taylor, D. W., Berry, P. C., & Block, C. H. (1958). Does group participation when using brainstorming facilitate or inhibit creative thinking? *Administrative Science Quarterly, 3*, 23–47.

evaluation from others may withhold ideas even though the group has been instructed to defer judgment. Some individuals in the group may loaf or "free ride" since members are evaluated as a group, or they may not feel that their contributions are important. Finally, members who participate more frequently often earn higher status which may intensify the reluctance of others to speak.

Because of the research indicating that individual brainstormers produce more ideas than group brainstormers, some experts have modified Osborn's method. Electronic brainstorming is designed to overcome the problems of production blocking and evaluation by having individuals type in their ideas at computer terminals. Group members work simultaneously to generate a master list, and the sources of ideas are not identified.[20] Brainwriting techniques ask group members to write down their ideas before sharing them with the group.[21] Other experts have abandoned brainstorming, preferring other idea generation techniques instead. Yet, it would be a mistake to reject group brainstorming altogether. Group brainstorming is a useful and enjoyable way to involve people in the problem-solving process. Individuals who might not take the time to think about a problem on their own will do so when asked to brainstorm in a group.

Morphological Analysis.   One way to encourage new ideas is to "force" together elements that seem to be completely unrelated. Morphological (form and structure) analysis, for instance, breaks the problem into its major parts and lists all the possible topics or subdivisions under each major heading.[22] Randomly combining these topics then generates new ideas that might solve the problem. An example of a morphological analysis is found below. If you were assigned to develop a new food product, you could decide that the major variables to consider are forms, kinds, properties, processes and packaging. By combining items from each list, you might determine that a low cost, freeze dried vegetable preserve packaged in a cup might be an exciting idea for a new product.

Variables for Food Businesses

Forms	Kinds	Properties	Processes	Packages
Preserves	Meat	Cost	Ferment	Bottle
Drink	Vegetables	Convenience	Freeze dry	Can
Chips	Fish	Nutrition	Compact	Pouch
Flake	Fruit	Taste	Blend	Foil/paper
Stew	Dairy	Texture	Form	Aerosol
Roll	Grains	Odor	Fry	Box
Soup	Nuts	Viscosity	Bake	Cup
Topping	Spices	Medicinal	Stir	Sack

Source: Miller, W. C. *The Creative Edge* (pg. 69), © 1987 by William C. Miller. Reprinted by permission of Addison-Wesley Publishing Company, Inc.

Idea Evaluation and Selection Techniques

Weighting Systems.   In order to select a solution, a group must evaluate its ideas against a set of criteria. The simplest approach is to develop a list of criteria first and then determine how each idea meets these standards. For example, a task force assigned to find a location for a new plant might decide that important considerations are local taxes, climate, housing, the workforce and transportation. The location that best satisfies the most criteria would be the most likely choice for the plant. However, this procedure does not take into consideration the fact that some factors may be more important than others. A more sophisticated approach is to give additional weight to selected criteria.[23] If tax rates are more important than transportation, then the task force might assign a weight of 4 to taxes and 1 to transportation. Each potential location could also be rated on how well it satisfies each criterion (1 = minimal satisfaction, 7 = highest satisfaction). To figure a total score for each potential plant location, the group would first multiply the weight of each criterion by its satisfaction rating. A location which received a satisfaction rating of 7 on taxes (which has a weight of 4) would earn a score of 28 on that item (4 X 7). The task force would then add up the scores from all the criteria to determine the overall score for that location. The site receiving the highest point total would be chosen as the location for the new plant.

Reverse Brainstorming.   When the costs of making a poor decision are high, reverse brainstorming is a useful way to identify possible weaknesses in a proposal. Following the rules of classical brainstorming, generate a list of the possible problems with a product or idea. Is it too expensive? Too complicated? Too difficult to design or manufacture? Then brainstorm solutions to each of these weaknesses. If the problems seem insurmountable, drop the idea and evaluate the next proposal using the same procedure.[24]

Problem Solving Formats

Synectics.   Synectics, a Greek word, means "the joining together of different and apparently irrelevant elements." Groups using the Synectics method generate ideas that appear at first to be unrelated to the problem at hand. Later in the process, group members use these ideas to generate creative solutions. The technique, co-developed by William Gordon and George Prince, has been used to develop new technologies and procedures in industry, government, education, the military and other settings.[25] The Kimberly Clark Corporation reduced the costs of packaging and shipping Kleenex after a Synectics group figured out how to squeeze most of the air out of the tissues. A Synectics group at Sunoco developed a way to dispense several different octanes of gasoline out of the same pump.

Choosing the right mix of members is the first step in the Synectics problem-solving method. A group's chances for creative success are much greater if members come from a variety of backgrounds and bring many different perspectives to the problem. The group leader and the group expert are the most important members of the Synectics team. The leader (appointed in advance to avoid leadership struggles which may detract from creativity) guides the discussion, encourages members to listen to one other and promotes a positive, nondefensive climate. A successful leader recognizes that no idea is completely good or bad but insists that group members comment on the positive aspects of previous ideas before finding fault or adding ideas of their own. The expert, usually the person requesting the group's help, clarifies the problem to be solved and evaluates ideas. An effective expert supplies the information the group needs while looking for positive elements in ideas that might seem "wrong" at first.

The stages of the Synectics method described below are best seen as guides, not as a series of required, inflexible steps. While designed for groups, the Synectics method can also be used by individuals.

> **Problem As Given (PAG).** The problem to be solved is stated, providing the starting point for the group's deliberations. The problem may be posed by an outside source or generated by the group itself. For example: "How can we reduce crime on campus?" or "How can we reduce the number of defects on our production line?"

> **Analysis and Explanation by Expert.** The expert describes the problem so that the entire group understands.

> **Immediate Suggestions.** Initial solutions are proposed. By expressing their immediate reactions, members gain a clearer understanding of the problem and prepare themselves for better alternatives that will emerge later in the discussion.

> **Goals As Understood (GAU).** Dream solutions or goals for the problem solving process are generated. The leader chooses one goal or aspect of the problem for the group to focus on. One group of architectural students, for example, dreamed of

having their own private studios. As a final project before graduation, they designed dormitory rooms that contained studio space.

Leader's Question. A question can spur analogical/metaphorical thinking; it is designed to encourage responses that help members see the problem in new ways. This question may request

- an *example* or direct comparison with parallel knowledge or technology. Often a leader asks for analogies from nature ("What is an example of a security system in the animal kingdom?"). The leader then selects one example for closer examination.

- a *book title*, a two-word phrase "that captures both an essence of and a paradox involved in a particular thing or set of feelings."[26] Some typical book analogies include:

  Progressive Regression for forest fire
  Connected Pauses for machine-gun burst
  Discrete Infinity for multitude of objects
  Impure Aggressor for acid

- a *personal analogy* or feeling of identification or empathy for an object, i.e. a molecule, animal, ocean wave, product. Group members imagine how it feels to be a living thing or inanimate object and speculate as to how they would act.

Force Fit. Seemingly irrelevant material developed by analogical thinking is applied or forced on the problem. Sometimes connections between the metaphors and the problem come naturally; at other times the leader must encourage members by suggesting possible associations or by soliciting further speculation. One group of geologists who wanted a better way to estimate the amount of oil contained in rock forced the idea of stroking a cat onto their geological problem. They concluded that freezing was the best way to "stroke" or calm oil so that they could get a more accurate measurement from their wells.

Viewpoint. A possible solution(s) to the problem which must be acceptable to the group expert who must know how to test it. Since most new ideas are rejected, several viewpoints are better than one.

Creative Problem Solving (CPS). The Creative Problem Solving (CPS) group format was developed by Sidney Parnes and his colleagues at the Creative Education Foundation at State University of New York at Buffalo.[27] This foundation, established by brainstorming pioneer Alex Osborn, studies the creative process, provides training in creative problem solving and holds annual creativity institutes. CPS consists of the six stages described and outlined in figure 5.1. Each stage begins with divergent activity which generates ideas and ends with convergent activity which refines and selects options. The CPS facilitator makes sure that the group defers judgment during divergent phases and that all ideas in each stage are recorded on a board or flip chart. CPS can be completed in one extended session or in a series of shorter sessions conducted over several days.

1. *Mess Finding.* The initial stage of the CPS process (also referred to as Objective Finding) narrows the focus of the group and gives it direction. A mess can be either a negative or positive situation (an opportunity). Highlighting outcomes and obstacles is one way to encourage divergence in this stage. Outcomes can be generated by constructing a list of "Wouldn't it be nice if (WIBNI) . . ." questions like "WIBNI students didn't have to take finals?" Obstacles can be identified through listing "Wouldn't it be awful if (WIBAI) . . ." statements. For example: "WIBAI all students had to take a comprehensive exam before they graduated?" The group converges by identifying important concerns and combining concerns that have common elements. The most important statement ("In what ways might students be evaluated more fairly?", for instance) is then taken to the next stage.

2. *Data Finding.* In this stage the group "takes stock of what they already know, or need to know, about the mess." [28] To stimulate divergence, the group can list what it wants or needs to know, sources for that information and a list of answers when the information has been gathered. Convergence comes when the group selects the most important pieces of information which define the problem more clearly.

3. *Problem Finding.* The divergent phase of problem finding generates as many different ways of expressing the problem as possible. The convergent phase of this step notes important areas of agreement and overlap and results in a problem statement that everyone can agree on. Problem statements should focus on one problem and should not include criteria which might impose limits on the ideas generated during the next stage.

Figure 5.1 Creative Problem-Solving (CPS) Process

PROBLEM SENSITIVITY
▼

DIVERGENT PHASE   **CONVERGENT PHASE**

Experiences, roles and   *diverge*   Challenge is accepted and
situations are searched for   **Mess**   systematic efforts undertaken
messes . . . openness to   **Finding**   to respond to it.
experience; exploring   *converge*
opportunities.

Data are gathered; the situa-
tion is examined from many   **Data**
different viewpoints;   **Finding**   Most important data are
information, impressions,   identified and analyzed.
feelings, etc. are collected.

Many possible statements of   **Problem**   A working problem statement
problems and sub-problems   **Finding**   is chosen.
are generated.

Many alternatives and   **Idea**
possibilites for responding to   **Finding**   Ideas that seem most promis-
the problem statement are   ing or interesting are selected.
developed and listed.

                                                         Several important criteria are
Many possible criteria are for- **Solution**   selected to evaluate ideas.
mulated for reviewing and   **Finding**   Criteria are used to evaluate,
evaluating ideas.   strengthen, and refine ideas.

                                                         Most promising solutions are
Possible sources of assistance   focused and prepared for
and resistance are considered;   **Acceptance**   action. Specific plans are
potential implementation steps   **Finding**   formulated to implement
are identified.   solution.

▲   NEW CHALLENGES   ▲

Source: Isaksen, S. G., & Treffinger, D. (1985). *Creative problem solving: The basic course*. Buffalo, NY: Bearly Limited. Used by permission.

4. **Idea Finding.** Brainstorming, forced relationships and other idea generation techniques can be used as tools to help the group list divergent ideas. The group then selects several ideas from the list for further consideration.

5. **Solution Finding.** The first step in solution finding is to generate a list of possible criteria (divergence) and then to select the most important criteria (convergence). Next, the group diverges again by modifying and combining the ideas carried over from the idea finding stage to build the strongest solutions possible. Finally, the group converges on the best solution. Weighting systems, reverse brainstorming and other evaluation and selection strategies can help the group make this determination.

6. **Acceptance Finding.** The goal of this final stage is to make sure that the solution will be accepted and implemented. Members need to consider such issues as obstacles to implementation, implementation strategies, resources, and timing. They then converge on a plan of action which details how the solution will be implemented. Implementation of the plan may, in turn, generate new challenges which start the Creative Problem Solving process over again.

Characteristics of Highly Creative Groups

Although groups taking a prescriptive approach to problem solving are generally more productive, using these creative problem solving techniques or formats will not guarantee success. Prescriptive approaches frequently ignore the social dimension of the group process. If members are tense or defensive, for instance, they're not likely to contribute their ideas no matter what agenda the group follows. When using a prescriptive strategy, a group may put too much trust in the method and lose sight of the fact that it is the quality of the group's interaction that ultimately determines whether the group will be productive.

With the limitations of the prescriptive approach to creative problem solving in mind, we offer the following description of the characteristics of highly creative groups. These characteristics, which highlight the important role that interpersonal relationships and effective communication play in groups, can act as a checklist for your small group. The more of these factors your group demonstrates, the more likely it is that the group will generate high quality, creative solutions.

Cooperative Orientation

Effective creative problem-solving groups have a cooperative orientation rather than an individualistic or competitive focus. A cooperative climate fosters the types of attitudes and behaviors needed for creative problem solving in groups. Communication, psychology, education and management scholars report that cooperative group members are more likely to:[29]

- send accurate messages and accurately interpret messages from others
- understand the perspectives of other participants
- be attentive and participate in the discussion
- be open to influence from others
- develop close relationships with others in the group
- develop a positive attitude toward the group's task and stay focused on the problem
- tolerate diverse opinions
- help other members perform more effectively
- identify errors in the reasoning of others in the group
- think clearly because they feel less stress
- take greater risks in thinking and expect more success
- provide more positive feedback to other members which promotes higher self-esteem

Assigning one joint product to a group instead of a series of individual products lays the foundation for a cooperative group atmosphere. A joint product promotes cooperation because participants can only achieve individual goals if others in the group reach their goals. Dividing the work fairly, rewarding the group as a whole (not individuals), and emphasizing shared values like a commitment to service or quality also contribute to the formation of a cooperative climate.[30] As a group member, you can encourage cooperation through the way that you interact with others. Communication behaviors which foster cooperation include proposing compromises or concessions, carrying through on promises, pointing out the need to cooperate, asking for help and accurately paraphrasing others' points of view.[31]

Concern for Excellence

Highly innovative groups demand excellence from their members by setting high standards. Standards set acceptable levels of performance; the higher the standards, the more pressure group members put on themselves and others in the group to perform. Standards also make it clear when the group and its members have either succeeded or failed. The project team that developed the Boeing 747 is one example of a creative group that maintained extremely high standards. (For another example of a creative project team, see the Creative Profile, page 140.) Boeing gave the team five years to develop the 747 and insisted that the new jet meet design criteria which were summarized in the Boeing Design Objectives Criteria Book. By holding to the high standards outlined in this manual, the team met both safety and design specifications and resisted the temptation to fly the plane before it was completely ready.[32]

The demanding environment created through adherence to high standards encourages members to seek better solutions to problems. Members of such groups do not rest on past performances or settle for mediocrity. Instead, they seek creative ideas which result in higher performance. High standards also generate discussion and conflict as members try to determine how to reach their goals. Conflict, as we'll see later, increases the flow of creative ideas. Groups with a concern for excellence are also more tolerant of diversity. As a result, many different viewpoints can be brought to bear on the problem.[33]

Supportive Climate

The climate of highly creative groups is supportive and nonjudgmental. Members feel that they can safely offer their opinions and ideas without being ridiculed. This encourages everyone to participate in the group's deliberations. When the level of participation is high, group members exchange more information, take more risks by offering a greater number of new ideas and are more committed to the group's ultimate decision.[34]

Psychologist Jack Gibb identifies six sets of communication behaviors which can either destroy or build a supportive climate in a small group. Gibb first noted these types of defensive versus supportive communication behaviors during an eight-year study of human relations training groups.[35] According to Gibb, members of defensive groups shift their attention from the problem to defending their images. Feeling threatened, they develop strategies

Creative Profile: Scientific Teamwork

We commonly associate scientific creativity with the eccentric scientist working alone in the laboratory. However, scientific discoveries are usually the result of group effort. The atomic bomb, for example, was developed by a team of scientists from many different disciplines. Even Thomas Edison, who is credited with such inventions as the electric light bulb, phonograph and microphone, was part of a research team.[1] One fascinating description of how teams of researchers make discoveries is found in the book *Brainstorming: The Science and Politics of Opiate Research* by Solomon Snyder who heads the neuroscience laboratory at the Johns Hopkins School of Medicine in Baltimore.[2] In 1972 Snyder received money from Richard Nixon's War on Drugs to fund research aimed at locating opiate receptors—the molecular sites in the brain which respond to heroin, morphine, codeine and other opiates. By locating these receptors, Snyder and his colleagues hoped to identify the causes of addiction which could lead to the development of nonaddictive drugs to relieve chronic pain.

Snyder relied heavily on a team of doctoral and postdoctoral students to carry out the receptor research program. Describing himself as a "colossal klutz," Dr. Snyder lets his student teams run all hands-on experiments in his lab. He devotes himself instead to developing ideas, supervising students and interpreting findings. According to Snyder, ideas are the key to scientific discovery:

> . . . basic medical research is not at all like the science one learns in high school or college. The important element in grown-up research is not technical virtuosity but original ideas. The best investigations are as creative as the most innovative artists and composers. Outstanding science demands the same kind of thinking processes as the most creative philosophy. (p. 161)

Snyder keeps a backlog of one hundred ideas and refines his list every week. After initial discussions with a prospective team member, he tries to select the idea that best matches the student's interests and skills. Some student researchers do best with details; others want to see how their work fits into the "big picture." The opiate project team consisted of eight to ten students from such fields as biochemistry, biophysics, pharmacology, mathematics, psychology and medicine. The composition of the team changed periodically as team members graduated or moved to other labs and other students took their places. When additional expertise was needed, Snyder asked colleagues from other laboratories to join the project.

The Johns Hopkins team made a series of significant discoveries. Each discovery, in turn, raised additional questions which led to further breakthroughs. In order to keep a "fresh, open mind to look at new questions," Snyder and his students were careful to write up their findings from one stage of the project before they moved on to the next. Team members first identified opiate receptors and pinpointed their location in the brain. In the process they developed a testing procedure that greatly reduced the time it takes to screen the effects of psychoactive drugs. The project group then provided more information about how the body's morphine (naturally produced by the human body) regulates such functions as pain and mood. These discoveries may yet lead to the development of new, nonaddictive drugs for the treatment of addiction, schizophrenia and pain.

Dr. Snyder concludes his description of the opiate receptor project with some observations about the social dimension of scientific research. The best scientists, argues Snyder, mix critical and creative thinking skills. They're most likely to learn about the creative aspect of science through communication with those who act as their mentors. He sums up the importance of scientific teamwork this way:

> Science, like other aspects of a culture, is a communal activity. The way in which scientists work together in teams is crucial to the discovery process. And the most important team of all is the one made up of a mentor and a student. (p. 189)

[1] Scheidel, T. (1986). Divergent and convergent thinking in group decision making. In R. Y. Hirokawa & M. S. Poole (Eds.), *Communication and group decision-making*, (pp. 113–130). Beverly Hills: Sage.

[2] Snyder, S. H. (1989). *Brainstorming: The science and politics of opiate research.* Cambridge: Harvard University Press.

for winning out over other group members or for escaping punishment. Listening also suffers in such an environment. Defensive group members not only distort the messages they send but also the messages they receive. They are less accurate perceivers of the verbal and nonverbal cues of others. Participants in supportive groups, on the other hand, are more effective listeners and put more of their energies into solving the problem. The result is higher creative productivity.

1. ***Evaluation vs. Description.*** Evaluative responses imply a judgment of the receiver. This judgment can be carried by message content ("What a stupid idea!") or through nonverbal cues like a sarcastic tone of voice or a smirk. Descriptive speech avoids the implication that the hearer needs to change in some way. Sending purely descriptive messages is difficult, however. A request for information ("When do you think you can be done?") can become evaluative if the speaker's facial expression suggests that the information is long overdue.

2. **Control vs. Problem Orientation.** Communicators who try to impose their viewpoints on others in the group and try to control the behavior of other group members provoke defensive reactions. By attempting to exert control, they imply that their fellow team members are inadequate. Communicators who signal a willingness to collaborate on an equal basis to solve the problem help build a supportive climate.

3. **Strategy vs. Spontaneity.** Group participants become defensive when they suspect that another member is using the group to achieve selfish goals like getting a higher grade or a promotion. They're most defensive when they suspect that the manipulator is hiding his or her intentions. Spontaneous behaviors (actions and comments which appear straightforward and honest instead of carefully planned) are much less likely to provoke defensive reactions.

4. **Neutrality vs. Empathy.** Neutral messages such as "Don't feel so bad" or "You will get over it" carry low emotional content and communicate a sense of detachment. They devalue (disconfirm) the worth of the receiver and promote defensiveness. In contrast, empathetic messages ("I understand"; "You must really have a problem with her") signal a sense of identification and confirm the worth of the receiver. Gibb suggests that using gestures and facial cues to express concern is a particularly powerful way to demonstrate empathy.

5. **Superiority vs. Equality.** Messages which communicate intellectual ("I got straight As in high school"), physical or status superiority highlight receivers' feelings of inadequacy. Recipients of such messages may tune out the speaker, become competitive ("I got better grades than you last semester"), or feel jealous. Though status differences typically exist in a group, they can be minimized if high-status individuals respect the abilities and opinions of other group members.

6. **Certainty vs. Provisionalism.** Dogmatic group members who claim to know all the answers quickly provoke defensive reactions in others. These individuals put themselves into the role of teacher and appear more interested in winning the argument than in solving the problem. They have very little tolerance for those who disagree with their ideas. Other group members commonly believe that dogmatic group members are trying to hide their feelings of inferiority by being inflexible. Provisional members, on the other hand, are willing to consider

other ideas and to change their opinions and attitudes as a result of group discussion.

Cohesive but Not Coercive

Highly creative groups recognize the difference between *cohesion* and *coercion*. While they emphasize collaboration, members of successful creative problem solving groups never make unanimity more important than effective problem solving. A group that makes cohesion its ultimate goal loses its ability to think both divergently and critically and resorts to coercion to pressure members to conform. Social psychologist Irving Janis developed the label "groupthink" to characterize groups that put unanimous agreement above all other considerations.[36] Groups that suffer from this syndrome fail to: consider all the alternatives, weigh the risks of their choices, work out contingency plans or discuss important ethical issues. In sum, these groups are ineffective creative problem solving teams. Janis sees such decisions as the Bay of Pigs invasion of Cuba, the United States' failure to anticipate the attack on Pearl harbor, the invasion of North Korea and the escalation of the Vietnam War as examples of groupthink in action. In each case, highly intelligent and skilled political leaders made terrible choices. By recognizing and responding to the symptoms of groupthink, these leaders might have been able to come up with more effective, creative solutions to world problems. Janis identifies the following as signs of groupthink:

> *Illusion of Invulnerability.* Groups that suffer from groupthink believe that they can do no wrong. Members are overly optimistic and are prone to take extraordinary risks. President Lyndon Johnson and his policy makers kept escalating the war in Vietnam because they believed that the North Vietnamese would back down. One of Lyndon Johnson's advisors later remarked: "We thought we had the golden touch."[37]

> *Rationalization.* Victims of groupthink construct rationalizations to protect themselves from feedback that would challenge their assumptions. In 1941, United States naval officers rationalized that the Japanese would never start a war with the United States, that any enemy carriers would be detected before attack, and that no warships anchored in Pearl Harbor could be sunk by torpedo bombs because the water was too shallow.

Belief in the Inherent Morality of the Group. Members of ingroups do not question the inherent morality of the group; they ignore ethical consequences. In discussions of the Cuban Bay of Pigs operation (which resulted in the death or capture of all the invading troops), President Kennedy's policy group rarely talked about the ethics of attacking a small neighboring country or of lying to the American public about the invasion. Later, during deliberations which safely ended the Cuban missile crisis, many of the same group members spent hours debating the morality of a surprise air attack. In the end, the group decided that such an option was not in the best, moral American tradition.

Stereotypes of Other Groups. When groupthink prevails, members tend to think of members of other groups as evil, weak or stupid. This was the case with Truman's advisors who didn't believe that the Chinese had the ability to respond decisively to the United Nations invasion of North Korea. As a result of this miscalculation, China entered the Korean conflict and the war ended in a stalemate.

Pressure on Dissenters. Victims of groupthink pressure members who disagree with the prevailing opinion in the group. When presidential advisor Bill Moyers arrived at one discussion of the Vietnam War, President Johnson welcomed him by saying: "Well, here comes Mr. Stop-the-Bombing."[38]

Self-Censorship. The groupthink syndrome encourages members to keep their doubts about group decisions to themselves. Perhaps as a result of being labeled as "Mr. Stop-the-Bombing," for example, Bill Moyers became a "domesticated dissenter" who only expressed reservations about a few details of the plan to escalate the war in Vietnam. Groupthink victims tend to minimize the importance of their doubts in order to reduce the dissonance they feel about keeping silent despite their reservations about the group's decisions.

Illusion of Unanimity. Victims of groupthink assume that the absence of conflicting opinions means that the entire group agrees on a course of action. Historian Aurthur Schlesinger (a participant in the Bay of Pigs planning sessions) had serious doubts about the invasion but he and others remained silent because they assumed that the group had consensus.

Self-Appointed Mindguards. Mindguards are group members who take it upon themselves to protect the group leader from dissenting points of view which might disrupt the group's consensus. President Kennedy's brother Robert took this role during the Bay of Pigs decision when he told Schlesinger: "You may be right or you may be wrong, but the President has made his mind up. Don't push it any further. Now is the time for everyone to help him all they can."[39]

Although Janis used national leaders to illustrate the dangers of groupthink, groups of ordinary citizens also put cohesion above effective problem solving. For example, members of cohesive class project groups often think that their groups are "best" and label other groups as inferior. They pressure dissenters who suggest different ways to complete the group project. In extreme cases, members of these groups may sabotage the projects of other project teams, confident that the goal of a higher grade for the group justifies their unethical behavior.

Janis makes several suggestions for reducing the likelihood of groupthink. As a leader, avoid expressing your preference for a particular solution. Instead, encourage every group member to be a critical evaluator and assign individual members the role of "devil's advocate" to argue against prevailing opinion. Divide regularly into subgroups and then come back to negotiate differences. Invite outside experts or colleagues to the group's meetings to challenge the group's ideas. Keep in regular contact with other groups. Roleplay the reactions of rival organizations and groups to reduce the effects of stereotyping and rationalization. After the decision has been made, give members one last chance to express any remaining doubts about the solution.

Minority Influence

The dangers of groupthink highlight the significant role that minority opinion plays in successful groups. The presence of individuals and subgroups who disagree with the majority can greatly increase a group's effectiveness.[40] When there is no minority, the attention of the group is focused on one point of view—the majority's. Group members have little motivation to examine the problem further. As a result, they disregard novel solutions and converge on one position. Minorities stimulate thought about the problem itself because they cast doubt on the prevailing opinion in the group. Members exert more effort when they must resolve the conflict between majority and minority solutions. They pay more attention to all aspects of the issue, consider more viewpoints, and use a wider variety of problem-solving strategies. This divergent thinking often leads to higher quality, more creative solutions. Being exposed to the dissenting views of minorities also encourages group members to resist conformity in other settings.[41]

Forming heterogenous groups made up of members who have significantly different backgrounds and perspectives is one way to encourage the emergence of minorities who stimulate creative thinking. Consider the case of a group assigned to reduce the number of product defects on an automobile assembly line. If this group includes members from sales, purchasing, management, the assembly line, engineering and maintenance, it is more likely to have a strong minority influence than if it is made up of just managers or assembly line workers. Appointing a "devil's advocate," as Irving Janis suggests, is another way to insure that a minority viewpoint is heard.

Productive Conflict

Conflict is one of the most important tools of productive creative problem-solving groups. As we've seen, highly creative groups encourage conflict by pursuing excellence, guarding against groupthink and fostering minority opinions. Members of these groups, however, engage in substantive rather than affective conflict. Substantive conflicts or controversies involve disagreements about ideas and solutions (the content of the discussion) while affective conflicts focus on the interpersonal relations between group members.[42] Substantive conflict is productive because it promotes a cooperative and supportive climate, reduces anxiety levels, increases the satisfaction of participants, helps members understand and appreciate each others' positions, stimulates thought about the problem, and results in a solution that integrates the thoughts of all group members.[43] Affective conflict has just the opposite effects. Conflict over personalities creates an unpleasant emotional atmosphere which frustrates members and diverts them from the task at hand. Groups in the midst of affective conflicts often engage in avoidance or escalation cycles. Members try to withdraw from the problem or escalate hostilities if the problem can't be ignored. Table 5.1 summarizes some of the symptoms of the avoidance and escalation cycles that characterize groups that are engaged in destructive conflicts.

Changing the behaviors that characterize avoidance and escalation is one way to encourage productive rather than destructive conflict; laying down some procedural ground rules

Table 5.1: Interaction Symptoms of Escalation or Avoidance Cycles

Symptoms of avoidance	Symptoms of escalation
Marked decrease in the group's commitment to solving the problem ("why would we care?")	An issue takes much longer to deal with than was anticipated
Quick acceptance of a suggested solution	Members repeatedly offer the same argument in support of a position
Members stop themselves from raising controversial aspects of an issue	Members over-inflate the consequences of not reaching agreement
People "tune out" of the interaction	Threats are used to win arguments
Unresolved issues keep emerging in the same or different form	Mounting tension is felt in the group
Discussion centers on a safe aspect of a broader and more explosive issue	The group gets nowhere but seems to be working feverishly
Little sharing of information	Name-calling and personal arguments are used
Outspoken members are notably quiet	Immediate polarization on issues or the emergence of coalitions
No plans are made to implement a chosen solution	Hostile eye gaze or less-direct eye contact between members
No evaluation is made of evidence that is offered in support of claims	Sarcastic laughter or humor as a form of tension release
	Heated disagreements that seem pointless or are about trivial issues

Source: From *Working Through Conflict: A Communication Perspective* by Joseph P. Folger and Marshall Scott Poole (p. 78). Copyright © 1984 by Scott Foresman and Company. Reprinted by permission of HarperCollins Publishers.

before the discussion begins is another.[44] As you begin your deliberations, encourage members to see conflict about ideas as a natural part of group discussion. Suggest that they use differences of opinion as a starting point for additional investigation. Urge members not to capitulate but to work toward consensus and to challenge any agreement that comes quickly and easily.

Summing Up

In this chapter, we laid the foundation for building more creative problem solving groups through describing the group process, surveying prescriptive problem-solving techniques and formats, and identifying the characteristics of highly creative groups.

We began by defining what a group is from a communication

perspective. A small group has a common purpose, interdependence, mutual influence, verbal and nonverbal communication, and a limited size. Small groups tackle many problems, but they only engage in creative problem solving when they solve complex, ill-structured problems. Ill-structured problems cannot be solved by using procedures that are currently in place. Solutions for this type of dilemma develop during group discussion. The Decision Emergence, Spiral and Multiple Sequence models are three descriptions of how solutions emerge through the group process.

Next we looked at prescriptive approaches to creative problem solving in groups. These are sets of guidelines or instructions designed to help groups avoid such common mistakes as offering premature solutions or failing to reach consensus. Prescriptive creative problem solving techniques can be classified according to their relationship to the three tasks that every group must accomplish in order to be successful: 1) redefining and analyzing the problem, 2) generating ideas, and 3) evaluating and selecting options. The 5Ws and H and Organized Random Search are problem definition and analysis strategies which help groups develop a new perspective on the problem. Brainstorming and Morphological Analysis enable groups to generate a large number of new ideas. Weighted Criteria and Reverse Brainstorming are techniques for selecting the idea(s) that will best solve the problem. Synectics and the Creative Problem Solving (CPS) format are two agendas that help groups accomplish all three tasks.

In the final section, we examined the characteristics of highly creative groups. These elements highlight the important role that interpersonal relationships and effective communication play in creative group problem solving. The more of these factors a group demonstrates, the more likely it will succeed. Highly innovative groups: share a cooperative orientation rather than an individualistic or competitive focus; demonstrate a concern for excellence by setting high standards; have a supportive rather than a defensive climate; recognize the difference between cohesion and coercion and take steps to avoid groupthink; encourage minorities to challenge the majority opinion of the group; promote substantive conflict about ideas.

Application Exercises

1. For the next week, keep a log of how much time you spend in groups at school, at work and in your personal life. Identify each

group as well as the specific problems discussed in each group session. What proportion of each group's time was devoted to creative problem solving? Compare your log with that of others in the class.

2. Which model best describes how solutions emerge during group discussion? Why? Find a partner and explain your position.

3. Select one of the prescriptive problem-solving approaches described in the chapter and use it in a group creative problem-solving session. Based on your experience, evaluate the advantages and disadvantages of this strategy.

4. If you've been assigned to a small group in this course, hold a group meeting to evaluate your team based on the list of characteristics of highly creative groups given in the text. As a group, develop strategies for improving the team's performance.

5. Create your own case study by describing a creative problem solving group to which you belong. Discuss the background of the group and describe its development. What prescriptive approaches has your group used? How would you rate the quality of the group's communication and the quality of its decision(s)? Write up your findings.

6. Develop a strategy for improving your communication skills as a small group member. What are your strengths? Weaknesses? How will you improve?

Endnotes

[1] See, for example:

Brilhart, J. K. (1982). *Effective group discussion* (4th ed.). Dubuque, IA: Wm. C. Brown.

Patton, B. R., Giffin, K., & Nyquist Patton, E. (1989). *Decision-making group interaction* (3rd ed.). New York: Harper & Row.

[2] Jensen, A. D., & Chilberg, J. C. (1991). *Small group communication: Theory and application*. Belmont, CA: Wadsworth p. 14.

[3] VanGundy, A. B. (1988). *Stalking the wild solution: A problem finding approach to creative problem solving*. Buffalo, NY: Bearly Limited.

[4] Churchman, C. W. (1971). *The design of inquiring systems: Basic concepts of systems and organizations*. New York: Basic Books.; VanGundy, A. B. (1988). *Techniques of structured problem solving* (2nd ed.). New York: Van Nostrand Reinhold Co.

[5] Fisher, A. B. (1970). Decision emergence: Phases in group decision making. *Speech Monographs, 37*, 53–66.

[6] Scheidel, T. M., & Crowell, L. (1964). Idea development in small discussion groups. *Quarterly Journal of Speech, 50*, 140–145.

[7] Poole, M. S. (1983). Decision development in small groups II: A study of multiple sequences in decision making. *Communication Monographs, 50*, 206–232.; Poole, M. S. (1983). Decision development in small groups III: A multiple sequence model of group decision development. *Communication Monographs, 50*, 321–341.

[8] Poole, M. S, & Roth, J. (1989). Decision development in small groups IV: A typology of group decision paths. *Human Communication Research, 15*, 323–56.

[9] Fisher, A. B. (1980). *Small group decision making* (2nd ed.). New York: McGraw Hill.

[10] See:

Larson, C. E. (1969). Forms of analysis and small group problem solving. *Speech Monographs, 36*, 452–455.

Hirokawa, R. (1985). Discussion procedures and decision-making performance: A test of a functional perspective. *Human Communication Research, 12*, 203–224.

[11] An excellent summary of both the strengths and weaknesses of prescriptive approaches can be found in Jensen & Chilberg, *Small group communication: Theory and application*, Ch. 2.

[12] VanGundy. *Techniques of structured problem solving*, Ch. 1.

[13] VanGundy, *Stalking the wild solution*, p. 6

[14] Parnes, S. J., Noller, R. B., & Biondi, A. M. (1977). *Guide to creative action* (rev. ed.). New York: Scribner.; Isaksen, S. G., & Treffinger, D. J. (1985). *Creative problem solving: The basic course*. Buffalo, NY: Bearly Limited.; VanGundy, *The techniques of structured problem solving*, Ch. 3.

[15] Williams, F. E. (1960). *Foundations of creative problem solving*. Ann Arbor, MI: Edwards Brothers.

[16] Osborn, A. F. (1957). *Applied imagination: Principles and procedures of creative thinking* (rev. ed.). New York: Charles Scribner's Sons.; Osborn, A. (1952). *Your creative imagination*. New York: Charles Scribner's Sons.

[17] Osborn, *Applied imagination*, p. 84.

[18] For excellent summaries of research related to brainstorming, see:

Lamm, H., & Trommsdorff, G. (1973). Group vs. individual performance on tasks requiring ideational proficiency (brainstorming): A review. *European Journal of Social Psychology, 3*, 361–388.

Jablin, F. M., & Siebold, D. R. (1978). Implications for problem-solving groups of empirical research on 'brainstorming': A critical review of the literature. *Southern Speech Communication Journal, 43*, 327–356.

[19] Diehl, M., & Stroebe, W. (1987). Productivity loss in brainstorming groups: Toward the solution of a riddle. *Journal of Personality and Social Psychology, 53*, 497–509.; Lamm & Trommsdorff; Jablin & Siebold.

[20] Gallupe, R. B., & Cooper, W. H. (1993, Fall). Brainstorming electronically. *Sloan Management Review*, pp. 27–36.

[21] Geschka, H. (1983). Perspectives on using various creativity techniques. In S. S. Gryskiewicz, J. T. Shields, & W. H. Shields (Eds.), *Selected readings in creativity (Vol. II)* (pp. 163–175). Greensboro, NC: Center for Creative Leadership.

[22] See:

Allen, M. S. (1962). *Morphological creativity*. Englewood Cliffs, NJ: Prentice-Hall.

Zwicky, F. (1969). *Discovery, invention, research through the morphological approach*. New York: MacMillan.

Miller, W. (1987). *The creative edge: Fostering innovation where you work*. Boston: Addison Wesley.

[23] VanGundy, *Techniques of structured problem solving*, Ch. 5.

[24] Whiting, C. S. (1958). *Creative thinking*. New York: Van Nostrand Rheinhold; VanGundy, *Techniques of structured group problem solving*, Ch. 5.

[25] The method's co-developers William Gordon and George Prince offer somewhat different descriptions of the steps of the Synectics process. Prince's description is offered here. See:

Gordon, W. J. (1961). *Synectics: The development of creative capacity.* New York: Harper & Row.

Prince, G. M. (1970). *The practice of creativity.* New York: Collier Books.

Many of the examples in this section of the chapter come from these two sources.

[26] Prince, p. 95.

[27] Issaksen, S., & Treffinger, D. (1985). *Creative problem solving: The basic course.* Buffalo, NY: Bearly Limited.; Treffinger, D. J., & Firestien, R. L. (1989, July-August). Update: Guidelines for effective facilitation of creative problem solving. *Gifted Child Today,* pp. 35–39.; Parnes, Noller, & Biondi, *Guide to creative action.*

[28] Treffinger & Firestien, p. 37.

[29] See:

Deutsch, M. (1973). *The resolution of conflict.* New Haven: Yale University Press.

Johnson, D. W. & Johnson, R. T. (1974). Instructional goal structure: Cooperative, competitive, or individualistic. *Review of Educational Research, 44,* 213–240.

Johnson, D. W., Maruyama, G., Johnson, R., Nelson, D., & Skon, L. (1981). The effects of cooperative, competitive, and individualistic goal structure on achievement: A meta-analysis. *Psychological Bulletin, 89,* 47–62.

Tjosvold, D. (1984). Cooperation theory and organizations. *Human Relations, 37,* 743–767.

[30] Tjosvold, D. (1986). Dynamics of interdependence in organizations. *Human Relations, 39,* 517–540.

[31] Johnson, D. W. (1974). Communication and the inducement of cooperative behavior in conflicts: A critical review. *Speech Monographs, 41,* 64–78.; Rubin, J. Z., & Brown, B. R. (1975). *The social psychology of bargaining and negotiation.* New York: Academic Press.

[32] Larson, C. E. & LaFasto, F. M. J. (1989). *Teamwork: What must go right/What can go wrong.* Newbury Park, CA: Sage, Ch. 7.

[33] West, M. A. (1990). The social psychology of innovation in groups. In M. A. West & J. L. Farr (Eds.), *Innovation and creativity at work: Psychological and organizational strategies* (pp. 309–333). Chicester, England: John Wiley & Sons.

[34] West, The social psychology of innovation in groups.

[35] Gibb, J. R. (1961). Defensive communication. *Journal of Communication, 11,* 141–148.

[36] Janis, I. (1982). *Groupthink* (2nd ed.). Boston: Houghton Mifflin.; Janis, I. (1971, November). Groupthink: The problems of conformity. *Psychology Today,* pp. 271–279.

[37] Janis, *Groupthink,* p. 105.

[38] Janis, *Groupthink,* p. 115.

[39] Janis, *Groupthink,* p. 40.

[40] For summaries of research on minority influence processes, see:

Moscovici, S. Mugny, G., & Van Avermaet, E. (Eds.) (1985). *Perspectives on minority influence.* Cambridge: Cambridge University Press.

Maas, A., & Clark, R. D. (1984). Hidden impact of minorities: Fifteen years of minority influence research. *Psychological Bulletin, 95,* 428–450.

[41] Nemeth, C. (1985). Dissent, group process and creativity: The contribution of minority influence. In E. Lawler (Ed.), *Advances in group processes* (Vol. 2, pp. 57–75). Greenwich, CT: JAI Press.; Nemeth, C., & Chiles, C. (1986). Modelling courage: The role of dissent in fostering independence. *European Journal of Social Psychology, 18,* 275–280.

[42] Guetzkow, H., & Gyr, J. (1954). An analysis of conflict in decision-making groups. *Human Relations, 7,* 367–381.

[43] See:

Hoffman, L. R., Harburg, E., & Maier, N. R. F. (1962). Differences and disagreements as factors in creative group problem solving. *Journal of Abnormal and Social Psychology, 64,* 206–214.

Tjosvold, D., & Johnson, D. W. (1977). Effects of controversy on cognitive perspective taking. *Journal of Educational Psychology* 69, 679–685.

Bell, M. A. (1974). The effects of substantive and affective conflict in problem-solving groups. *Speech Monographs, 41*, 19–23.

Johnson, D. W., & Johnson, R. T. (1979). Conflict in the classroom: Controversy and learning. *Review of Educational Research, 49*, 51–70.

Tjosvold, D. (1985). Implications of controversy research for management. *Journal of Management, 11*, 21–37.

[44] Hall, J., & Watson, W. H. (1970). The effects of normative intervention on group decision-making performance. *Human Relations, 23*, p. 304.

Quotations

Scheidel, T. (1986). Divergent and convergent thinking in group decision making. In R. Y. Hirokawa & M. S. Poole (Eds.), *Communication and group decision-making*, pp. 113–130. Beverly Hills: Sage.

von Oech, R. (1983). *A whack on the side of the head*. New York: Warner Books.

6 | Creative Organizational Communication

Nothing fails like success.

Richard Pascale

PREVIEW

- ► Communicating and Organizing
- ► The Learning Organization
    Modifying Mental Models
    Building Blocks of the Learning Laboratory
- ► Becoming a Change Master
    Innovation Strategies
    Leading Creativity
- ► Summing Up
- ► Application Exercises

Creativity is the key to organizational survival. The needs of customers and clients, public tastes, the nature of the workforce, governmental regulations, technology and other factors shift constantly. To survive, organizations must cope with changes and initiate changes of their own through the development of new products, services, programs, manufacturing processes and marketing strategies. Organizations that don't respond creatively to change are doomed. As a result, individuals often live longer than organizations. Only two percent of all corporations in the United States, for example, and four percent of all federal agencies live to be fifty years old.[1] Even companies large enough to be ranked among the "Fortune 500" are threatened. One-third of the industrial firms on this list disappeared between 1970 and 1983.[2]

In this chapter we'll suggest ways to encourage the creative communication which is essential to the health of organizations. We'll see how organizing is a communication process, describe learning organizations, and outline strategies for becoming a change master.

Communicating and Organizing

Any discussion of creative organizational communication should be based on an understanding of the relationship between communicating and organizing. To clarify the connection between communication and organizations, we'll rely on the observations of University of Michigan social psychologist Karl Weick.[3] Weick believes that individuals organize themselves in order to process equivocal (ambiguous) information from the environment. By interacting with one another, they reduce the uncertainty generated by messages that can be interpreted in many different ways. Pickup basketball games provide one example of how organizing diminishes the discomfort caused by ambiguity. Players meeting for the first time are faced with a series of questions: "How should we form teams?" "How long will the games be?" "Will defensive or offensive players call their own fouls?" "How good are the other players in the group?" They feel more comfortable once they establish rules and procedures and learn more about the skills of the other participants.

According to Weick, members of organizations are connected to each other through communication loops called double interacts. A double interact consists of an act, a response and an adjustment.

Consider the three-step pattern that could result when a college or university announces a tuition increase. Administrators act by proposing increased fees. Students respond by complaining about the higher costs. School officials may then adjust by asking for less money.

Weick rejects the widely accepted belief that organizations are the products of careful, rational planning. Instead, he argues, we act now and make sense of what we did later. Organizations evolve through a process of enactment—selection—retention. He describes the first step in the process this way:

> There is no such thing as experience until the manager does something. . . . Experience is the consequence of activity. The manager literally wades into the swarm of "events" that surround him [her] and actively tries to unrandomize them and impose some order. The manager acts physically in the environment, attends to some of it, ignores most of it, talks to other people about what they see and are doing. As a result the surroundings get sorted into variables and linkages and appear more orderly.[4]

Weick contends that the worst decision a manager can make is to decide not to act. Doing something is far better than doing nothing. He also notes that managers act in ways that provoke reactions that reconfirm their original actions. For example, if they anticipate trouble from employees, they often have their suspicions confirmed. Expecting insubordination, they may act in an authoritarian manner—giving orders and refusing to listen to employee concerns. The "problem" workers respond to what they see as callous treatment by ignoring directives and filing grievances.

The second step in the change process—selection—involves the interpretation of actions. Organizational members engage in retrospective sense making by selecting the most appropriate meanings after events have occurred.[5] When processing routine messages, managers and workers typically rely on recipes or formulas called assembly rules (e.g. "lower sales mean no Christmas bonuses"; "tenure decisions must be made by the board of trustees"; "if complaint letters come in, send them to the public relations department"). However, when faced with highly equivocal information, members must engage in more communication in order to reach an acceptable level of uncertainty. The death of a college president, for instance, triggers a flurry of communication activity. To determine what this unusual event means to the future of the organization, faculty, staff and students hold informal discussions, call one another, send E-mail messages and attend special meetings.

Committing events to organizational memory through retention is the third and final step in the evolutionary cycle. Although many actions are forgotten, those that are recalled tend to be repeated. Companies that have boosted sales in the past by cutting prices are likely to do so again. Manufacturers who previously emphasized marketing will be reluctant to put additional money into product development instead.

By focusing on the organizing process rather than on static organizational structures, Weick highlights the fact that organizations are themselves the products of communication. Schools, businesses, religious congregations, social agencies and other organizations are created through the actions and interpretations of their members. Communication is not something that takes place within an organization—it IS the organization. Yet, the same processes which bring organizations into being often discourage further creativity. Both selection and retention can blind members to the changes they need to make in order to survive. They follow existing rules and repeat what's been done in the past when they should be developing new interpretations and strategies instead. In the end they become victims of their symbolic creations—a danger we described in chapter 1.

To prosper, organizations must strike the necessary balance between stability and creativity. They can only function effectively if members know their roles and use established procedures to carry out such tasks as claim processing, engineering, filing and budgeting. At the same time, they must continually change or find themselves faced with extinction. Some scholars suggest that organizations can meet the competing demands for order and change by becoming learning laboratories. In the next section we'll take a closer look at organizations as learners.

The Learning Organization

Learning organizations take a systematic approach to change by continually recreating themselves through the application of new insights and ideas. These organizations are particularly skilled at generating and acquiring knowledge and at using this information to modify their behavior. They try to resolve the tension between stability and creativity by blending what they believe to be the best of the old and the new. Transforming an existing organization into a learning laboratory is a two-stage process. Organizational members must first challenge their current ways of thinking; then, new building blocks or practices must be put into place.

> A learning organization is a place where people are continually discovering how they create their reality. And how they can change it.
>
> Peter Senge

Modifying Mental Models

Most of an organization's memory is stored in the minds of its members rather than in its official written records. Organizational learning expert Peter Senge uses the term **mental models** to refer to the knowledge, beliefs and assumptions that workers and managers carry around in their heads.[6] Mental models direct the thoughts and actions of communicators and derive much of their power from the fact that individuals rarely take a careful look at what they believe. Guided by unchallenged and often faulty assumptions, they overlook potential problems and opportunities. Consider the case of General Motors. The automobile giant lost much of its market share to foreign imports in the 1970s and 1980s because it assumed that American consumers were only concerned about styling, not quality. The mental model of GM and other American automakers kept these organizations from competing effectively with the Japanese and Europeans who recognized that American consumers had become more interested in a car's reliability. In recent years GM has dramatically reduced product defects and won back some of its former customers. If executives at General Motors had examined their mental models in the 1970s and acknowledged then that they believed that Americans cared only about style, they might have shifted their focus to quality much sooner and maintained their share of the American market.

> With over 50 foreign cars already on sale here, the Japanese auto industry isn't likely to carve out a big slice of the U.S. market for itself.
>
> *Business Week*, August 2, 1968

The problem of faulty assumptions is compounded when, in addition to blindly accepting their own beliefs, communicators use defensive routines to keep others from challenging their mental models. Defensive routines are thoughts and actions which protect "usual ways of dealing with reality."[7] One defensive strategy is to defeat opponents through debate. In this type of routine, neither party learns from the other because each is more interested in winning than in gathering information. Another defensive routine puts the emphasis on "saving face." In this case, conflict is submerged because participants believe that ignoring conflict is best for individuals and the organization. Communicators who don't deal publicly with conflict send out mixed messages. While their words indicate agreement, their tone of voice, facial expressions and body posture signal disapproval.

The use of defensive routines creates a competitive, distrustful communication climate and encourages the organization to emphasize stability at the expense of creativity. When members protect their current ways of thinking, they don't see the need for change. They are content to live with the status quo, particularly when the organization is enjoying success. Significant shifts in strategy come only when existing mental models are cast into doubt.

> We understand that the only competitive advantage the company of the future will have is its managers' ability to learn faster than their competitors. So the companies that succeed will be those that continually nudge their managers towards revising their views of the world.
>
> Arie P. De Geus, Planning Director, Royal Dutch Shell

Learning organizations help members identify and challenge their mental models. Individuals in these organizations use reflection and inquiry communication skills which reduce the use of defensive routines and encourage the examination of assumptions. The end result is greater organizational creativity. Reflection skills center on thinking about how we think. The Left-Hand Column exercise is one way to identify our intrapersonal communication patterns.[8] To complete this exercise, select a recent communication encounter which didn't produce the learning that you wanted. Write out what you and the other person said in the right hand column. Record what you were thinking *but did not say* in the left-hand column. The Left-Hand Column exercise reveals many of the assumptions we make about others. In the example, the colleague sounds supportive, but the underlying assumption is that Sandy lacks confidence and initiative. Sandy's refusal to admit that the presentation went poorly is taken as proof that Sandy lacks initiative. Jean doesn't really express an opinion about the presentation or what was reported about it. The problem is never discussed and thus cannot be resolved. Neither Sandy nor Jean have the opportunity to learn and improve.

The Left-Hand Column Exercise

Imagine Jean's exchange with a colleague, Sandy, after a big presentation to the boss on a joint project. Jean missed the presentation, but had heard that it was poorly received.

Jean: How did the presentation go?

Sandy: Well, I don't know. It's really too early to say. Besides, we're breaking new ground here.

Jean: Well, what do you think we should do? I believe that the issues you were raising are important.

Sandy: I'm not so sure. Let's just wait and see what happens.

Jean: You may be right, but I think we may need to do more than just wait.

Now, here is what the exchange looks like with the "left-hand column":

What Jean is Thinking	*What is Said*
Everyone says the presentation was a bomb.	**Jean:** How did the presentation go?
Does she really not know how bad it was? Or is she not willing to face up to it?	**Sandy:** Well, I don't know. It's too early to say. Besides, we're breaking new ground here.
	Jean: Well, what do you think we should do? I believe that the issues you were raising are important.
She really is afraid to see the truth. If she only had more confidence, she could probably learn from a situation like this.	**Sandy:** I'm not so sure. Let's just wait and see what happens.
I can't believe she doesn't realize how disastrous that presentation was to our moving ahead.	**Jean:** You may be right, but I think we may need to do more than just wait.

Source: Senge, P. (1990). *The fifth discipline: The art of the learning organization.* New York: Doubleday/Currency, pp. 195–196. Used by permission.

Recognizing leaps of abstraction is a particularly important reflection skill. As we indicated in chapter 4, confusing inferences and judgments with facts is one of the most common creative roadblocks. We frequently jump from observations to generalizations, and then we accept the generalizations as facts. For example, some police officers know for a "fact" that citizens have little respect for the law. Why? Because they frequently observe lawbreakers. One way to avoid a dangerous leap of abstraction is to ask why you believe what you do and to identify the information upon which your generalization is based. Whenever possible, test the generalization. In the interaction between Sandy and Jean described above, both the observation and the generalization could be in error. The presentation might have gone well (after all, the source of the information may be incorrect), or Sandy might have confidence and initiative but lack the necessary skill to make an effective presentation.

In addition to identifying our intrapersonal communication, we need to be able to identify the mental models of others. Inquiry opens up the door to collaborative learning. Asking questions (one of the creative word tools described in chapter 4) uncovers the observations and generalizations of other communicators. Probing for the reasons behind a decision or action can also reveal the inconsistencies in another person's position. The key is to practice reciprocal advocacy and inquiry. Put forth proposals but be willing to reveal your reasoning process and try to find out more about the mental model of the other party. Effective inquiry tactics include 1) asking for the reasons behind another person's position or proposal, 2) encouraging others to explore your view or to introduce another perspective (i.e. "Can you see a problem with my reasoning?"), 3) identifying the logic behind your perspective, and 4) encouraging others (and yourself) to talk about what might be blocking effective communication.

Building Blocks of the Learning Laboratory

Revealing and challenging current ways of thinking is the first step in building learning organizations; incorporating practices that encourage continuous learning is the second. According to Robert Garvin of the Harvard Business School, there are five building blocks that make up the learning laboratory. These five major activities include:

1. **Systematic problem solving.** Members of learning organizations take a systematic approach to solving dilemmas. Rather

than relying on their instincts or gut-level reactions, they use interviews, surveys, statistical analysis and other scientific tools to discover new information which can be incorporated into the problem solving process.

2. ***Experimentation.*** Organizational learners continually seek out and test new knowledge through ongoing programs and demonstration projects. Ongoing programs consist of small experiments which gradually increase the knowledge base. Employees of the Corning company, for instance, constantly test new materials and mixtures to develop better glass. Workers at Chaparral Steel develop new mold designs by using water to simulate the flow of molten steel.[10] Demonstration projects are larger and more complex than ongoing programs. Project designers generally start from "scratch" at one site because their programs challenge current organizational practices. If successful, the tactics used in the demonstration project are generally adopted by the organization as a whole. GM learned about creative work teams, quality and customer service through its Saturn plant which manufactured cars in Tennessee rather than in Detroit. The company is now trying to incorporate these lessons into all of its operations. A detailed description of a demonstration project sponsored by General Electric is found in the Creative Dilemma on page 162.

3. ***Learning from past experiences.*** Learning organizations reflect on their successes and failures and then record these lessons so that future employees can learn from them. The British Petroleum company set up a post-project appraisal unit to review six projects a year. In addition to reporting to the board of directors, the group wrote up case studies and revised company planning guidelines based on its findings.

4. ***Learning from others.*** A great deal of learning comes from looking outside the organization. Taking a systematic approach to learning from outside sources is sometimes referred to as "benchmarking." In the benchmarking process, members of one organization study the practices of other more effective organizations in hopes of identifying procedures that will improve the performance of their group. Xerox (the company that created the concept of benchmarking) has used the procedure to improve its billing, warehousing and manufacturing processes. Customers are also a rich source of learning. Sony, Motorola and other learning organizations routinely send managers and employees out to meet with customers to see how company products are being used and to determine consumer needs.

Creative Dilemma:
Building a New Compressor at General Electric

Introducing a major innovation often leads to a series of changes. One change generally leads to another and then another. At each step in the process, innovators must learn new skills and make important decisions. Failing to learn or making a poor choice can kill the creative idea and spell disaster for the organization.

General Electric faced just such a series of changes and related learning challenges and decisions when it introduced a new refrigerator compressor. The compressor, a pump that produces cold air, is a refrigerator's most important and expensive component. U.S. companies had long been the world leaders in the compressor and refrigerator markets, and executives at GE dismissed the idea that foreign manufacturers could pose a serious threat to their business. However, in the early 1980s companies from Japan and Italy began manufacturing better, cheaper compressors. Some U.S. firms, like Whirlpool, began to manufacture compressors overseas to take advantage of lower labor costs. General Electric could either 1) buy compressors from competitors or suppliers overseas, or 2) produce a higher quality compressor in the United States that would sell for less than those made in foreign countries. Some at GE argued that buying the compressor part from other firms—called sourcing—was regrettable but inevitable. They didn't believe that the company could ever catch up to the competition. To them, sourcing was the best way to guarantee the survival of the product line. Others disagreed. They pointed out that sourcing would put the company at the mercy of suppliers, some of whom were competitors. By buying from others, GE would lose its edge as the market leader in its largest line of products. The firm decided to go against industry trends and to pursue the second option.

Under the leadership of its refrigerator manufacturing director Tom Blunt, the Major Appliance Building Group (MABG) began to develop a rotary compressor which required fewer parts than the traditional reciprocating compressor. The company used a version of the rotary compressor in its air conditioners but had never applied the design to refrigerators because refrigerators work compressors much harder. To keep costs down, the compressor would have to be manufactured in one of the most automated factories in the world. In addition, design specifications required that the parts of the compressor work together at a friction point as narrow as .01 of the width of a human hair. No mass-produced product had ever been manufactured at such an extreme tolerance level.

Blunt put together a group of 40 people to design the new factory (price tag: $120 million) which would be located in Columbia, Tennessee, 200 miles from manufacturing headquarters in Louisville. The team was largely made up of current company engineers who had little experience with automation. The manufacturing director was convinced that these engineers could develop the factory if they had the backing of management. According to Blunt: "Some of the engineers here were the brightest people I had ever seen. They had degrees coming out of their ears. But they'd never been allowed to do anything." Blunt's most important rule: never allow anyone on the team to say that it couldn't be done.

Process and product engineers worked together to develop the new factory design, putting steps of the manufacturing process on large pieces of paper and taping them on corridor and office walls. Then they readjusted the sheets of paper to determine how to integrate such functions as grinding, loading and materials handling. The next step was to adapt current machinery to the higher demands of the new factory. Most vendors didn't believe that their products could meet the more exacting specifications. To adapt old machines to new tasks, Blunt and his team "played around with them." Hundreds of changes were made on each machine, and GE had to develop its own sensing and gauging systems in order to achieve the rapid adjustments the manufacturing process demanded.

In addition to modifying equipment, GE had to train employees for work in the new automated environment. The company built a large training center and asked workers to spend 120–400 hours without pay learning new job skills. To the surprise of some managers, the work force gladly sacrificed personal time to attend training sessions. Many employees believed that learning how to operate an automated system was the only way to keep their jobs. Others were motivated by the chance to acquire new skills and saw the company's investment in their training as a sign that GE believed in their potential. Managers also had to learn new behaviors. They began to listen more closely to the ideas of assembly workers and encouraged employees to write training manuals and to solve their own problems. Responsibility for success or failure rested on the work group, not on any one individual.

The new plant opened on schedule and soon exceeded cost and quality expectations. But twenty-two months later a small percentage of the larger rotary compressors began to fail. A trouble shooting team isolated the problem and came up with a better design. At first, company officials offered to replace any broken compressor at no cost to the customer. Then Roger Schipke, MABG head, decided to temporarily halt production of the rotary compressor and to return to using the old reciprocating compressor part until the new design could be put into place. He reasoned that every compressor failure was a blow to the company's reputation. Later, at a cost of $150 million, the company decided to recall all of its original rotary compressors, even those that were still working properly.

Based on their experience with the rotary compressor, some GE executives suggest that in the future any new technology should be introduced gradually rather than all at once. Limited field testing, for example, might have revealed the design flaw and reduced losses. Overall, however, the company is pleased with its choice to produce in America rather than to buy or to manufacture overseas. Many of the lessons learned at the Columbia plant and at other demonstration projects have been adopted by the organization as a whole. CEO Jack Welch wants to "take out the boss element" at General Electric by reducing the power of managers and by helping employees think for themselves. Teams of managers and workers from every division now use process mapping to improve quality and to increase productivity.

Discussion Questions

1. Did GE make the right decision to build a new compressor rather than source or manufacture overseas?

2. How did Blunt and GE foster a learning climate? What mistakes, if any, were made?

3. Would you have continued to produce and sell the original compressor as the better design was being put into place? Why or why not? Would you have replaced every compressor, even those that had not broken?

Sources:

Magaziner, I. C., & Patinkin, M. (1989, March–April). Cold competition: GE wages the refrigerator war. *Harvard Business Review*, pp. 114-124.
Magaziner, I. C., & Patinkin, M. (1989). *The silent war: Inside the global business battles shaping America's future.* New York: Random House, Ch. 3.
Stewart, T. A., (1991, August 12). GE keeps those ideas coming. *Fortune*, pp. 41-49.
Fetterman, M. (1991, July 15). 'CEO of the Year' will focus on soft stuff. *USA Today*, 1b-2b.

5. ***Transferring knowledge.*** Learning organizations spread knowledge around through the use of reports, tours, personnel transfers and training programs. Reports and tours are popular ways to transfer learning, but they can't adequately communicate complex concepts. Moving knowledgeable individuals from one department or facility to another is often a more effective way to transfer information. Training programs which are tied directly to implementation can also promote wider learning. GTE, for example, gives managers two months to develop quality plans for their units based on what they learn during a three-day training session. Whatever transfer method is used, organizational learning can be measured through testing attitudes and knowledge, by observing behavior to see if managers and employees act differently, and by monitoring organizational performance to

determine if such factors as profitability, quality and delivery times improve.

Becoming a Change Master

If we're to function effectively in learning organizations, we must act as "change masters" who not only generate and promote our own creative ideas but also encourage others to develop their creative abilities. Our personal success and the success of the organizations we join will depend on how well we use both innovation and leadership strategies. In this final portion of the chapter, we'll take a closer look at tactics that can help us become more effective change agents.

Innovation Strategies

In the organizational setting, coming up with the creative idea is just the first step. Other people must be convinced to support the project, and the idea must be put in a tangible form which is then adopted by the organization as a whole. Rosabeth Moss Kanter, an expert on organizational innovation, outlines a number of strategies that change masters use to see an innovation (the new concept, physical object or practice that is the product of creative thinking) through from its inception to its adoption.[11]

Kaleidoscope Thinking. Kanter uses the kaleidoscope metaphor to illustrate the lateral thinking styles of organizational innovators. Kaleidoscope thinkers take existing data and generate new patterns in much the same way that twisting a kaleidoscope puts the fragments in the device into new formations. Kaleidoscope thinkers are able to develop new associations because they gather information from a variety of sources. In their quest for knowledge they visit other departments, study in different fields and so on.

Coalition Building. Organizational innovators almost never have enough resources of their own to make their ideas become reality. They need to find additional money, time, space, materials, workers and information. In addition, others must "buy into" their ideas if they are to succeed. Introducing a new product, for instance, requires participation from designers, engineers, production personnel, office staff, the sales force and others. Securing resources and a broad base of support requires coalition building. Coalition formation generally starts when innovators take their symbolic "tin cups" and "beg" others for help. While colleagues usually expect something in return for their contributions, once they've put something in the "cup" contributors feel a sense of ownership in the project. Their feedback may modify the original idea to make it more attractive.

Teamwork. Teamwork is particularly important when it comes time to translate a creative idea into a concrete object like a prototype or model. Project developers need freedom from outside interference to complete this task successfully. Work teams frequently move to isolated locations (sometimes referred to as "reservations" or "skunkworks") and carefully control their contact with outsiders. Team members engage in boundary management. They gather information and resources from other units but, at the same time, release only the information that the team wants to share with the rest of the organization. Boundary management also requires keeping in touch with the members of coalitions formed earlier and dealing with those who oppose the innovation. Opponents generally try to derail innovations by using passive tactics like making petty criticisms or failing to respond to requests. Occasionally, however, critics become more active—as in the case of a manager who challenges an innovation because it interferes with a pet project. Team members should be alert to such criticism and should be prepared to protect the project until it reaches the point where it can stand or fall on its own merits.

Because innovations seldom develop as expected, project teams also need flexible guidelines. Cost overruns, unanticipated delays, modifications, and secondary innovations (the additional adjustments needed to make the innovation work) are an integral part of the innovation process. Work teams need lots of leeway when it comes to finances, time and modifications.

Persistence. There is a point in the history of every new project or idea when problems mount up and innovators are tempted to quit. As Kanter points out, "*everything* looks like a failure in the middle."[12] At this juncture, persistence literally means the difference between success and failure. Giving up spells the end of the innovation process; continuing on frequently pays off. For example, the development of one highly successful consumer product was dubbed "Project Lazarus" because it was resurrected four times by determined employees who refused to take no for an answer.

Persistence is required even after the product or procedure has been developed and is ready for use. Organizational members frequently ignore innovations they did not develop; researchers call this the Not Invented Here (NIH) syndrome. Change masters overcome resistance by encouraging the organization to demonstrate its commitment to the innovation publicly through funding and corporate statements.

Sharing the Credit. Wise change agents make sure that everyone who helps in the innovation process gets recognized and rewarded for their efforts. Sharing credit and rewards strengthens feelings of ownership in the idea and encourages participation in upcoming projects. One significant reward is the opportunity to be on future creative teams. Team members typically enjoy the intense learning, challenge, and comraderie associated with developing an important new idea. They look forward to collaborating again on a future innovation. Tom West, who led a new computer development team for Data General, labeled this reward "pinball." According to West: "You win one game, you get to play another. You win with this machine, you get to build the next."[13] While the opportunity to innovate again is enough for some, the best approach is to offer *both* the freedom to create and enough financial rewards to keep creators from leaving the organization. AT & T, for example, offers creative team members performance rewards and "stock" in the group's venture.[14] (See the Creative Profile on the next page for an in-depth look at how one highly creative organization encourages and rewards innovation.)

Leading Creativity

We suggested earlier that acting as a change master means leading the creative efforts of other people at the same time we shepherd our own innovations. Leading creativity in the organizational context takes developing a vision, tolerating failure, focusing attention on innovation and empowering others.[15]

1. **Develop a Vision.** Visions are descriptions—symbolic portraits—of what the organization should be like in the future (e.g. "the largest manufacturer of ball bearings in the United States"; "a provider of high-quality service to children and their families"; "a major urban research university"). A vision inspires commitment and directs the creative efforts of followers by indicating what types of new ideas are needed. It becomes the unifying force which binds organizational members together. Employees of innovative organizations like Rubbermaid, Wal-Mart and Hewlett-Packard make decisions based on whether or not they help achieve the vision.

Warren Bennis and Burt Nanus interviewed ninety highly successful leaders from government, education, business, music and

Creative Profile: Innovating at 3M

Many of us associate innovation with computer manufacturers, defense contractors, robotics and other high tech industries. Yet, one of most innovative companies in America manufactures such mundane products as tape and sandpaper. At the Minnesota Mining and Manufacturing Company headquartered in St Paul, Minnesota, innovation has been essential to the company's success since its earliest days. 3M started when a group of investors bought a piece of land so that they could mine corundum, the abrasive that makes sandpaper scratchy. When the investors discovered that the land didn't hold any corundum, they had to create new products or quit. The firm's first successful inventions were an abrasive cloth for metal finishing and a waterproof sandpaper used for polishing exterior auto finishes. Now the company manufactures sixty thousand products, including Post-it notes, Scotchgard fabric protector, overhead projectors, heart-lung machines, insulating materials and light fixtures.

At 3M, attention is clearly focused on new product development. Staff members can spend up to 15 percent of their time on new products—called "bootlegging"—and managers must ensure that 25 percent of each division's profits are generated by products introduced during the past five years. 3M Genesis Grants fund ideas that are not claimed by any one division. New venture teams made up of volunteers from several different departments guide the development of new projects and are guaranteed job security at their previous statuses should the innovation fail. Those who create and sponsor new ideas get a chance to manage those products like their own businesses when they come to market. The company also honors important innovators through special awards and selection into the Carlton Society—an innovator's hall of fame.

3M keeps divisions small (division managers must know each staff person's first name, for example) and relies on peer review rather than formal rules to guide performance. Information is constantly shared through seminars, company trade shows, and informal idea sessions which often include customers. Although as many as 60 percent of its new ideas fail, 3M doesn't seem to mind. According to former CEO Allen Jacobson: "Outsiders say we are very lenient in rewarding failure." Like its emphasis on innovation, toleration of failure is strongly rooted in 3M's history. Early company inventor Francis Okie kept his job at 3M even though he suggested that sandpaper could be sold to men as a replacement for razor blades! Later Okie went on to invent the waterproof sandpaper that helped 3M survive.

3M's focus on innovation should serve it well in the years to come. The company continues to spend nearly twice the U.S. average for research and development. Recent innovations include a new type of insect repellant, a more durable face mask for dentists, and a hearing aid with many different volume settings. However, 3M now prioritizes innovative ideas, investing heavily in those projects that seem to have the greatest earnings potential while paying less attention to products that will likely serve small markets. This approach seems to overlook the fact that "minor" inventions can become major profit centers. 3M Post-it notes, developed to hold bookmarks in place using an adhesive from an earlier, unsuccessful experiment, currently generate over $300 million annually in sales. A new filter created by a 3M chemist to clean lubricants in metal shops now filters water, paint, beer and many other products.

Discussion Questions

1. Should 3M focus on fewer ideas or continue to encourage as many ideas as possible?
2. Can other companies become as innovative as 3M if they do not have the same type of innovative history?
3. Create a list of the ten most innovative companies in America. What criteria should be used when making such a list?
4. Can the 3M approach to innovation be adapted to nonprofit organizations like federal agencies? Why or why not?

Sources:

Dubashi, J. (1992, February 18). 3M: New talent and products outweigh the costs. *Financial World*, p. 19.

Mitsch, R. AA. (1992, September-October). R & D at 3M: Continuing to play a big role. *Research Technology Management*. pp. 22-25.

Mitchell, R. (1989, April 10). Masters of innovation: How 3M keeps its new products coming. *Business Week*, pp. 58-63.

Mitchell, R. (1989, Innovation Issue). Mining the work force for ideas. *Business Week*, p. 121.

Keeping the fires lit under the innovators. (1988, March 28). *Fortune*, p. 45.

Katauskas, T. (1990, November). Follow-through: 3M's formula for success. *Research and Development*, pp. 46-52.

sports and found that these leaders spent a good deal of time talking with employees, clients, other leaders and consultants before developing their visions.[16] Based on their research, Bennis and Nanus suggest that if you want to create a vision, you should begin with careful study of your organization's: 1) past—to determine the reasons for its successes and failures, 2) present—to determine current strengths, weaknesses and resources, and 3) future—to identify possible long-term social, political, economic, intellectual and environmental changes. The key is to interpret or structure this information in such a way as to construct a realistic vision which fits with the norms of the group and motivates followers. The vision should take longer to achieve than the typical long-range plan but be reachable within the careers of those who currently work in the organization (ten years, for example).

2. ***Tolerate Failure.*** Despite their best efforts, even the most skilled and persistent innovators sometimes fail. Creative leaders believe that failure is an important learning tool since those who don't fail aren't trying or learning. General Johnson, founder of the Johnson & Johnson Company, once noted: "If I wasn't making mistakes, I wasn't making decisions."[17] IBM's first president, Thomas Watson, shared the same philosophy. After making a $10 million blunder, a young executive walked into his office and began the conversation by saying, "I guess you want my resignation." Watson answered: "You can't be serious. We've just spent $10 million educating you!"[18]

Effective leaders refuse to dwell on failure since concentrating on what can go wrong makes failure much more likely. Bennis and Nanus call this positive approach to failure the Wallenda Factor after the famous tightrope aerialist, Karl Wallenda. Wallenda was successful as long as he focused all of his energy on tightrope walking. He fell to his death in San Juan, Puerto Rico in 1978 after worrying for months about the danger of this particular tightrope walk. When he concentrated on *not falling*, rather than on walking, he was "virtually destined to fall."[19]

3. ***Focus Attention on Creativity*** Leaders who want to encourage creativity make the generation of new ideas, products and procedures the focus of organizational attention. First, they invest their own time in innovation activities. The founder of the Honda corporation, for example, worked directly with new employees in project start ups. Next, they encourage creativity through measurement, rewards and punishments.[20] Subordinates are more likely to generate and support innovations if rewards depend on developing new products, services and cost saving-techniques, and if promotions, raises and other benefits are withheld when innovative goals are not met. Finally, creative leaders use stories, rituals and other important symbols to reinforce creative values. Stories that feature creative heroes dramatize the organization's commitment to innovation. The fact that 3M inventor Francis Okie was not fired for suggesting that men shave with sandpaper (see the Creative Profile, page 168) reinforces the notion that 3M tolerates eccentricity and failure. Okie's eventual success suggests to employees that persistence pays big dividends. Like stories, rituals also focus organizational attention. Rituals are repeated patterns of behavior like weekly staff meetings or the

annual barbecue. In particular, rituals that mark important changes in status or roles (called rites of passage) or rituals that raise the standing of members (referred to as rites of enhancement) demonstrate the group's commitment to creativity. Promotion announcements, company celebrations, awards ceremonies, notes in the company newsletter and other rituals which publicly acknowledge creative individuals and activities are powerful reminders that creativity is a central concern of the organization.[21]

4. **Empower Others.** Successful change masters empower creators by giving them access to funds, materials, time and organizational support which facilitates the generation, development and diffusion of innovations. Empowerment also means helping followers to believe in their own abilities, to develop what psychologist Albert Bandura calls the efficacy expectation.[22] Followers who believe that they can deal with the people, events and situations in their environments—who have a sense of self-efficacy or personal power—are more likely to take initiative and to persist in the face of difficult circumstances. Subordinates who believe that they have limited self-efficacy—who feel powerless—will be less inclined to offer new ideas or to see them to completion. Feelings of powerlessness come from such organizational factors as an impersonal bureaucratic climate, authoritarian supervision, unrealistic goals, too many rules, repetitive tasks, lack of resources and limited opportunities for advancement.

> Innovative companies provide the freedom to act, which arouses the desire to act.
>
> Rosabeth Moss Kanter

To help followers develop a sense of efficacy, creative leaders eliminate organizational factors which create feelings of powerlessness. They seek to create lateral rather than hierarchical structures by keeping their operating units small, reducing levels of authority, cutting back on rules, paying less attention to status and so forth. For example, the Gore-Tex company divides its plants when they employ over 200 people and allows any staff person to take ideas or complaints to anyone else in the firm. This highly profitable organization also downplays titles. Each of the corporation's 5,300 employees is called an "associate."[23] Ideas incubate more readily in such an atmosphere than in more traditional organizations which emphasize authority. In one high tech business, for instance, new products had to be reviewed by 223 committees before they went to market![24]

Along with modifying organizational structures, the leaders of learning organizations supply important information which builds followers' perceptions of their personal power. Leaders empower followers when they:[25]

- provide positive emotional support, particularly during times of stress and anxiety. Stress, fear and other negative factors reduce feelings of personal efficacy. The impact of these factors can be diminished through group support and through the use of films, speakers, seminars and other devices to build excitement and confidence. Play can also produce a positive emotional climate. One new manager broke the tension in his division by starting a squirt gun fight with his staff. This act signalled that having fun was okay in a difficult work situation and that he had a more informal managerial style than his predecessor.

- offer words of encouragement. When leaders praise followers, they "persuade" subordinates that they are capable of handling difficult tasks. The most effective leaders spend time every day praising others in meetings, in the lunchroom, in speeches and so on. According to Irwin Federman, who heads a successful technology company called Monolithic Memories, "This business of making another person feel good in the unspectacular course of his [her] daily comings and goings is, in my view, the very essence of leadership."[26]

- model successful performance themselves or provide opportunities to observe others who are successful. Knowing that someone else can handle a task makes it easier for a worker to continue to learn the same task even after repeated failures.

- structure tasks so that followers experience initial success. Initial victories build expectations for future triumphs. Effective leaders structure tasks so that they become increasingly complex. Completing one part of the job is followed by training and then greater responsibilities.

Summing Up

In this chapter we looked at ways to encourage creative organizational communication. We started by examining the relationship between communicating and organizing. Individuals organize themselves in order to process ambiguous information from the environment and are connected with each other through communication cycles called double interacts. Organizations evolve as members act to impose order on events (enactment), interpret their actions (selection), and then commit those acts to memory (retention).

To prosper, organizations must balance the need for stability and creativity. They must function in an orderly fashion on a day-to-day basis but develop new strategies in response to changing conditions. One way to achieve this balance is by building learning organizations. Learning organizations continually recreate themselves through the application of new insights and ideas to modify existing behavior. Transforming an existing organization into a learning organization is a two-step process. First, organizational members must challenge their current ways of thinking called mental models. Modifying mental models involves reflection (examining our own assumptions and beliefs) and inquiry (finding out what others really think). Second, new building blocks or practices must be put into place. The building blocks of the learning laboratory are systematic problem solving, experimentation, learning from past experiences, learning from others and transferring knowledge.

In order to function effectively in learning organizations, we need to act as change masters. Change masters promote their own innovations while encouraging others to develop their creative abilities. Important innovation strategies include kaleidoscope thinking, coalition building, teamwork, persistence and sharing the credit. Leading the creative efforts of others requires: 1) the development of a vision for the organization which motivates followers and guides their creative efforts; 2) toleration of failure; 3) focusing attention on creativity through the use of time, measurement, rewards, punishments, stories and rituals; 4) empowering followers through sharing resources, eliminating organizational factors which generate feelings of powerlessness, providing emotional support, using words of encouragement, modeling and structuring tasks for success.

Application Exercises

1. Do you agree with Karl Weick that organizational members act first and then make sense of their actions later? Why or why not? Be prepared to explain your reasoning to the rest of the class.

2. As a group project, profile a learning organization in your community. Compare this organization to similar organizations that are more traditional. Describe the way in which members challenge current mental models and follow the five practices described in the chapter.

3. Write up your own version of the Left-Hand Column exercise described on page 159. How did your assumptions contribute to the lack of learning in this situation? Is there a significant difference between what you say you believe and how you act? Now describe what you think the other person was thinking in this same situation. How does his/her mental model differ from yours?

4. Trace the development of an organizational innovation. Identify important developmental stages and the innovative strategies used during the adoption process.

5. Develop a plan for empowering someone you lead. How will you share information and authority? Provide emotional support? Encouragement? Successful models? Structure tasks to ensure initial success? Write up your findings. As an alternative, describe how a leader empowered you.

Endnotes

[1] Starbuck, W. H. (1983). Organizations as action generators. *American Sociological Review, 48*, 91–102.

[2] De Geus, A. P. (1988, March–April). Planning as leading. *Harvard Business Review*, pp. 70–74.

[3] Weick, K. (1979). *The social psychology of organizing* (2nd ed.). Reading, MA: Addison-Wesley.; Weick, K. E. (1989). Organizing improvisation: 20 years of organizing. *Communication Studies, 40*, 241–248. (For a brief introduction to Weick's information systems approach, see: Griffin, E. (1994). *A first look at communication theory* (2nd ed.). New York: McGraw Hill, Ch. 23.)

[4] Weick, *Social psychology of organizing*, p. 148.

[5] Weick, *Social psychology of organizing*, p. 221.

[6] Senge, P. M. (1990). *The fifth discipline: The art and practice of the learning organization*. New York: Doubleday/Currency.; Senge, P. M. (1990, Fall). The leader's new work: Building learning organizations. *Sloan Management Review*, pp. 7–24. See also:

Kim, D. H. (1993, Fall). The link between individual and organizational learning. *Sloan Management Review*, pp. 37–49.

[7] Argyris, C. (1985). *Strategy, change and defensive routines*. Boston: Pitman, p. 5. For more information on defensive routines, see: Argyris, C. (1990). *Overcoming organizational defenses: Facilitating organizational learning*. New York: Allyn and Bacon.

[8] Senge. *The fifth discipline*, pp. 195–196.

[9] Garvin, D. A. (1993, July–August). Building a learning organization. *Harvard Business Review*, pp. 78–91. Most of the examples in this section come from Garvin's article.

[10] Leonard-Barton, D. (1992, Fall). The factory as learning laboratory. *Sloan Management Review*, pp. 23–38.

[11] Kanter, R. M. (1988). Change-master skills: What it takes to be creative. In R. L. Kuhn (Ed.), *Handbook for creative and innovative managers*, (pp. 91–99). New York: McGraw-Hill.; Kanter, R. M. (1988). When a thousand flowers bloom: Structural, collective, and social conditions for innovation in organizations. *Research in Organizational Behavior, 10*, 169–211.; Kanter, R. M. (1983). *The change masters*. New York: Simon and Schuster, Ch. 6.

[12] Kanter, Change-master skills, p. 94.

[13] Kidder, T. (1981). *The soul of the new machine*. Boston: Little, Brown and Company, p. 228.

[14] Kanter, R. M. (1989). *When giants learn to dance*. New York: Simon and Schuster.

[15] Many of the concepts discussed in this section of the chapter are covered in more detail in:

Hackman, M. Z., & Johnson, C. E. (1991). *Leadership: A communication perspective*. Prospect Heights, IL: Waveland Press.

[16] Bennis, W., & Nanus, B. (1985). *Leaders: The strategies for taking charge*. New York: Harper & Row. For a list of questions to consider when constructing a vision, see: Nanus, B. (1992). *Visionary leadership*. San Francisco: Jossey Bass.

[17] Peters, T. J., & Waterman, R. H. (1982). *In search of excellence* New York: Harper & Row, p. 223.

[18] Garvin, p. 86.

[19] Bennis and Nanus, p. 70.

[20] Schein, E. H. (1985). *Organizational culture and leadership*. San Francisco: Josey Bass, Ch. 10.

[21] Trice, H. M., & Beyer, J. M. (1985). Using six organizational rites to change culture. In R. H. Kilmann, M. J. Saxton, & R. Serpa (Eds.), *Gaining control of the corporate culture* (pp. 370–399). San Francisco: Jossey Bass; Trice, H. M., & Beyer, J. M. (1984). Studying organizational cultures through rites and ceremonies. *Academy of Management Review, 5*, 653–669.

[22] Bandura, A. (1977). Self-efficacy: Toward a unifying theory of behavioral change. *Psychological Review, 84*, 191–215.

[23] Weber, J., Driscoll, L., & Brandt, R. (1990, December 10). Farewell fast track. *Business Week*, pp. 192–197.

[24] Peters and Waterman, pp. 17–18.

[25] Management theorists Jay Conger and Rabindra Kanungo have adapted Bandura's strategies for empowering others to organizational settings. Our discussion of empowerment is based on material taken from:
Conger, J. A., & Kanungo, R. N. (1988). The empowerment process: Integrating theory and practice. *Academy of Management Review, 13*, 471–482.
Conger, J. (1989). Leadership: The art of empowering others. *The Academy of Management EXECUTIVE, 3*, 17–24.

[26] Conger, *Leadership: The art of empowering others*, p. 20.

Quotations

Pascale, R. T. (1990). *Managing on the edge*. New York: Simon and Schuster.

Senge, P. (1990). *The fifth discipline: The art and practice of the learning organization*. New York: Doubleday/Currency.

Power, C. (1984). *The experts speak: The definitive compendium of misinformation*. New York: Pantheon Books.

De Geus, A. P. (1988). Planning as leading. *Harvard Business Review*, pp. 70–74.

Kanter, R. M. (1983). *The change masters*. New York: Simon and Schuster.

7 | Creative Written Communication

Your manuscript is both good and original; but the part that is good is not original, and the part that is original is not good.

Samuel Johnson

PREVIEW

► The Writing Process

► Strategies of Highly Creative Writers
Strategy 1: Tinker with the Problem (Explore It Carefully)
Strategy 2: Extended Planning and Goal Setting
Strategy 3: Continuous Practice
Strategy 4: Revise, Revise, Revise

► Overcoming the Blank Page: Breaking Writer's Block
The Sources of Writer's Block
Breaking Writer's Block
Idea Generation Techniques

► Creative Writing and the Computer

► Summing Up

► Application Exercises

As you've discovered by now, your success as a student depends on the quality of your written communication. Grades in many courses are based on term papers, abstracts, essay questions, lab reports, analysis papers, book reviews and other written products. What you may not realize, however, is that written communication is just as important to your career success. The typical American worker spends over one day a week engaged in writing. Those employed in professional and technical occupations (jobs which are largely filled by college graduates) devote the most time to written communication.[1] When deciding whom to hire, personnel managers look for applicants who can both speak and write effectively.[2]

Most writing assignments pose problems which demand novel solutions. This means that written communication of every kind—fiction or nonfiction, informative or persuasive—must be creative if it is to be effective. Even writers faced with routine tasks like producing business letters or press releases must find new ways to present their ideas. In this chapter, we'll focus on writing as a form of creative communication and describe techniques that can help you become a more creative writer. First we'll examine the writing process itself. Then we'll identify the writing strategies of highly creative writers and suggest ways to overcome writer's block. Finally, we'll look at how you can make the best use of the computer as a creative writing tool.

The Writing Process

Any model of the writing process must account for the fact that writing is more demanding than speaking. Although we utter thousands of spoken words every day with relative ease, writing takes concentrated effort. Written communication takes more time to produce and has to conform to a greater number of rules (spelling, punctuation, etc.). Writers must pay close attention to how they express ideas because they create permanent records which can be reread by audiences.

Stage models describe the composing process as a series of distinct steps or stages. The Pre-Writing/Writing/Rewriting Model is one example of the linear approach to composition.[3] According to this model, each stage of the writing process is marked by a special set of activities which distinguishes it from the other stages. Pre-Writing is the thinking and planning that happens before writing begins; writing is the recording of thoughts on paper; rewriting consists of revising and editing the text. Pre-writing is the most important stage in this model because the quality of the final product largely depends on how much effort the writer puts into planning.

The Conception/Incubation/Production model is another linear approach to writing.[4] In this model, the composing process begins with conception—the events leading up to the decision to write. Sometimes a writer makes a quick decision to write when faced with an assignment; in other cases he or she chooses to write after mulling over an idea for some length of time. Deciding just what to write is the second important task of the conception stage. To determine how to proceed, the writer draws upon such factors as written or oral instructions, the potential audience, and previous experiences with similar writing tasks. The next step is planning or incubation. In this stage, the author concentrates on aspects of the topic isolated during the conception stage, organizes content and lets the project incubate by diverting conscious thought to other tasks. The actual writing (which involves choices about how to start, which words to use, how to structure the composition, and what corrections and improvements to make) is carried out during the production stage.

Stage models identify the tasks that writers must perform in order to complete a writing assignment successfully. Every writer must plan, gather and assemble information, record words on paper, and revise. In addition, these theories focus attention on the thinking that occurs before ideas appear on paper or on a screen. Stage models provide an oversimplified view of the composing process, however. Composing is recursive rather than linear. Instead of following a series of clear-cut steps, writers continually shift between planning, writing and rewriting. They may plan, write, and revise, for example, and then plan, write and revise again.

To address the limitations of linear models, Linda Flower and John Hayes of Carnegie Mellon University developed the Cognitive Process Model diagrammed on page 180.[5] The arrows in the diagram indicate that there is a continuous interchange between the major elements of the model and that writing activities occur in many different sequences, not just one. (For more information on how these researchers gathered data to support their model, see the Creative Dilemma on page 181.)

The **task environment** in the Cognitive Process Model incorporates "everything outside the writer's skin that influences the performance of the task."[6] This includes such factors as the topic of the assignment, the intended audience, and information that

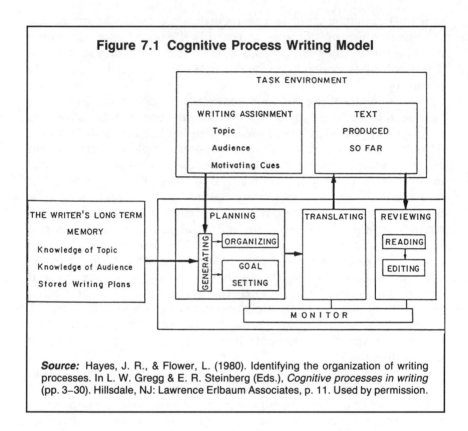

Figure 7.1 Cognitive Process Writing Model

Source: Hayes, J. R., & Flower, L. (1980). Identifying the organization of writing processes. In L. W. Gregg & E. R. Steinberg (Eds.), *Cognitive processes in writing* (pp. 3–30). Hillsdale, NJ: Lawrence Erlbaum Associates, p. 11. Used by permission.

influences a writer's motivation. For example, students usually put more effort into the final paper if the instructor emphasizes that it represents a high percentage of the final grade. After writing begins, the document itself becomes a major part of the task environment. The newly created text provides the foundation for further writing and rewriting.

The writer's **long-term memory** contains information about the topic, the audience and how to write. Consider how these elements interact when faced with the assignment described in the Creative Dilemma: "Write an article describing your college major for the newspaper at your former high school." To complete this project, you will need to call upon your knowledge of 1) your major, 2) characteristics of the readers of your high school newspaper, and 3) the format of newspaper articles.

The writing process itself consists of planning, translating and reviewing. The function of the **planning** process, which involves generating, organizing and goal-setting, is to build an internal

Creative Dilemma: Understanding Your Writing Habits

In chapter 2 we described a series of process tracing studies directed by cognitive scientists at Carnegie Mellon University. Researchers conducting these studies asked problem solvers to record their thoughts out loud as they worked. In one such project, writing expert Linda Flower, along with John R. Hayes and others, had writers talk into microphones as they composed. The investigators then analyzed recordings of these verbal reports (protocols) to identify important elements of the writing process. Later, composition instructors began to use the same strategy to identify the writing problems of their students. Verbal protocols can reveal if a writer edits prematurely, for instance, or has trouble deciding which direction to take.

The following assignment (which is modelled after those used by the Carnegie Mellon researchers) will give you insights into your writing habits. In addition, your verbal protocol may reveal factors which block your writing or make it uncreative and ineffective. Follow all directions carefully.

Write an article for the newspaper at your former high school describing your college major. As you complete the assignment, try to *say everything out loud as you are thinking and writing.* Even irrelevant comments are acceptable. You won't capture every thought, but be as complete as possible. Tape your comments and play them back after the essay is written (reserve up to an hour to complete the assignment). If you can, find a partner and compare tapes.

Discussion Questions

1. Did speaking out loud make it harder for you to write?
2. What did you learn about how you write from this exercise?
3. Can you identify any potential trouble spots in your writing based on your protocol?
4. How does your approach to writing compare to that of your partner?

Sources:

Flower, L., & Hayes, J. R. (1981). A cognitive process theory of writing. *College Composition and Communication, 32*, 365–387.; Hayes, J. R., & Flower, L. (1980). Identifying the organization of writing processes. In L. W. Gregg & E. R. Steinberg (Eds.), *Cognitive processes in writing.* Hillsdale, NJ: Erlbaum.

Harris, M. (1985). Diagnosing writing-process problems: A pedagogical application of speaking-aloud protocol analysis. In M. Rose (Ed.) *When a writer can't write* (pp. 166–181). New York: Guilford Press.

representation of the final product. Generating is the act of retrieving information from long-term memory. Retrieving one piece of information from memory activates a chain or cluster of related items. For example, when you search your memory for the characteristics of a reader of your high school newspaper, you probably retrieve a host of items, such as the reader's age, interests, problems, physical appearance and hobbies. Organizing involves selecting the most relevant information retrieved from memory and putting this material into an outline, a series of points or some other writing plan. Goal-setting determines the structure of the writing plan. Procedural goals relate to how to write the paper ("I'll put my strongest point last"), while substantive goals relate to the paper's content or purpose ("I want to demonstrate that I understand both the strengths and weaknesses of capitalism"). Goals also serve as criteria for judging text during the editing process.

Translating refers to the conversion of ideas into sentence form. As we noted in our discussion of inner speech in chapter 4, ideas are stored in words or phrases in memory. The writer's job is to unpack the information embedded in these words or phrases and to translate it into a clearly organized, understandable piece of writing. The task of translation is extremely complex, requiring writers to choose the correct words, use proper grammar and spelling, follow a logical sequence and so on. However, translation becomes less demanding with practice. When spelling, sentence construction and grammar become somewhat automatic, more attention can be paid to such issues as writing style and organization.

Reviewing consists of reading and editing in order to improve the written product. When editing, the writer identifies and corrects violations of the rules of writing, inaccurate meanings, and problems in meeting goals. Brief episodes of editing may occur at any time during the writing process. More systematic review generally occurs when an author sets aside time for evaluation after completing translation.

The **Monitor** in the Cognitive Process Model refers to the way in which the writer oversees the writing process and decides to shift from one subprocess to another. Generally, the generating and editing processes interrupt other subprocesses. Individuals have a variety of writing styles. Some writers compose and edit one sentence at a time; others write as rapidly as possible and return later for thorough review.

Strategies of Highly Creative Writers

Identifying the habits of highly creative writers can provide us with a powerful tool useful in improving our own writing skills. By adopting the strategies of successful writers, we can become more creative as well. Creative writers tinker with the problem (explore it carefully), develop extended plans and goals, practice constantly, and revise, revise, revise.

Strategy 1: Tinker with the Problem (Explore It Carefully)

In chapter 5 we emphasized the importance of problem definition, noting that the key to solving a problem often lies in how the problem is defined. Problem formulation plays a particularly important role in written communication because many writing tasks are loosely (ill) structured.[7] Consider your last term paper, for example. Chances are, your instructor provided very few guidelines when making this assignment. She or he may have specified the general topic area (perhaps one of the subjects covered in class), how long the paper should be, what style manual you should use when citing sources and a due date. The rest of the details were probably left up to you. You had to select and narrow the topic, locate resources, organize the paper and draw appropriate conclusions. Linda Flower highlights the important role that writers play in constructing the problems they solve by comparing a writing assignment to a more mundane chore:

> . . . consider the way two car owners I know see the task of "washing the car." In owner A's image, you need to wash the car when the dirt is so thick you can't see the color and somebody has written "wash me" on the back window. His goals: save the body, save face, remove the top layer of dirt. This job is saved for weddings and funerals. His strategies: wait for a warm day, give it a hose, and sponge once over—a 12-minute task. In owner B's image of "washing the car," this task is called for when a salt spray, an afternoon shower, or a dusty road sullies his cream puff. His goal: to see his reflection. His strategies: go to the high-priced car wash for hot soap and a blow dry, vacuum the carpets, do the windows, dust the ashtray, hose the underbody, wax the chrome wheels, and touch up with Poly-Guard. If two representations of a simple task like "washing the car" can differ so greatly, what happens when people have to represent a more complex rhetorical problem to themselves?[8]

Creative writers devote more time to exploring or tinkering with a problem. In this regard, they're like the successful Chicago artists described in chapter 2 who, when given a studio filled with painting supplies and objects to draw, spent more time tinkering with the objects before painting them.[9] Remember that these artists touched the items, picked them up, rearranged them and turned them over before they began to draw. They didn't settle for sketching a traditional arrangement and even when they began to paint, they were willing to reformulate the problem as they completed their drawings. In the same way, highly creative writers explore a writing problem carefully, considering such elements as the effect they want to have on readers, how they want to project themselves and arrange their ideas, and how they can present their thoughts in interesting ways. These writers resist the temptation to define the problem as 1) simply summarizing information, or 2) completing an assignment with as little effort as possible. In addition, they modify their interpretations as they write. By formulating complex, unique problems, creative writers generate better, more creative papers. This suggests that if we want to improve our writing, we should begin by giving more thought to the problem itself.

Strategy 2: Extended Planning and Goal Setting

Creative writers use what they know about their topics, their audiences and writing strategies to build complex, sophisticated goals.[10] Highly creative writers not only specify what they want to include in the final product, they also develop a purpose and theme and generate a skeleton structure. Because they have a clear plan of attack, they are more likely to construct papers which are coherent and have the desired effect on their readers. The effort that creative writers put into extended planning generates new perspectives on the problem. Less creative writers (often writers with less experience) focus almost all of their attention on content. They spend very little time constructing goals related to the purpose of the paper or to the audience. As a consequence, their papers merely restate information.

Strategy 3: Continuous Practice

We noted earlier that translating thoughts to sentences is a difficult chore which taxes the mental capacity of the writer. When most of a writer's attention is focused on such fundamentals as spelling, grammar and sentence construction, little cognitive capacity is left for dealing with other concerns. Through practice, highly creative writers have mastered the basics of the translation process and can concentrate on larger issues such as how to seize and hold the reader's attention. Creative writers advise novices to write at every opportunity. Here's what free lance magazine writer Peter Leschak has to say about the importance of writing practice:

> The major difference between bad writers and good writers usually boils down to how much they write. Writing is a craft, and you improve by doing. As long as you can physically make words appear on paper or on a screen, you can write. How well you do so will largely be determined by how hard you work at it.[11]

The importance of continuous writing practice is another reminder that, as we pointed out in chapter 1, generating and developing ideas is hard work. In writing, as in other forms of creative communication, success comes after persistent, extended effort. (One successful writer describes the difficulties and joys of writing in the Creative Profile on page 187.)

Strategy 4: Revise, Revise, Revise

Unlike spoken communication, written communication gives us the opportunity to change what we've said. Once we've spoken, there's no way to take back our words—no matter how inappropriate or damaging they were. When we write, we can read over our words and change them or throw them away. Creative writers recognize the importance of revision. Novelist Hima Worlitzer notes: "One of the great pleasures of writing is revision, the second and third and fourth chance you hardly ever get in any other area of your life."[12]

> Rewriting is when playwriting really gets to be fun. . . . In baseball, you only get three swings and you're out. In rewriting, you get almost as many swings as you want and you know, sooner or later, you'll hit the ball.
>
> Neil Simon

In addition to taking revision seriously, creative writers use revision strategies that are significantly different from the tactics of their less creative counterparts. The following table highlights the differences in the way that ineffective/uncreative and effective/creative writers revise.[13]

Uncreative Writers	**Creative Writers**
Often avoid revision, believing that revision is unnecessary or too difficult.	Recognize the need for revision and continually rewrite.
Focus on sentence-level problems: spelling, word choice, grammar and punctuation.	Focus on larger problems: arguments, theme, overall structure, if the paper meets the needs of the audience.
Most interested in correcting minor problems in the paper.	Most interested in how the entire paper fits together.
Go through the paper once.	Reread the paper many times, looking for different problems each time.
Edit from beginning to end without going back to revise earlier sections.	Return to earlier sections when later revisions require adjustment.
Final product not significantly different or better.	Final product substantially changed, improved, and more creative.
Perspective on the problem unchanged after revision.	New perspective on the problem emerges through the revision process.

Overcoming the Blank Page
Breaking Writer's Block

Almost everyone who writes experiences writer's block—the inability to start writing or to finish a writing project. As many as 10 percent of all college students suffer this problem regularly, and even experts admit that they are occasionally at a loss for words.[14] If you've experienced writer's block, you know how frustrated you feel when you want or need to write but can't find anything to say. You've done your homework and you are committed to the project. Yet, no matter how hard you try, you just can't get started. You produce a few sentences, write a lot of sentences that don't lead anywhere, or complete a number of paragraphs and grind to a halt. After staring a few hours at a sheet of paper or computer screen, you understand what Flaubert meant when he said: "You don't know what it is to stay a whole day with your head in your hands trying to squeeze your unfortunate brain so as to find a word."[15]

The Sources of Writer's Block

Before we identify the sources of writer's block, we first need to clarify the difference between pausing and blocking. Periods of delay are a natural part of the writing process. Writers pause while composing to search their memories, to organize their thoughts,

Creative Profile: Annie Dillard

Most professional writers specialize in either fiction or non-fiction—producing novels and short stories, for example, or essays and biographies. Annie Dillard is an exception to this rule. Not only is Dillard a Pulitzer Prize winning essayist (*Pilgrim at Tinker Creek*), she is also a successful poet (*Tickets for a Prayer Wheel*) and novelist (*The Living*).

Annie Dillard reflects on her experiences as an author and makes some observations about the writing process in a short book entitled *The Writing Life*. In it, she quickly dispels the idea that writing is easy; Dillard finds that just getting started is difficult. Almost anything can serve as a distraction to keep her from writing: singing birds, beautiful landscapes or softball games. To help her focus on her writing, Dillard frequently works in such spartan settings as lonely cabins and library study rooms. Once, when she found herself watching cows and people instead of writing, she sketched the scene outside her window, drew the blinds for good, and hung up the picture!

The key to writing is intense, persistent effort, according to Dillard. She notes that although William Faulkner wrote *As I Lay Dying* in six weeks in his spare time, most authors spend two to ten years on a major project. During that period they must return daily to their work and reassert their mastery over it. Otherwise the project, like a lion caged in the writer's study, gets stronger and harder to control. "If you skip a day," she warns, "you are, quite rightly, afraid to open the door to its room. You enter its room with bravura, holding a chair at the thing and shouting 'Simba!'" (p. 52)

Although the writing life is not glamorous, Dillard argues that it does have its rewards. Writing provides an interesting, even "exhilarating" challenge to the writer who has the freedom to select the task, the materials and the pace of the work. All the decisions about how the project should develop are ultimately in the hands of the author. Moments of creative insight—when new ideas, sentences and sonnets seem to emerge from nowhere after days of searching—more than make up for the drudgery of writing. Dillard describes these peak moments this way:

At its best, the sensation of writing is that of any unmerited grace. It is handed to you, but only if you look for it. You search, you break your heart, your back, your brain, and then—and only then—it is handed to you. From the corner of your eye you see motion. Something is moving through the air and headed your way. It is a parcel bound in ribbons and bows; it has two white wings. It flies directly at you; you can read your name on it. If it were a baseball, you would hit it out of the park. It is that one pitch in a thousand you see in slow motion; its wings beat slowly as a hawk's. (p. 75)

What advice does Dillard give other writers? Don't hold anything back:

One of the few things I know about writing is this: spend it all, shoot it, play it, lose it, all, right away, every time. Do not hoard what seems good for a later place in the book, or for another book; give it, give it all, give it now. . . . Anything you do not give freely and abundantly becomes lost to you. You open your safe and find ashes.

After Michelangelo died, someone found in his studio a piece of paper on which he had written a note to his apprentice, in the handwriting of his old age: "Draw, Antonio, draw, Antonio, draw and do not waste time." (pp. 78–79)

Discussion Questions

1. What is the most difficult aspect of writing for you? The most rewarding?

2. Is the key to writing intense daily effort? Why or why not?

3. When writing, have you ever experienced the sensation of "unmerited grace" described by Dillard?

Source: Dillard, A. (1989). *The writing life.* New York, Harper & Row.
Other books by Annie Dillard include:
Pilgrim at Tinker Creek.
Teaching A Stone to Talk.
An American Childhood.
Tickets for a Prayer Wheel.
The Living.
Living by Fiction.
Encounters with Chinese Writers.
Holy the Firm.

and to analyze what they've already written. These short pauses play an essential role in writing. Blocking, on the other hand, is marked by long periods of inactivity in which writers produce little if anything—despite their best efforts. Composition teachers, psychologists, communication scholars and writing consultants offer a variety of explanations for writer's block. Some are listed below.

Poor Work Habits. A great many writers have trouble getting started because they don't set aside regular time to write. Since writing is hard work, almost any other activity becomes an excuse not to write. Before long, the writing project is postponed or forgotten. Composing in the wrong environment also leads to blocking. Concentrating on a writing task is difficult in settings that are cluttered, noisy or filled with distractions.[16]

Writing Apprehension. Just as some people fear public speaking and other forms of oral communication, others experience anxiety about written communication.[17] Those who are highly apprehensive about writing prefer majors and professions that require less written work. When high apprehensives do write, they write less than low apprehensives and their work is generally rated lower in quality. Apprehensive writers engage in negative self-talk that centers on how much they hate or fear writing and on how much they fear rejection and disapproval of what they write.[18] The relationship between apprehension and blocking is reciprocal. Anxiety interferes with the writing process, and experiencing writer's block makes writers more anxious about future writing assignments. To determine if apprehension is causing you to block, take the Writing Apprehension Test on the following page.

Unrealistic Expectations. Unreasonable beliefs about writing and one's own writing ability can interfere with the writing process. Some people mistakenly assume that the writing should be easy; they get bogged down when they discover that it's not. Others can't get started because they believe that what they write must meet impossibly high standards.[19]

Faulty Writing Tactics. Blocking can also be caused by using the wrong strategies when writing. In a study of student writers conducted at UCLA, Mike Rose discovered that those who block frequently (high blockers) are more likely to use these tactics when given an assignment for class:[20]

- *Incremental planning.* Earlier we noted that less creative writers spend less time planning than their creative counterparts. Incremental planning (sitting down to compose a paper without giving much thought to the final product) is also characteristic of high blockers. They plan as they write and can't adapt their plans when new information comes along.

- *Conformity to rigid, wrong or conflicting rules.* High-blockers adhere to a set of absolute rules like "You should always put the thesis statement at the end of the first paragraph," or "You should never employ passive verbs." They let these rigid rules dictate their writing style instead of responding to the demands of the situation or the audience. In some instances, the rules themselves ("Every essay should have three main points") aren't valid. In other cases, one rule ("Avoid the passive voice when writing") may conflict with another ("Keep the 'I' out of academic writing").

Figure 7.1 Writing Apprehension Test

Directions: Below are a series of statements about writing. There are no right or wrong answers to these statements. Please indicate the degree to which each statement applies to you by marking whether you (1) strongly agree, (2) agree, (3) are uncertain, (4) disagree, or (5) strongly disagree with the statement. While some of these statements may seem repetitious, take your time and try to be as honest as possible.

_____ 1. I avoid writing.

_____ 2. I have no fear of my writing being evaluated.

_____ 3. I look forward to writing down my ideas.

_____ 4. My mind seems to go blank when I start to work on a composition.

_____ 5. Expressing ideas through writing seems to be a waste of time.

_____ 6. I would enjoy submitting my writing to magazines for evaluation and publication.

_____ 7. I like to write my ideas down.

_____ 8. I feel confident in my ability to clearly express my ideas in writing.

_____ 9. I like to have my friends read what I have written.

_____10. I'm nervous about writing.

_____11. People seem to enjoy what I write.

_____12. I enjoy writing.

_____13. I never seem to be able to write down my ideas clearly.

_____14. Writing is a lot of fun.

_____15. I like seeing my thoughts on paper.

_____16. Discussing my writing with others is an enjoyable experience.

_____17. It's easy for me to write good compositions.

_____18. I don't think I write as well as most other people.

_____19. I don't like my compositions to be evaluated.

_____20. I'm no good at writing.

To determine your score on the WAT, complete the following steps:

1. Add the scores for items 1, 4, 5, 10, 13, 18, 19, and 20.

2. Add the scores for items 2, 3, 6, 7, 8, 9, 11, 12, 14, 15, 16, and 17.

3. Complete the following formula: WAT = 48 − (total from step 1) + (total from step 2).

Your score should be between 20 and 100. If your score is below 20 or above 100, you have made a mistake in computing the score.

Source: Richmond, V. P., & McCroskey, J. C. (1992). *Communication: Apprehension, avoidance, and effectiveness* (3rd ed.). Scottsdale, AR: Gorsuch Scarisbrick, pp. 121–122. Used by permission.

- *Premature editing.* High-blockers pay much more attention to their language and grammar as they compose their first drafts. Concentrating on surface issues instead of on underlying ideas can interfere with the writing process. The problem of premature editing is magnified when writers try to complete an assignment in one draft. Trying to find the "perfect" phrase on the first try can result in writing paralysis.

Breaking Writer's Block

You probably noted one or more obstacles that block your writing from the factors described above. You'll need to address these problem areas if you want to reduce the frustration generated by blocking. To get you started, a list of strategies specifically targeted to each of these causes of writer's block is given below. This list is not exhaustive. In fact, we hope you'll add your strategies to ours (see Application Exercise 5, page 200).

Problem	Solution
Poor Writing Habits	Set aside time to write on a regular basis.
	Find a quiet, uncluttered writing environment away from the phone, roommates, family, pets, and other distractions.
Writing Anxiety	Form a peer editing group to give you friendly feedback about your writing.
	Identify negative self-talk ("Nobody will like this paper") that generates anxiety and modify such discouraging messages ("Even if some readers don't like what I've written, at least I will encourage them to think more about my topic").
	Work with a counselor or teacher to develop a plan for reducing your anxiety.
Unrealistic Expectations	Recognize that writing is a challenging but manageable task.
	Strive for an acceptable final product—not a perfect one.
Incremental Planning	Take time to preplan the entire concept.
	Develop a general outline based on your initial conceptualization; modify your plan as you write.

Rigid, wrong, or contradictory rules	Follow only a few, flexible rules that encourage you to keep going (e.g. "Don't worry about spelling but keep writing."; "When a new idea comes, insert it in the paper.").
	Become an "opportunistic writer" who changes the paper's structure and content as better ideas emerge during the writing process.

Idea Generation Techniques

In addition to implementing one or more of the suggestions described above, you may also want to try some procedures that have been specifically designed to spark the flow of creative writing ideas. Useful idea generation techniques include freewriting, open-ended writing, tagmenics, talk to your reader, idea manipulation, associative listing, and clustering.

Freewriting. Freewriting is perhaps the simplest of all writing idea generation techniques.[21] To freewrite, force yourself to write without stopping for ten minutes. Keep writing no matter what. Don't worry about logic, grammar, spelling, sudden topic changes or anything else. If you can't think of anything to put on paper, then write "I can't think of anything to say," or begin with a sentence taken from a newspaper story or novel. If you can't think of what to say next, repeat the last word or phrase over and over until something else occurs to you. Filling the entire page with the same sentence is better than saying nothing at all.

Freewriting is a useful strategy both for breaking writer's block and for developing writing skills. Writing expert Peter Elbow, the leading proponent of the technique, argues that freewriting is the best way to practice writing.[22] According to Elbow, freewriting:

- teaches writers to separate composing from editing
- is a good way to warm up for a real writing assignment
- forces writers to write when they don't feel like writing
- teaches writers how to write without stopping to think about grammar, rules, spelling and so on
- serves as an outlet for feelings that might distract from the task at hand
- generates new topics to think and write about
- frequently produces an excellent product

Open-Ended Writing. Open-ended writing is particularly useful when you feel that you have something to say but aren't sure what form the final product will take.[23] For example, if you're angry about rising tuition rates, you may not know just how to express your frustrations. The final product of the open-ended writing process may be a letter to the college president, an article in the school paper or a short story.

Open-ended writing consists of alternating divergent and convergent phases. Begin by writing for fifteen to twenty minutes. Then stop and look over your writing to discover the center or focus of what you've written (i.e. "tuition rates are rising faster than inflation"). Write this main point down in a sentence and use that sentence as the starting point for the next concentrated writing session. Repeat the process, letting your writing lead you into new directions. Continue this cycle until you have a clear idea of what your final product will be.

Tagmenics. Tagmenics is a systematic method for generating different perspectives on a subject or problem.[24] View your subject as a particle (a separate thing), a wave (something that changes over the course of time), and a field (a component of a larger situation or context). Record your observations from each one of these perspectives. For instance, if you want to write about the family, you might note these thoughts which could give you new insights into your topic:

- When viewed as a particle, every family is unique. No two families have the same hobbies, beliefs, rules or problems.

- When viewed as a wave, the family experiences the constant stress of change. Children grow up and move away, parents age and retire, family members may get ill or die.

- When viewed as a field, a family is at the mercy of outside forces. Crime, drug use and unemployment can destroy families.

Talk to Your Reader. This strategy recognizes that producing speech is easier than producing prose and that the best ideas often come when we talk to someone else.[25] Imagine yourself walking into your reader's office, dorm room or living room and having to make your case in few minutes. Give your message out loud and then *write it down.* To extend this technique, visualize yourself in a variety of situations, such as in front of a hostile audience or with a group of friends in the breakroom at work. Anticipate the questions, objections and interpretations of your listeners. Talking out loud forces you to get started and puts the emphasis on generating ideas rather than on generating polished sentences or phrases. Editing comes later.

Idea Manipulation. Idea manipulation is a set of techniques that can be used to rearrange elements of a topic to come up with new ideas.[26] Pause for a moment and think of your favorite course. Imagine that your assignment is to write about this class. Here's how each of the idea manipulation techniques could be applied to this writing project.

- *Identify Dependent Variables.* Note the most significant elements of the subject. These will serve as your dependent variables—the elements you want to focus on as you write. Are they your classmates? The instructor? The content of the course?

- *Generate Critical Cases.* The purpose of this step is to generate good examples (critical cases) to compare with the topic. Describe a poor course, an average one, another class in the same department as your favorite one.

- *Compare Similar Cases (Analogize).* Comparing cases is a good way to discover what underlying factors account for their similarity on the dependent variable. If you decided earlier that the instructor was the key dependent variable, then note what the instructors in your best courses have in common. The use of humor? Competence? Friendliness?

- *Compare to Dissimilar Cases (Contrast or Differentiate).* Identifying the differences between critical cases generates new ideas that would be missed if only similar examples were examined. When contrasting two cases that are significantly different, try to account for the differences. If you looked forward to one class in your major but dreaded attending another, what made one so positive and the other so negative?

- *Simulate.* Simulation consists of taking the same subject and creating different scenarios by adding different variables. Would the class have been so outstanding if the instructor had used different teaching methods, graded differently, or if the class had met in a different location at a different time of the day?

- *Taxonomize.* Taxonomizing is the process of locating all the factors or constraints that separate critical cases. Characteristics of excellent courses might include a friendly instructor, interesting subject matter, a comfortable classroom, and high quality students. Poor courses might be characterized by poor teaching, boring subject matter, depressing classrooms, and class members who don't get along.

• *Dimensionalize.* This step structures the categories identified above. Each factor is then located along the appropriate dimension(s). For instance, instructor behaviors can be placed along such dimensions as friendly/unfriendly, fair/unfair, competent/incompetent. The behaviors of the professor in your favorite course are probably located at the positive end of each continuum (friendly/fair/competent).

Associative Listing. Associative listing consists of writing down words associated or connected with a particular topic.[27] Each word on the list can activate a cluster of ideas related to the subject or can bring one idea back to mind when needed. Listing words takes less time than writing sentences and therefore is less likely to slow down the production of new ideas. Associative listing can be completed in one session, but this technique works best if a series of lists is created during several sessions and then combined into one master list. Here is a list of words that might be generated by the subject of professional basketball:

coaches	injuries
salaries	dunks
Chicago Bulls	passing
announcers	dribbling
fans	fast breaks
travel	television contracts
Olympic competition	trades
equipment	NBA arenas
ticket prices	famous players

Selecting the words "famous players" from this list could activate such related subtopics as the Basketball Hall of Fame, how the game has changed, superstars of the past and so on. Each of these subtopics can provide a subject for a paper or a new angle on the general topic of famous professional basketball players.

Clustering. Like associative listing, clustering is based on making connections between related ideas. However, while associative listing relies solely on verbal symbols which are processed by the left brain, clustering (which is a version of the mind mapping strategy described in chapter 3) is based on visual patterns which are identified by the right brain.[28] First write a nucleus word such as a term with strong emotional meaning or the topic of an assigned paper, near the middle of a blank sheet of paper and circle it. Then record any related words radiating out from your nucleus word. Each new word should be circled and connected by a line to the previous circle. If you have a new, unrelated thought, start again at the nucleus and continue in a different direction. When your right brain recognizes a pattern in your cluster (generally in a couple of minutes), you'll have a sense that you know what you want to say and are ready to write. Write for eight minutes and then bring your piece full circle by tying your conclusion back to your introduction. Here's an example of what one student wrote when clustering:

Figure 7.3 Clustering Example

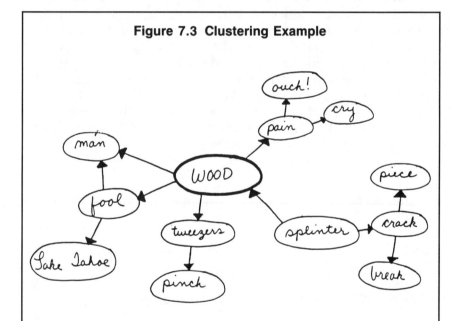

Splinter is a terrible word. Its sound is synonymous with the sensation: jagged, sharp, piercing. I remember vacationing in Tahoe. The pier was old, worn, and wooden; the boards as rough as a face full of scabs. Running along it, my foot caught the attention of an angry spike of wood, injecting itself cleanly and deeply into the ball of my foot. If I screamed it was not from the pain initially felt, but from anticipated sensations. It's not the hole the shot makes but the length of the slim sword that brings pain.

Laurie Welte

Source: Rico, G. (1983). *Writing the natural way.* Los Angeles, CA: J. P. Tarcher, p. 39. Used by permission.

Once you're comfortable with clustering, you can use the technique to help you develop goals and structure for papers, poems, speeches and presentations. Clustering can also be a helpful tool for revision. If you're not comfortable with a first draft, you may want to cluster again to see if a new focus and pattern emerge.

Creative Writing and the Computer

Over the past twenty years, the computer has replaced the typewriter as a writing tool. Computer labs are some of the busiest places on campus and a growing number of colleges and universities require that students purchase their own computers.

The speed and flexibility of computers and word processors account for their popularity. Computer-assisted writers can modify and print text in a fraction of the time it takes to alter and produce a document on a typewriter. Before the advent of computers, typewriter users relied on "cut and paste" editing. If they wanted to change the position of paragraphs in a rough draft, they literally cut the page into pieces, rearranged the paragraphs and taped or pasted them back together. They were reluctant to make even minor changes after typing the final draft because a single correction (adding a footnote, for instance) could force them to retype an entire page. With a computer, writers can rearrange paragraphs, correct mistakes and print the text in a few minutes. As a result, computer users get more enjoyment out of writing, and they generate longer papers.[29]

Despite the computer's many advantages as a writing tool, computer-assisted writers don't always produce higher quality text. A number of investigators report that writing produced on the computer is not significantly better than writing generated by other means.[30] There are number of factors hampering the creativity of computer writers. First, novice computer users must learn how to use the computer at the same time they're composing, and the quality of their writing suffers. Second, computer writers may not always get the training they need to write effectively. Writers do best when they receive assignments and training which are specifically adapted to the computer program and system they're using.[31] Third, there are some disadvantages to writing on a computer. Since the screen only displays one page at a time, writers don't get an overall sense of what they've written and have trouble recalling the exact location of paragraphs. Reading text on a screen also takes longer than reading text on paper.[32] Fourth, many computer writers retain the old, bad habits they had before they switched to the new technology. They begin writing without clearly defining the problem or planning, continue to make only minor revisions and so on. Fifth, the writer, not the computer, ultimately determines the quality of the final product. Computer writers, like writers who use pens or typewriters, must plan, translate and revise. The computer alone will not transform a poor writer into a good writer.

If you want to make the most of the computer as a creative writing tool, you'll need to avoid the pitfalls described above. Start by getting the experience and training you need. Once you've mastered your computer's hardware and software, you can devote full attention to writing. If possible, enroll in writing courses taught on computers in the classroom. Next, use the computer to implement the creative writing strategies described earlier in this chapter. Try out software programs like IdeaFisher, MindLink and Inspiration 3.0 which help writers tinker with the problem, generate ideas and develop goals and plans.[33] Practice writing on the computer and, as you revise, take advantage of the computer's ability to change text. Experiment by moving paragraphs and sections and by typing several versions of the same sentence or paragraph. Print a hard copy of your text to get an overall picture of what you've written. Finally, look for opportunities to interact with others as you write. Form a peer editing group which will give you feedback on your writing. Work with others in the group on joint writing projects. Computers facilitate interaction between writers. By connecting computer terminals and exchanging disks, writers can comment on each other's writing and work together on projects.[34] Collaborative writing is becoming increasingly common in technical fields as well as in business and industry.

Summing Up

In this chapter we focused on writing as a form of creative communication. We discussed two models which describe writing as a linear series of distinct steps or stages. In the Pre-Writing/Writing/Rewriting model, pre-writing refers to the thinking and planning that occur before writing begins, writing is the recording of thoughts on paper, and rewriting consists of revising and editing the text. In the Conception/Incubation/Production model, initial decisions about when to write and what to include make up the conception stage. Planning and information gathering take place during incubation, and sentences are constructed during the production stage. The Cognitive Process Model views writing as recursive rather than linear. According to this model, writers don't follow a single sequence but shift repeatedly between writing activities. Important elements of the Cognitive Process Model include the task environment, the writer's long-term memory, planning/translating/reviewing, and the cognitive monitor which oversees the composing process.

Adopting the strategies of highly creative writers can help us become more effective writers as well. Creative writers tinker with the writing problem (explore it carefully), develop extended plans and goals before they write, master the basics of writing through continuous practice, and revise repeatedly to develop final drafts that are significantly different and more creative than their first drafts. Nearly all writers experience writer's block—the inability to begin or to continue writing. Common sources of writer's block include: poor writing habits (not setting aside time to write or trying to write in the wrong environment); apprehension about writing; unrealistic expectations (believing that writing should be easy; setting impossibly high standards or being too critical of our writing); faulty writing tactics (incremental planning, following rigid, wrong or conflicting rules, premature editing). Addressing these obstacles is one way to break writer's block; using idea generation strategies is another. Idea generation techniques include freewriting, open-ended writing, tagmenics, talk to your reader, idea manipulation, associative listing, and clustering.

The computer has replaced the typewriter as a creative writing tool. Although the computer makes writing faster, easier to change and more interactive, computer-generated writing is not necessarily better than writing produced by hand or on a typewriter. Computer writers are often inexperienced or poorly trained and equally subject to poor writing habits. To make maximum use of the computer, we need to get the training and experience we need, use the computer to implement creative writing strategies and search for ways to interact with others as we write.

Application Exercises

1. Interview a professional in your field to determine the type of writing you can expect to do when you graduate. Find out:
   - how much time he or she spends writing during a typical week
   - the types of writing (letters, memos, radio spots, articles, etc.) the job requires
   - intended audiences
   - the strategies this person uses to generate creative ideas

2. Build your own model of the writing process or construct one in a group. Present your model to the class for feedback.

3. Write a short summary paper describing your strengths and weaknesses as a writer based on material presented in the chapter. Develop a plan for becoming a more creative writer.

4. Create your own set of strategies for dealing with the causes of writer's block. Are there other sources of writer's block not identified in the chapter?

5. Choose two idea generation techniques described in the chapter and use them to generate ideas for your next major writing assignment.

6. Pair off with someone else in the class and describe how you use the computer when you write. Has using the computer changed your writing habits? Is your writing better? Faster? More creative? How can you make better use of the computer as a writing tool?

Endnotes

[1] Faigley, L., & Miller, T. P. (1982). What we learn from writing on the job. *College English, 44*, 557–569.

[2] Curtis, D. B., Winsor, J. L., & Stephens, R. D. (1989). National preferences in business and communication education. *Communication Education, 38*, 6–14.

[3] Rohman, D. G. (1965). Pre-writing. The stage of discovery in the writing process. *College Composition and Communication, 29*, 106–112.

[4] Britton, J., Burgess, T., Martin, N., Mcleod, A., & Rosen, H. (1975). *The development of writing abilities* (11–18). Hampshire, England: Macmillan Education, Ch. 2.

[5] Flower, L., & Hayes, J. R. (1981). A cognitive process theory of writing. *College Composition and Communication, 32*, 365–387.; Hayes, J. R., & Flower, L. (1980).

Identifying the organization of writing processes. In L. W. Gregg & E. R. Steinberg (Eds.), *Cognitive processes in writing* (pp. 3–30). Hillsdale, NJ: Lawrence Erlbaum Associates.
6 Flower & Hayes, Identifying the organization of writing processes, p. 12.
7 Flower, L., & Hayes, J. R. (1980). The cognition of discovery: Defining a rhetorical problem. *College Composition and Communication, 31*, 21–32.
8 Flower, L. (1989). *Problem solving strategies for writing* (3rd. ed.). San Diego, CA: Harcourt Brace Jovanovich, p. 76.
9 Getzels, J. W., & Csikszentmihalyi, M. (1976). *The creative vision: A longitudinal study of problem finding in art.* New York: Wiley.
10 Carey, L. J., & Flower, L. (1989). Foundations for creativity in the writing process. In J. A. Glover, R. R. Ronning, & C. R. Reynolds (Eds.), *Handbook of creativity* (pp. 283–303). New York: Plenum Press.
11 Leschak, P. (1991, November). The five-step creativity workout. *Writer's Digest,* pp. 26–29.
12 Wolitzer, H. (1991). Twenty questions. In R. Pack & J. Parini (Eds.), *Writers on writing* (pp. 281–292). Hanover, NH: University Press of New England, p. 289.
13 See, for example:
Sommers, N. (1980). Revision strategies of student writers and experienced adult writers. *College Composition Communication, 31*, 378–388.
Faigley, L, & Witte, S. (1981). Analyzing revision. *College Composition and Communication, 32*, 400–414.
Bartlett, E. J. (1982). Learning to revise: Some component processes. In M. Nystrand (Ed.), *What writers know: The language, process and structure of written discourse* (pp. 345–363). New York: Academic Press.
Beach, R., & Eaton, S. (1984). Factors influencing self-assessing and revising by freshmen. In R. Beach & L. Bridwell (Eds.), *New directions in composition research* (pp. 149–170). New York: Guilford.
14 Rose, M. (1984). *Writer's block: The cognitive dimension.* Carbondale, IL: Southern Illinois University Press.
15 Rose, *Writer's block,* p. 1.
16 Mack, K., & Skjei, E. (1979). *Overcoming writing blocks.* Los Angeles: J. P. Tarcher.
17 For a comprehensive review of writing apprehension research, see: Daly, J. A. (1989). Writing apprehension. In M. Rose (Ed.), *When a writer can't write* (pp. 19–82). New York: Guilford Press.
18 Boice, R. (1985) Cognitive components of blocking. *Written Communication, 2*, 91–104.
19 Minninger, J. (1980). *Free yourself to write.* San Francisco: Workshop for Innovative Teaching.
20 Rose, M. (1980). Rigid rules, inflexible plans, and the stifling of language: A cognitivist analysis of writer's block. *College Composition and Communication, 31*, 389–401.; Rose, *Writer's block.*
21 For more information on freewriting, see:
Elbow, P. (1981). *Writing with power: Techniques for mastering the writing process.* Oxford, England: Oxford University Press.
Elbow, P. (1973). *Writing without teachers.* New York: Oxford University Press.
Minninger, *Free yourself to write.*
Boice, R., & Meyers, P. A. (1984). Two parallel traditions: Automatic writing and free writing. *Written Communication, 3*, 470–490.
22 Elbow, *Writing with power,* Ch. 2.
23 Elbow, *Writing with power,* Ch. 7.
24 Pike, K. (1964). A linguistic contribution to composition. *College Composition and Communication, 15*, 82–88.; Pike, K. (1964). Beyond the sentence. *College Composition and Communication, 15*, 129–135.; O'Looney, J. A., Glynn, S. M., Britton, B. K., & Mattocks, L. F. (1989). Cognition and writing: The idea generation

process. In J. A. Glover, R. R. Ronning, & C. R. Reynolds (Eds.), *Handbook of creativity* (pp. 305–321). New York: Plenum Press.

[25] Flower, *Problem solving strategies for writing*, p. 104.

[26] Collins, A., & Genther, D. (1980). A framework for a cognitive theory of writing. In L. W. Gregg & E. R. Steinberg (Eds.), *Cognitive processes in writing* (pp. 51–72). Hillsdale, NJ: Lawrence Erlbaum Associates.

[27] O'Looney, Glynn, Britton, & Mattocks, Cognition and writing.

[28] Rico, G. (1983). *Writing the natural way*. Los Angeles: J. P. Tarcher.

[29] Bangert-Drowns, R. L. (1989). *Research on wordprocessing and writing instruction*. Paper presented at the American Educational Research Association, San Francisco, CA.; Holdstein, D. (1987). *On composition and computers*. New York: Modern Language Association.; Hawisher, G. E. (1989). Research and recommendations for computers and instruction. In G. E. Hawisher & C. L. Selfe (Eds.), *Critical perspectives on computers and composition instruction* (pp. 44–69). New York: Teachers College Press.

[30] See, for example:

Valeri-Gold, M., & Deming, M. P. (1991). Computers and the basic writer: A research update. *Journal of Developmental Education, 14*, 10–12, 14.

Pearce, C. G., & Barker, R. (1991). A comparison of business communication quality between computer written and handwritten samples. *Journal of Business Communication, 28*, 141–151.

Varner, I. I., & Gregg, P. M. (1988). Microcomputers and the writing process. *Journal of Business Communication, 25*, 69–79.

Hawisher, G. E. (1987). The effects of word processing on the revision strategies of college freshmen. *Research in the Teaching of English, 21*, 145–149.

Hawisher, G. E., & Fortune, R. (1989). Word processing and the basic writer. *Collegiate Microcomputers, 7*, 275–284.

[31] Sommers, E. (1985). Integrating composing and computing. In J. L. Collins & E. A. Sommers (Eds.), *Writing on line* (pp. 1–10). Upper Montclair, NJ: Boynton/Cook.

[32] Haas, C. (1989). "Seeing it on the screen isn't really seeing it": Computer writers' reading problems. In G. E. Hawisher & C. L. Selfe (Eds.), *Critical perspectives on computers and composition instruction* (pp. 16–29). New York: Teachers College Press.; Haas, C., & Hayes, S. R. (1986). What did I just say? Reading problems in writing with the machine. *Research in the Teaching of English, 20*, 22–25.

[33] For reviews of these software programs see: Zilber, J. (1990, May). IdeaFisher and Mindlink. Two packages define a new generation of software: Brainstorming tools. *MacUser*, pp. 67–68.

Miley, M. (1991, December). Inspiration 3.0. *MacWorld*, p. 195.

[34] Daiute, C. (1985). *Writing and computers*. Reading, MA: Addison-Wesley.

Quotations

Lindskoog, K. (1989). *Creative writing*. Grand Rapids, MI: Academic/Zondervan.
Mack, K., & Skjei, E. (1979). *Overcoming writing blocks*. Los Angeles: Tarcher.

8 | Creative Persuasive Communication

It takes two to speak the truth—one to speak, one to hear.

Henry David Thoreau

PREVIEW

- ► Creative Influence
    Persuasion versus Coercion
- ► The Process of Persuasion
    Source
    Message
    Channel
    Receiver
- ► Interpersonal Persuasion
    Bargaining
    Negotiation
- ► Mass Persuasion
    Persuasive Campaigns
    Creative Public Relations
    Creative Advertising
- ► Summing Up
- ► Application Exercises

Creative Influence

Imagine yourself in the following situations: trying to convince a friend, who is tired from a long week of school, to go to a movie Friday night; working to resolve a labor dispute; developing an advertising campaign for a new soft drink. What do these scenarios have in common? Each involves one of the most creative of all communication activities—influencing others. Whether your communication involves a few well-chosen words regarding the value of relaxing at the movie theater or a detailed set of strategically developed and tested advertising messages, getting others to respond as you would like them to requires creative communication.

In this chapter we will focus on the process of influence known as persuasion. We will look at how persuasion works and focus on interpersonal persuasive tactics used in bargaining and negotiation. We will also explore creative ways to persuade large numbers of people through persuasive campaigns, public relations, and advertising.

Persuasion versus Coercion

To begin, let's look at the process of persuasion as it differs from another form of influence—coercion. Persuasion can be defined as the process of influencing the thoughts and/or behavior of others. Persuasive influence allows for choice on the part of the receiver. With persuasion, we are afforded options. Coercion, on the other hand, leaves an individual with few, if any, options.

For example, a friend of yours has chosen a particular course of study and tells you the virtues of majoring in this discipline. The job prospects after graduation are excellent; the coursework is challenging and exciting; the faculty are internationally recognized and often involve students in their research projects. While there are many different majors from which you might choose, you decide to select the same major as your friend, based on the information provided. This is an example of persuasion.

Compare this experience to the following. After two years as an undeclared undergraduate, you are informed by the campus advising office that you must select a major. You are also informed that due to your low grade point average there is only one department which will accept you. Your "choice" then becomes to select that major or to transfer to another university. Assuming that you cannot or will not transfer, you must accept the only available major. This is an example of coercion. Which situation will result in more positive feelings? Undoubtedly, you would respond more favorably to the major you chose as a result of persuasion than to the major you were coerced into accepting.

Coercion requires little creativity. To force someone to take action by delivering a reprisal for non-compliance involves only brute force. On the other hand, persuasion requires creative communication. To construct and present a compelling argument necessitates original thought. Let's look at the persuasion process in detail.

The Process of Persuasion

There are many different approaches for looking at the persuasive process. One of the earliest and most widely cited approaches was developed at the end of World War II at Yale University by Carl Hovland and his associates. This approach, which focuses extensively on communication variables, is known as the Yale Approach.[1]

The Yale Approach is based on two assumptions. First, persuasion involves *learning* new attitudes. Attitudes refer to our likes and dislikes. You probably have attitudes about the superiority of one fast food restaurant over another, the President of the United States, this textbook, your local sports team, and literally thousands of other people, places, things, and ideas. Sufficient rewards must be provided to learn a new attitude. For instance, you will choose a new favorite restaurant if the food is good, and the price is reasonable—and your old favorite failed to meet those standards. The second assumption of the Yale Approach is that a new attitude can only be accepted when it is compatible with a person's worldview.[2] One cannot be persuaded to think or act in a manner which is not in sync with his or her rational and logical view of the world.

Hovland and his associates argued that the extent to which a person will be persuaded to change an attitude by a message depends on a chain of learning responses. These learning responses operate in five stages: attention, comprehension, acceptance, retention, and action.[3] Changing attitudes requires the use of creative communication techniques in each of these five stages.

- **Attention.** In this stage the persuader must grab the target person's notice. Advertisers accomplish the gaining of attention by increasing the volume on television and radio advertisements; by using highly attractive men and women to sell products; and by using production techniques such as quick cuts and unusual angles to make television advertisements more interesting.

- **Comprehension.** After attention has been gained, the message must still be understood in order to be effective. Advertising campaigns have failed when target audience members were not able to comprehend the message. In the late 1980s the Reebok shoe company ran a series of ads claiming that Reebok shoes enabled wearers to state their individuality. The ads claimed Reebok shoes "Let UBU." UBU was intended to be understood as "you be you." Unfortunately, many consumers didn't make that connection and found the ads confusing.

- **Acceptance.** In the acceptance stage, the target assents to the message that is comprehended.

- **Retention.** After the message is accepted, it must be remembered. Advertisers realize the importance of having their persuasive messages retained; that is why they bombard us with multiple persuasive messages. Test yourself to see how well you remember the advertising messages to which you are regularly exposed. What are the ingredients of a McDonalds Big Mac sandwich? Which company uses the advertising slogan Go For It? What soft drink is for those members of the new generation who wish to be young? You probably remember these persuasive messages and many, many more.

- **Action.** The Yale researchers believed that a target person must take action, if fully persuaded. That action might include buying a Big Mac sandwich, a pair of Nike shoes, or a Pepsi. Others argue that the action step is not necessary for persuasion to take place—those researchers maintain that merely changing the way an individual thinks is enough.

Each of these five stages is theoretically important. However, the Yale researchers and those who followed have focused most on the acceptance stage. Acceptance is influenced by four key components of the communication process: the source, the message, the channel, and the receiver.[4] These four components of the persuasive process are among the most heavily researched areas in the persuasion literature.

Source

Important factors influencing the effectiveness of the source of a persuasive appeal and subsequently the acceptance of the appeal are: source credibility, similarity, and physical attractiveness.

Source credibility. Source credibility is what the listener believes about the speaker.[5] This level of belief is attributed solely in terms of listener perceptions. Credibility levels fluctuate from audience to audience, from situation to situation, and from topic to topic. Three primary dimensions of credibility have been identified—expertise (referring to knowledge, intelligence, and competence), trustworthiness (referring to character, honesty, and consistency), and dynamism (referring to confidence, activity, and assertiveness).[6]

Perceptions of source credibility are an important determinant of the effectiveness of a persuasive appeal. In one study, several persuasive speeches were created to convince student subjects they could function adequately with less sleep. Some speakers advocated that people could function without any sleep, others told students they needed one hour per night, two hours per night, three hours per night, and so on, up to eight hours per night. The researchers exposed student subjects to texts of one of the speeches—telling half the subjects that the message they were reading was written by a Nobel Prize-winning psychologist and the other half of the subjects that the message was written by the director of the local YMCA. Participants were later asked how many hours of sleep they believed a person needed to function adequately. The subjects were far more likely to reflect the number of hours advocated by the higher credibility psychologist than the lower credibility YMCA director.[7]

Research on the impact of source credibility on the effectiveness of persuasive appeals is not entirely consistent with the findings of the sleep study cited above. Not every study has found that sources with higher credibility are more persuasive than sources with lower credibility. Other factors such as pre-existing attitudes and stereotypes may minimize the impact of source credibility.[8] However, if you wish to influence others it is important to cultivate an image as a credible source of information. You can accomplish this by working to be perceived as more expert, trustworthy, and dynamic.

Advertisers often try to capitalize on the credibility of celebrities by hiring them to endorse their products. The most effective celebrity endorsements appear to be those in which the celebrity and the product are matched in some way.[9] This match further enhances the celebrity's credibility. For example, we would expect former NBA basketball player Michael Jordan to be an *expert* about Nike basketball shoes; sports announcer John Madden to be a *trustworthy* and straightforward source of information about Ace home improvement and hardware products; and talk show host Kathie Lee Gifford to be a *dynamic* spokesperson for Carnival Cruise Lines. When the reputation of a celebrity is tarnished, credibility is reduced and the company employing the celebrity spokesperson will be quick to sever the relationship. This was the case with three former Pepsi celebrity endorsers: boxer Mike Tyson and pop stars Madonna and Michael Jackson. A product is only as credible as the celebrity to which it is linked.

Similarity. Sources perceived to be similar to the recipients of their message have been shown to be more effective at persuasion. One researcher found that people were more likely to buy paint from a salesperson who had previously used the same type and amount of paint as they were planning to buy.[10] The impact of source similarity appears to intensify when the issue is personal and involves value judgements and opinions (which brand and model of computer is best, for example).[11] Persuasion experts Erwin Bettinghaus and Michael Cody offer the following conclusions regarding the impact of source similarity on persuasion:

- Similarity is likely to be most useful if it satisfies some personal need or concern of the receiver.
- The similarity between the source and the receiver should be relevant to the persuasion topic.
- Similarity is important in producing the desired persuasive effects if it increases liking and/or trust for the source.
- Similarity involves a range of characteristics which can enhance the effectiveness of a persuasive appeal, including similarity of attitude, occupation, speech patterns and dialects, and ethnicity. Similarity in attitudes, however, is the only factor which produces consistently increased persuasiveness.[12]

In sum, we need to seek to establish a perception of similarity with the target of a persuasive appeal. This can be accomplished by emphasizing similarities in attitudes and in other characteristics.

Physical attractiveness. A number of research investigations have found that physically attractive communicators are more effective persuaders than their less attractive counterparts. In one such study, students asked to sign a petition banning the serving of meat in university dining halls were significantly more likely to comply when the request was made by a physically attractive source than when the same request was made by a physically unattractive individual.[13]

The relationship between physical attractiveness and persuasion is complex. Generally, physical attractiveness appears not to directly affect persuasive outcomes, but rather does so indirectly, by means of its influence on a receiver's liking for the source.[14] Advertisers exploit the relationship between physical attractiveness and persuasion. Magazine, billboard, and television advertisements are filled with highly attractive men and women representing a wide variety of services and products. Although physically attractive sources of persuasive messages appear to create feelings of identification with receivers, research suggests that physical attractiveness by itself does not guarantee the success of a persuasive appeal.

> Beauty is a mystery. You can neither eat it nor make flannel out of it.
>
> D. H. Lawrence

Message

A variety of message factors influence the acceptance of the persuasive appeal. Among the most important are message repetition, message sidedness, and fear appeals.

Message repetition. A single exposure to a persuasive message is not likely to produce a significant persuasive effect. For this reason message repetition is a common persuasive strategy. Persuaders use message repetition to familiarize receivers with persuasive appeals. Think of some commonly advertised products such as Coca-Cola, Chevrolet automobiles, and Levis blue jeans. How familiar are you with the advertisements for these products? They are probably extremely familiar to you because you are bombarded with the messages on a daily basis. In fact, it is hard to imagine a twenty-four hour span in your life in which you would not be exposed to some form of advertisement for one of these products. You would have to avoid television, radio, magazines, newspapers, and billboards just for starters. You would also need to avoid vending machines, cars driving by, and walking behind anyone wearing blue jeans. You would likely need to retreat to some secluded location in the wilderness to be completely isolated from messages about these three products. And that's just three of the literally thousands of advertising messages to which you are exposed on a regular basis.

Advertisers repeat their messages because repetition enables the receiver to become more familiar with a product and receivers tend to like what is familiar to them. When receivers are frequently exposed to the same message, they eventually tend to reach a point of saturation. At this point, continued exposure to the message is no longer effective. The saturation point is known as the "wear-out threshold." This is why advertising campaigns and slogans change on a regular basis. Bettinghaus and Cody offer the following conclusions concerning message repetition:

- Repetition is useful in establishing new products and brands in the market.
- A group of commercials should not wear out as fast as a single commercial.
- Only good commercials reach the wear out threshold. A commercial that is ineffective will quickly decrease in effectiveness the more frequently it is aired. Good commercials increase in effectiveness the more they are aired until the point of saturation.
- An advertising slogan (for example, Tastes Great! Less Filling!) will not wear out as quickly if a series of advertisements differing in content are used in conjunction with the slogan.
- Advertisements which require greater levels of involvement from receivers (such as the Taster's Choice instant coffee romance series) wear out less quickly than simple or straightforward advertisements.[15]

Message sidedness. As the saying goes, there are two sides to every story. In persuasion this is referred to as message sidedness. A persuader has the option to present one side of his or her argument or to address opposing points of view by presenting two sides of the argument. Research suggests it is most beneficial to present one side of the argument when the audience is generally in favor of the persuader's point of view or when the argument is the only one which will be presented. Both sides of an argument should be presented when the audience initially disagrees with the persuader, or when it is likely that the audience will hear the other side from another source.[16] Kamins and his colleagues suggest that two-sided arguments are effective for increasing the credibility of celebrities used in advertisements. Since receivers know that celebrities are paid for their endorsement, they may become suspicious when a celebrity has only positive things to say about a product or service. By discussing both the positive and negative features of the product or service, the celebrity may be perceived as more credible and likable by receivers.[17]

Fear appeals. The use of fear to modify thoughts and behaviors is a common persuasive technique. Graphic illustrations depicting the results of drinking and driving; hospital scenes in which drug users are portrayed hooked to life-support apparatus; photographs of the decayed lungs of cigarette smokers, and graphic images of aborted fetuses to discourage abortion are all examples of persuasive fear appeals. The effectiveness of such appeals depend on the intensity of the appeal, the nature of the solution, and the specificity of the recommended action.

> Let them hate so long as they fear.
>
> Lucius Accius

In general, research suggests that moderate fear appeals are most persuasive.[18] Receivers are likely to repress their responses to highly intense fear appeals due to their extreme discomfort or anxiety. When presented with a highly intense fear appeal (such as the depiction of severely injured drunk driving accident victims), a receiver may deal with his or her apprehension by asserting, "That can't happen to me." Very mild fear appeals, on the other hand, may be dismissed as inconsequential.

For a fear appeal to be successful, the persuader must supply a reasonable alternative to the fearful consequences.[19] A persuasive fear appeal designed to minimize the spread of AIDS and other sexually transmitted diseases would not be effective if it offered the suggestion "avoid all sexual contact" as the solution to the problem. For most individuals, "avoid all sexual contact" is not a reasonable solution to the exigency caused by the fear appeal. An effective fear appeal would offer alternatives for minimizing the spread of AIDS that are generally perceived as more reasonable, such as using condoms, selecting sexual partners more carefully, or having sex only in a monogamous relationship.

Well developed fear appeals offer specific recommendations.[20] A fear appeal which suggests that receivers should "be careful" when having sex would not be effective. Since receivers are not given specific recommendations (how should one be careful?), they are likely to ignore the fear appeal. If a receiver can't solve the problem, then why should he or she worry about it? Again, specific suggestions like use a condom when engaging in any kind of sexual activity, avoid sexual contact with high-risk partners, or be monogamous provide specific recommendations which enable the receiver to avoid the fearful consequence.

The effects of fear appeals are often short-lived. Researchers have noted that the persuasive impact of a fear appeal begins to dissipate within twenty-four hours.[21] Further, evidence suggests that fear appeals by themselves are not very persuasive. Such appeals seem to be most effective when used in combination with other persuasive strategies.[22]

Channel

Several factors influence the channel through which the persuasive appeal is delivered. The most important of these factors in terms of acceptance is the choice of the medium for delivery of the persuasive appeal.

> The medium is the message.
>
>   Marshall McLuhan

Choice of medium. The persuasiveness of a message varies based on complexity and the medium selected for presentation. Generally research suggests that more complex messages are more persuasively presented in written form, while simple messages are more persuasively presented in video or audio form (see table 8.1).[23] These findings may explain why so many politicians create television and radio advertisements which center around short sound bites as opposed to more substantive comments. It may also explain why the charts, graphs, and figures presented by presidential candidate Ross Perot in 1992 left so many voters feeling bewildered.

Daniel O'Keefe suggests that the degree to which the receiver can control the pace of presentation of the message has more impact

Table 8.1
Attitude Change as a Function of Medium Selected and Message Complexity

Medium	Message Complexity	
	Simple message	Complex message
Written	low	high
Audiotape	moderate	low
Videotape	high	low to moderate

on persuasability than the medium in which the message is presented.[24] For example, O'Keefe argues that a complex message could be effectively presented in the video or audio format if the receiver had the ability to slow down, stop, or replay the message. This activity would be analogous to rereading material presented in written form and would enable the receiver to deal more effectively with complex information. This persuasive strategy is used by the makers of Buick automobiles. Buick offers free videotapes to consumers detailing the latest test results of their products. The consumer can review the information at home which allows the receiver the opportunity to control the pace of presentation and, as such, enables the incorporation of more detailed information.

Receiver

Several factors influence the receiver's acceptance of any persuasive appeal we create. The most important of these factors are the receiver's personality characteristics and his or her degree of involvement with the communication issue.

Personality characteristics. Research suggests a variety of individual personality characteristics influence a receiver's susceptibility to a persuasive message. These findings can be confusing and, at times, contradictory. However, the following general conclusions can be supported:

- Receivers with high self-esteem are generally more resistant to influence than receivers with moderate or low self-esteem.[25]
- Receivers with high self-esteem may be more influenced by a high level fear appeal than receivers with low self-esteem.[26]
- Highly intelligent receivers pay greater attention to the quality of a persuasive argument than less intelligent receivers. As such, more intelligent receivers are more effectively persuaded by convincing arguments.[27]
- Highly dogmatic (closed-minded) receivers are more likely to respond to persuasive appeals based on traditional values which serve to maintain the status quo (Keep America free—resist gun control) than to logical or information-based appeals (There were over 1,400 accidental deaths caused by firearms in the United States last year—now is the time for strict gun control).[28]
- High self-monitoring receivers (those who look to others for social cues) are more likely to be persuaded by appeals that focus on images of glamour, success, status, excitement, and sex. Low

self-monitoring receivers (those who are highly individualistic and independent) are more likely to be persuaded by persuasive appeals which emphasize quality and value.[29]

Involvement with the communication issue. The degree to which a receiver feels commitment or involvement with an issue influences his or her persuasability. When a receiver feels a high degree of involvement, he or she is more likely to spend time scrutinizing a persuasive argument. Further, when highly involved receivers listen to arguments that are counter to their initial position, they generate a greater number of counterarguments than do less involved receivers.[30]

Interpersonal Persuasion

Many of the examples cited thus far are from the world of advertising. Certainly creativity and persuasion play a key role in the development of advertising campaigns. We will focus in detail on creative advertising later in this chapter. Creativity and persuasion, however, play an equally important role in allowing us to meet interpersonal needs. We call this day-to-day application of creative persuasive techniques, interpersonal persuasion. Two interpersonal persuasive strategies are bargaining and negotiation. Bargaining involves a win-lose clash of wills. This type of persuasive encounter may take place when you return an unwanted item to a local department store, purchase an automobile, or buy trinkets from a street vendor. Negotiation involves problem solving. In negotiation the goal is to develop mutually advantageous (win-win) resolutions to problems. Examples of negotiation might include a husband and wife deciding where to go on vacation, two roommates deciding on the distribution of living space, or team members dividing aspects of a major project. Negotiation is a more creative process than bargaining. There are times, however, when it is advantageous to bargain with others.

Bargaining

Roger Fisher, William Ury, and Bruce Patton of the Harvard Negotiation Project suggest two models of bargaining: hard bargaining and soft bargaining.[31] Hard bargaining is designed to maximize outcomes. Unfortunately, gains in outcomes often come at the expense of the relationship. If you are on a vacation in Mexico and you encounter a street vendor selling unique pottery, you will likely use the hard bargaining approach. If the price of the pottery is marked at twenty dollars, you will probably counter with a bid which is significantly lower—say three dollars. The vendor will respond to your offer—lowering the price to eighteen dollars—and the hard bargaining game is on. According to Fisher, Ury, and Patton hard bargaining involves the following:

- An adversarial relationship
- Extreme, often unfair, positions
- A win-lose clash of wills
- Demands for concessions
- Threats
- Deception
- Mistrust[32]

> If you don't get what you like then you will be forced to like what you get.
>
> George Bernard Shaw

The hard bargaining strategy involves three basic steps:

1. **Open with an extreme position.** Your initial demands should be more extreme than those you expect to agree to. Your initial position should not be so extreme, however, that it discourages the other party from engaging in bargaining. You might use this technique when purchasing an automobile. Your initial offer is likely to be significantly lower than the sticker price listed on the vehicle you wish to purchase.

2. **Make small grudging concessions.** Do not make any significant concessions until the other party does. If the salesperson tells you that he or she could not possibly sell the vehicle for the price you offer, add a small amount—perhaps $100—to your offer.

3. **Use viable threats.** The most common threat is for a bargainer to suggest that he or she will withdraw from bargaining if the other party does not make more significant concessions. You might tell the salesperson that you cannot afford to make a payment of $220 per month, but if the salesperson can figure a way to get your payment down to $200 a month you'll buy the automobile. If not you'll go somewhere else.[33]

Many people are uncomfortable with hard bargaining. They dislike the adversarial nature of this approach and are concerned about the damage that hard bargaining techniques inflict on relationships. As a result, they choose to use soft bargaining. Soft bargaining emphasizes the necessity of reaching agreement. Soft bargainers are quick to offer concessions and are concerned primarily with maintaining relationships. According to Fisher, Ury, and Patton, soft bargaining involves the following:

- A friendly relationship
- Frequent concessions
- A search for agreement
- A willingness to lose the dispute to preserve the relationship
- Open disclosure
- Trust[34]

The soft bargaining strategy involves three basic steps:

1. ***Make numerous offers and concessions.*** Provide many alternatives and be willing to change your position easily. An example of this might be two neighbors negotiating payment for the construction of a fence bordering both properties. Fearing damage to the relationship, one neighbor might engage in soft bargaining by offering the other neighbor a number of options for contributing to the purchase of materials and helping with construction.

2. ***Trust the other party completely.*** To avoid confrontation the soft bargainer must trust the other party. If the neighbor who agreed to help with the fence is late with his or her payment for materials or does not assist with construction as agreed, the soft bargaining neighbor must trust that the promised actions are forthcoming.

3. ***Yield as necessary to avoid confrontation.*** The primary goal of soft bargaining is to avoid confrontation. To do so often requires the soft bargainer to yield to pressure applied by the other party. If the neighbor who agreed to help with the fence tells the soft bargaining neighbor that he or she is unable to follow through with their earlier stated financial commitments, then the soft bargainer will yield to this fact in an attempt to preserve the relationship.[35]

Soft bargaining is most often a losing strategy. Soft bargainers are particularly vulnerable to hard bargainers. Although soft bargainers may preserve the relationship with the other party, the use of this concession-oriented style is not the only method available for dealing with problems in a manner that respects interpersonal relationships. A more creative approach to dealing with interpersonal needs is negotiation.

Negotiation

As noted earlier in the chapter, negotiation is a problem solving process which seeks win-win resolutions. As such, the negotiation process depends on the implementation of creative solutions. Fisher, Ury, and Patton suggest a four-step approach, called Principled Negotiation, which enables problem solvers to reach solutions satisfactory to both parties.[36]

> Let us never negotiate out of fear, but let us never fear to negotiate.
>
> John F. Kennedy

1. ***Separate the people from the problem.*** Avoid defining negotiation situations as a test of wills. Focus instead on working together toward a common goal—resolving the issues at hand. Build trust to diffuse strong emotions and keep conflict from escalating.

2. ***Focus on interests, not positions.*** A negotiating position is the negotiator's public stance ("I want $40,000 a year in salary"). An interest, on the other hand, is the reason why the negotiator takes that position ("I need to earn $40,000 so that I can save the downpayment for a house"). Focusing on positions can blind you and the other negotiator to the fact that there are many creative ways to meet the underlying need or interest. The company in the example above might pay less in salary and yet meet the employee's need for housing by offering a low cost home loan. For an example of the importance of focusing on interests as opposed to positions, see the Creative Profile on page 218.

3. ***Invent options for mutual gain.*** Spend time brainstorming solutions that can meet the needs of both negotiators (see chapter 5). The more options that are generated, the greater the likelihood of reaching a win-win resolution. Win-win resolutions allow both parties in a negotiation to claim victory. Too often negotiators assume a "fixed pie" model when resolving differences of opinion. The fixed pie model looks at

Creative Profile: Negotiation at Camp David

In September 1978, President Jimmy Carter invited the leaders of Egypt and Israel to the presidential retreat at Camp David in Maryland's Catoctin Mountains. At Camp David, Carter, Egyptian President Anwar Sadat, and Israeli Prime Minister Menachem Begin met to negotiate a mideast peace settlement. The compound at Camp David provided a calm and relaxing venue. Both Sadat and Begin and their delegations were housed in rustic cabins located within sight of one another. Still, representatives from both sides were initially tense as they cautiously worked to crack the eight-month deadlock in Egyptian-Israeli negotiations. Often Carter himself would shuttle back and forth from Sadat's cabin to Begin's cabin presenting offers and counteroffers.

Some two weeks into the negotiations signs of progress were noticeable. One issue, in particular, on which the two sides came to agreement was the disposition of the Sinai Peninsula. Israel had occupied the Egyptian Sinai since the Six Day War of 1967. At the outset of the Camp David negotiations, Israel insisted on keeping some of the Sinai. Egypt, on the other hand, wanted the entire Sinai returned to Egyptian sovereignty. Proposal after proposal was offered for dividing the Sinai. Each offer, however, was deemed unacceptable by one side or the other. Finally, the negotiators looked beneath the initial positions held by Egypt (we want all of the Sinai) and Israel (we will give back part of the Sinai) and began to focus on underlying interests. This was the turning point.

Israel's interest involved security; Israelis did not want Egyptian tanks deployed on their border ready to roll across at any time. Egypt's interest involved sovereignty; the Sinai had been part of Egypt since the time of the Pharaohs. Further, Egyptians had been displaced from their homes after the 1967 Israeli takeover. Since Israel had no interest in maintaining sovereignty over the Sinai or in having Israeli citizens settle in the area, a solution became clear. Israel would return the Sinai to Egypt, allowing Egyptians to control an area where they had a historic claim and allowing them to return to their homes. Egypt, in return, would demilitarize large areas of the Sinai, removing tanks and other offensive military weapons and personnel from near Israel's border. These demilitarized areas, in many cases, would come under United Nations control.

By looking beyond initial positions and focusing on underlying interests, both sides emerged from the negotiations as winners. Further, agreements regarding the Sinai served as a springboard for additional problem solving between Egypt and Israel. Although the mideast remains a "hot spot" today, relations between Egypt and Israel are generally quite good. This demonstrates the long-term value of identifying interests and seeking resolutions that meet the needs of both parties.

Discussion Questions

1. What role do you think working in a relaxing setting, such as Camp David, plays in developing creative solutions to problems?

2. How effective is it to have someone play the role of mediator, shuttling back and forth as President Carter did, in tense negotiations? Can you think of any other creative strategies which might be useful in this situation?

3. The negotiators at Camp David clearly focused on interests, not just positions. Can you identify any of the other aspects of Principled Negotiation used at Camp David? Did the negotiators separate the people from the problem, invent options for mutual gain, or use objective criteria?

4. Attempts at compromise (simply dividing the Sinai into Egyptian and Israeli-governed sections) failed at Camp David. Success came only when the negotiators uncovered a collaborative win-win resolution which met the needs of both parties. What are the advantages and disadvantages of compromise? Of collaboration? When is it most appropriate to compromise? To collaborate?

Sources:

Camp David—and after. (1978, September 18). *U.S. News & World Report*, pp. 16–19.

Fisher, R., Ury, W., & Patton, B. (1991). *Getting to yes* (2nd ed.). New York: Penguin, pp. 41–42.

Mideast tangle. (1978, September 25). *U.S. News & World Report*, pp. 26–29.

problem solving as being analogous to cutting pieces of pie. This model assumes there is only one pie. The winner is the party with the most pie at the end of the negotiation. By inventing options for mutual gain, creative negotiators realize there need not be a single pie. Indeed, both parties in a negotiation can walk away with a whole pie of their own. The negotiation of the Sinai Peninsula land dispute presented in the Creative Profile is a classic example of how both sides in a negotiation can come away as winners.

4. ***Insist on using objective criteria.*** Find a set of criteria that both parties can agree on when determining the terms of the settlement. This reduces the possibility that one party will force the other into accepting an unsatisfactory solution. In most cases, negotiators will be comfortable with an agreement that corresponds to widely accepted norms. Such standards can range from used car price books to mortgage appraisals to legal precedents for insurance settlements.

Roger Fisher and another member of the Harvard Negotiation Project, Scott Brown, suggest that Principled Negotiation works best when negotiators are unconditionally constructive.[37] Being unconditionally constructive when you negotiate means you should do things that are good for the relationship and good for you, whether the other party reciprocates or not. Fisher and Brown identify six basic elements in being unconditionally constructive.

Rationality. To varying degrees, emotions affect all of our relationships. Emotions run the gamut from those we think of as positive (such as love, admiration, and respect) to those we tend to think of as negative (such as hate, frustration, and anger). When our emotions get too powerful, they can cloud our judgement. The rational negotiator balances his or her emotions with reason. To do this you should develop an awareness of your emotions. Instead of simply reacting emotionally, you should try, instead, to acknowledge your emotional state. For example, if the behavior of the other party in a negotiated settlement angers you, talk about your anger, don't just display it.

2. **Understanding.** Even if a negotiator is rational, he or she will not be prepared to solve a problem until the problem is fully understood. Misunderstandings frequently contribute to failed negotiations. Further, misunderstandings usually strain relationships. Fisher and Brown offer the following example of how a misunderstanding can affect a relationship:

> In 1962, [Soviet] General Secretary Nikita Khrushchev, addressing the United Nations in New York, made a now infamous speech. Pounding a shoe on the podium, he proclaimed, "We will bury" the Western capitalist countries. Most Americans interpreted this as a threat; a statement that the goal of the Soviet Union was to bomb the United States into oblivion. After the U.S. press widely reported the "threatening" language, scholars and Soviet officials pointed out that in Russian the phrase did not imply a threat, but simply expressed a belief that the Soviet system would outlive the Western system. A healthy young Russian might easily say, "I will bury my father," meaning, "I expect to be around after he is gone."[38]

This type of cultural misunderstanding becomes increasingly common as negotiators deal more frequently with parties from other nations. Before attempting to solve a problem you must be certain that you understand the other person's point of view.

3. **Communication.** To have a working relationship you must have open, honest communication. To improve your communication as a negotiator it is important to remember three principles: there is always something to talk about, listening is more important than telling, and consistency is critical.

It is a mistake to assume there is nothing to talk about when negotiations are at an impasse. Avoiding interaction does nothing to solve a problem. In 1985, United States Secretary of State George Shultz boycotted a meeting of foreign ministers to protest New Zealand's decision to bar U.S. nuclear-armed warships from New Zealand ports. New Zealand prime minister David Lange, realizing his participation in the meeting prompted Shultz's decision not to attend, recognized that reducing communication would not solve the problem when he stated, "the important point about a long-standing alliance is that the members must be able to talk out their differences."[39]

Many negotiators assume it is most important for them to tell the other party where they stand. Building a productive working relationship, however, involves listening more than telling. Listening provides negotiators with valuable information and demonstrates to the other party that a negotiator is committed to problem solving.

To be effective, communication must be consistent. Negotiators must follow through on promises, be consistent in their words and deeds, and avoid telling one thing to one person or group and something different to another. Inconsistent messages undermine the trust that others have for us and inhibit effective problem solving. To realize the devastating effect of inconsistent communication, we need only look at the harsh criticism President George Bush was subjected to when he promised "No new taxes" and later recanted.

4. **Reliability.** Trust is probably the most important element of a good working relationship. As noted above, inconsistency reduces trust. Behaviors that can destroy trust include engaging in erratic and unpredictable behavior, breaking promises, and being deceptive or manipulative. By avoiding these types of behaviors we can promote an image of reliability which will encourage others to have more trust in us.

5. **Persuasion, not coercion.** The tactics a negotiator uses when dealing with the other party have a significant effect on the quality of the interaction. Coercive tactics damage relationships and weaken our resolve to come to consensus. If people are creatively persuaded rather than unthinkingly coerced, both the outcome and the degree of compliance are improved.

6. **Acceptance.** To negotiate successfully you must accept the other party. Negotiation cannot take place without some degree of

mutual respect. The conflict between the Israelis and the Palestinians is an example of the importance of acceptance. Although the conflict is still not fully resolved, it was only after both sides recognized and accepted one another that some progress could be made toward resolving differences.

Mass Persuasion

Mass persuasion provides some of the most recognizable examples of creative persuasion. This persuasion takes place in the public context and generally involves the use of organized persuasive campaigns. Such campaigns can generally be conceptualized as fitting into one of four broad categories: political campaigns (campaigns for a political office or referendum); commercial product campaigns (campaigns for consumer goods); campaigns revolving around an idea, issue, or cause (an anti-smoking campaign, for example); and campaigns revolving around corporate images and advocacy (campaigns which focus on an audience's overall opinion of the corporation or a social issue such as protection of the environment rather than a specific product).[40]

> Corporate advertising requires creative genius to penetrate the indifference with which people regard most corporations.
>
> David Ogilvy

Persuasive Campaigns

A persuasive campaign is an "organized and sustained attempt at influencing groups or masses of people through a series of messages."[41] Everett Rogers and Douglas Storey surveyed over forty years of campaign research. Based on their analysis, they identified the following as characteristics of successful campaigns.[42]

Pretest messages and identify market segments. Organizers of effective campaigns rely on research to help them shape messages. The producers of *Sesame Street*, for instance, pretest their programs to determine how they will be received by preschool audiences. Doing market research prior to a campaign reveals what audiences currently believe, if receivers understand the campaign, and which campaign messages are best suited to particular segments of the market.

Expose a large segment of the audience to clear campaign messages. Message exposure is a prerequisite for campaign success. Audiences must be aware of campaign messages before they can act on the information contained in those messages. Similarly, it is important that messages are clear. As noted in the Reebok UBU example discussed earlier in this chapter, when receivers do not understand a message there is little opportunity for persuasive impact.

> Making the simple complicated is commonplace; making the complicated simple, awesomely simple, that's creativity.
> Charlie Mingus

Use media which are most accessible to target groups. Successful campaigns utilize those media which are most accessible to audiences. Products targeted to 18–25 year-old consumers, for example, are more often found on radio and television outlets that are popular with younger audiences, such as rock and roll radio stations and television networks like MTV, ESPN2, and Fox.

Use the media to raise awareness. The media are most effective when used to provide important information, stimulate interpersonal conversations, and recruit additional people to participate in the campaign. Media messages raise awareness and get people talking about the merits of politicians, products, organizations, and causes. The media play such an important role in shaping public opinion that almost all organizations from small colleges to multinational corporations hire public relations specialists to help place stories in newspapers, magazines, and on radio and television broadcasts.

Rely on interpersonal communication, particularly communication between people of similar social backgrounds, to lead to and reinforce behavior change. Interpersonal communication networks play a particularly important role in persuasive campaigns designed to change people's behaviors. Behavioral change is more likely when the desired behaviors are modeled by others. The national crime prevention campaign that urges listeners and viewers to "Take a Bite Out of Crime" is one example of how media and interpersonal channels can complement each other. Although many people learn about crime prevention behaviors through the campaign's media spots, listeners put these behaviors into action only after they become involved in neighborhood watch groups.

Use high credibility sources. Successful campaigns use highly credible representatives. As we noted in relation to commercial advertising earlier in this chapter, a campaign is only as credible as the individuals who speak on its behalf.

Direct messages at the individual needs of the audience. Audiences are most influenced by messages aimed directly at personal needs. Effective political campaigns emphasize how the candidate will help the voter by lowering taxes, providing more jobs, building better roads, lowering crime, and so on. Campaigns for popular products link the purchase of the item with a specific need felt by the audience.

Emphasize positive rewards rather than prevention. Many campaigns (such as the one urging us to wear seat belts) try to help audiences avoid future, unwanted events. These campaigns often fail because the consequences of noncompliance are uncertain. In the case of safety belts, many of us drive without them because we don't believe we will ever be in a serious auto accident. Effective campaigns emphasize the immediate positive rewards that come from adopting a belief, value, or behavior. Campaign planners may use our fear of suffering a heart attack to encourage us to start a regular exercise program. However, we are more likely to adopt a regular exercise routine if campaign messages emphasize weight loss, stress reduction, and other immediate, positive benefits.

Creative Public Relations

Public relations presents a unique challenge to the creative communicator. Public relations involves research, media relations, product publicity, and public affairs, among other duties.[43] Each of these responsibilities requires creativity in order to effectively influence both internal and external audiences. However, the public relations task which may require the greatest creativity is dealing with crisis. The need for crisis communication strategies was realized after the near meltdown of the Three-Mile Island nuclear plant in the late 1970s. In the years since, a significant number of organizations have developed crisis communication plans.[44] Advertising executives James Gregory and Jack Wiechmann offer a six-step model for dealing creatively with crisis:[45]

1. ***Be prepared, have a plan of action.*** Crisis, whether caused by an emergency (such as the indictment of a top company official) or an accident (such as a chemical leak or oil spill) must

be anticipated. Some organizations have detailed emergency manuals which specify appropriate actions in the event of a crisis. Other companies even simulate crisis situations to test responsiveness. The creative techniques discussed in chapter 5 can be useful here.

2. ***Build a crisis management team.*** A trained team of decision-makers from across organizational functions should be on call at all times to handle any crisis situation which might arise. In the event of a crisis, members of this team should be prepared to identify the impact of the crisis on their department or unit. By brainstorming "worst-case" effects, the team can begin to develop a strategy which minimizes negative outcomes. In smaller organizations a single individual may replace the crisis team.

3. ***Respond quickly to crisis.*** A rapid response is important in a crisis situation. Although crisis managers need to be careful not to respond hastily, decisive communication issued soon after the event is most often the hallmark of effective crisis management. Johnson & Johnson demonstrated the value of a quick response when they immediately decided to withdraw Tylenol from the marketplace and cancel advertising after tainted Tylenol capsules resulted in several deaths in the Chicago area in 1982. Exxon, on the other hand, reacted slowly to the grounding of its tanker *Valdez* off the Alaska coast in 1989. This delayed response led to intense and prolonged media speculation and criticism.

4. ***Work cooperatively with the media.*** Crises can be managed more effectively with the cooperation of the media. The media are vital in telling a story of a crisis situation to government, financial, consumer, and other influential groups. During the Tylenol crisis, Johnson & Johnson held a video newsconference simultaneously with reporters from major cities. Further, Johnson & Johnson staff were available around the clock to answer telephone inquiries regarding the Tylenol situation.

5. ***Don't panic.*** Whether a crisis situation goes according to plan or not, it is important to be flexible. Crisis managers must be careful not to let the stress of a crisis situation inhibit their creativity. They must avoid letting a disaster panic them down blind alleys.

6. ***Take out image insurance.*** The organizations that are most prepared to deal with crisis are those that already have a positive public image. When rumors surfaced in 1993 that

injection needles were found in cans of Pepsi, there was relatively little consumer reaction. This is primarily attributable to the positive image that Pepsi had in the marketplace and consumer confidence in the inherent safety of Pepsi products.

Creative Advertising

One of the most creative forms of influence is advertising. Creative ideas are the lifeblood of successful ad campaigns. When advertisements lack creativity, they are much more likely to be lost amid the myriad of messages to which we are regularly exposed. Those advertisements, on the other hand, which capture our attention and imagination are far more likely to be remembered and acted upon. James Marra uses the acronym ADNORMS to describe the essence of creative advertising ideas. ADNORMS stands for adaptability, durability, newness, oneness, relevance, memorability, and simplicity.[46]

Adaptability. When advertisements are adaptable, they can utilize all the available media. The most creative advertisements are suited to a variety of media such as billboards, point of purchase, magazines, radio, and television. McDonald's recent campaigns linked to hit movies such as *Jurassic Park* and *The Flintstones* are a prime example of highly adaptable advertising. These campaigns present messages through a variety of media as well as through point of purchase promotions offering "super-sized" drinks, sandwiches, and orders of french fries.

Durability. When advertising ideas are durable, they sustain an image over long periods of time. Clear, unmistakable, and appropriate brand images offer durability. Advertising icons like the Marlboro man, Colonel Sanders, and the Maytag repairman are examples of creative advertising concepts which demonstrate durability.

Newness. The most creative advertisements are novel. They present ideas in an interesting, and often unexpected, way. Being the first to present a particular message or the first to present a message in a particular manner enables an advertiser to demonstrate newness. Apple Computer's well-known "1984" television commercial, in which groups of young people are seen smashing images of George Orwell's Big Brother, served to represent the challenge of upstart Apple to industry-leader IBM. The advertisement, which cost $500,000 to produce and only aired once on network television, was selected by the editors of *Advertising Age* as the commercial of the decade for the 1980s.[47]

Creative Dilemma: Developing Creative Advertisements

James Marra suggests the use of the acronym ADNORMS to describe the essence of creative advertising ideas. Develop an advertisement (print, radio, or television) for the products or services listed below. Try to incorporate as many of the ADNORMS characteristics as possible into your advertisement.

Adaptability   Relevance

Durability   Memorability

Newness   Simplicity

Oneness

- Fizzy, a new citrus cola soft drink
- Maxair Deluxe vacuum cleaners
- International World Airlines, an airline carrier with nonstop service to Europe
- Dewey, Cheetem, & Howe, a law firm specializing in personal injury
- Pecs Palace, a health club for the serious weightlifter
- Gasco unleaded gasoline
- The Raptor GT, a new sports car
- Burger Village, a fast-food chain
- Adventureland amusement park
- Blotz beer
- Crispies potato chips
- Ultravision televisions and VCRs

Discussion questions

1. Are some of the ADNORMS characteristics more important than others? Are some easier to achieve?
2. Do certain products seems to be more suited to a particular medium (print, radio, or television)?
3. What strategies are most effective in developing creative advertising ideas? (You may want to review the discussion of the creative process in chapter 3 to answer this question).
4. How effective is humor as an advertising technique? What types of products or services should not be advertised humorously?

Oneness. When advertising ideas have oneness they are bound by a singular core idea or theme. This focus makes it much easier for audience members to understand and remember an advertising message. The Federal Express slogan, "When it Absolutely, Positively Has To Be There Overnight," is a good example of an advertising message which communicates a singleminded commitment.

Relevance. An advertisement is relevant to the extent that it has meaning for the target audience. Ads that tell audience members what they can hope to gain from the use of a particular product or service enhance involvement on the part of the audience. Testimonials for weight loss products, exercise apparatus, and self-help programs, for example, often include creative appeals to the relevance of the product or service.

Memorability. The longer an advertisement sticks in the target audience's mind, the more memorable it is. A variety of factors, including the other aspects of the ADNORMS model, contribute to the memorability of an advertisement.

Simplicity. Simple advertisements are clear and instantly meaningful. Ideas are presented in an uncluttered fashion and the audience is not required to engage in any unwanted effort in order to comprehend the message.

ADNORMS represent the standards of quality found in the most creative of advertising ideas. Of course, not all ads satisfy all the requirements. In most cases, one or more of the ADNORMS characteristics are missing. The more standards that are met, the more creative the advertisement. Try to use the ADNORMS model to generate your own creative advertisements in the Creative Dilemma on page 227.

Summing Up

In this chapter we focused on creative persuasive communication. We began by looking at the difference between persuasion and coercion. Persuasion can be defined as the process of influencing the thoughts and/or behavior of others. This process involves choice. Coercion, on the other hand, involves forced compliance and offers few, if any choices.

There are many different approaches for looking at the persuasive process. One of the most widely discussed frameworks for looking at persuasion is the Yale Approach. The Yale Approach suggests that the extent to which a person will be persuaded depends on a chain of learning responses. These learning responses operate in five stages: attention, comprehension, acceptance, retention, and action. Each of the these stages is important. The acceptance stage, however, has generated the most interest from researchers.

Acceptance is influenced by four key components of the communication process: the source, the message, the channel, and the receiver. Several factors influence the effectiveness of the source of the persuasive appeal. Among the most important are source credibility, similarity, and physical attractiveness. Important factors impacting the persuasive message include message repetition, message sidedness, and fear appeals. The most important channel factor is choice of the medium for delivery of the persuasive appeal. Important receiver factors include personality characteristics and the receiver's involvement with the communication issue.

Creativity and persuasion play a vital role in allowing us to meet our interpersonal needs. Two interpersonal persuasive strategies are bargaining and negotiation. Bargaining involves a win-lose clash of wills. Negotiation involves problem solving and seeks win-win solutions. There are two models of bargaining: hard and soft. Hard bargaining is designed to maximize outcomes at the expense of relationships. Many people are uncomfortable with hard bargaining and choose soft bargaining instead. Soft bargainers are quick to offer concessions and are concerned primarily with maintaining relationships. Soft bargaining is often a losing strategy.

A more creative approach to dealing with interpersonal problems is negotiation. Principled Negotiation is a four-step model of negotiation: 1) separate the people from the problem; 2) focus on interests, not positions; 3) invent options for mutual gain; and 4) insist on using objective criteria. Principled Negotiation works best when negotiators are unconditionally constructive. To be unconditionally constructive a negotiator must: be rational, gain understanding, communicate openly and honestly, be reliable, use persuasive (not coercive) tactics, and be accepting.

Mass persuasion takes place in the public context and generally involves the use of organized persuasive campaigns. Successful campaigns pretest their messages and identify market segments, expose a large portion of the audience to campaign messages, use media which are most accessible to target groups, rely on the media to raise awareness, utilize interpersonal communication to bring about behavior change, employ high credibility sources, direct messages at individual needs, and emphasize positive rewards rather than prevention.

Public relations requires a high level of creativity. The public relations task which may require the greatest degree of creativity is dealing with crisis. To deal with a crisis most effectively: be prepared, build a crisis team, respond quickly, work cooperatively with the media, don't panic, and take out image insurance.

One of the most creative forms of influence is advertising. The essence of creative advertising can be summed up in the acronym ADNORMS: adaptability, durability, newness, oneness, relevance, memorability, and simplicity.

Application Exercises

1. Develop a persuasive presentation. Try to analyze strategies for maximizing the effectiveness of your presentation based on characteristics of the source, message, channel, and receiver.

2. Analyze your personal response to persuasive fear appeals. Determine if low, moderate, or high fear appeals are most persuasive to you. What factors, if any, influence your response?

3. Generate a list of the strengths and weaknesses of the hard bargaining, soft bargaining, and Principled Negotiation approaches. Identify situations in which each approach would be most useful.

4. Engage in a negotiation using the Principled Negotiation approach. Analyze the results of your interaction. Were you unconditionally constructive? Did you achieve a win-win outcome? How did the other party react to you? Discuss your experience in class.

5. Analyze an organizational crisis situation in which you were involved or heard about somewhere else. How effective was the organization at dealing with the crisis? How many of the six suggestions offered by Gregory and Wiechmann did the organization follow?

6. Identify your ten favorite advertisements. Look for patterns. Do these ads use similar creative strategies? Deal with similar products? Compare your lists with others in class to generate a list of the ten best-liked advertisements in your class.

Endnotes

[1] For a detailed description of the Yale Approach see:

Hovland, C. I., Janis, I. L., & Kelley, H. H. (1953). *Communication and persuasion.* New Haven: Yale University Press.

[2] Hovland, Janis, & Kelley, pp. 10–11.

[3] As reported in:

Smith, M. J. (1982). *Persuasion and human action.* Belmont, CA: Wadsworth, pp. 214–215.

[4] These four components of the communication process were originally attributed to Harold D. Lasswell. See:

Lasswell, H. D. (1948). The structure and function of communication in society, In L. Bryson (Ed.), The *communication of ideas* (pp. 37–51). New York: Harper & Row.

[5] Lulofs, R. S. (1991). *Persuasion: Contexts, people, and messages.* Scottsdale, AZ: Gorsuch Scarisbrick, p. 154.

[6] Brembeck, W. L., & Howell, W. S. (1976). *Persuasion: A means of social influence* (2nd ed.). Englewood Cliffs, NJ: Prentice Hall.

[7] Bochner, S., & Insko, C. A. (1966). Communicator discrepancy, source credibility, and opinion change. *Journal of Personality and Social Psychology, 4,* 614–621.

[8] See, for example:

Aronson, E., & Golden, B. (1962). The effect of relevant and irrelevant aspects of communicator credibility on opinion change. *Journal of Personality, 30,* 135–146.

[9] Kahle, L. R., & Homer, P. M. (1985). Physical attractiveness of the celebrity endorser: A social adaptation perspective. *Journal of Consumer Research, 11,* 954–961.

[10] Brock, T. C. (1965). Communicator-recipient similarity and decision change. *Journal of Personality and Social Psychology, 1,* 650–654.

[11] See, for example:

Cantor, J., Alfonso, H., & Zillman, D. (1975). The persuasive effectiveness of the peer appeal and a communicator's first-hand experience. *Communication Research, 3,* 293–310.

Goethals, G. R., & Nelson, R. E. (1973). Similarity in the influence process: The belief-value distinction. *Journal of Personality and Social Psychology, 25,* 117–122.

[12] Bettinghaus, E. P., & Cody, M. J. (1994). *Persuasive Communication* (5th ed.). Fort Worth: Harcourt Brace, pp. 131.

[13] Chaiken, S. (1979). Communicator physical attractiveness and persuasion. *Journal of Personality and Social Psychology, 37,* 1387–1397.

[14] O'Keefe, D. J. (1990). *Persuasion: Theory and research.* Newbury Park, CA: Sage, pp. 154.

[15] Bettinghaus & Cody, pp. 66–68.

[16] Lumsdaine, A. A., & Janis, I. (1953). Resistance to counter propaganda produced by one-sided and two-sided presentation. *Public Opinion Quarterly, 17,* 311–318.

[17] Kamins, M. A., Brand, M. J., Hoeke, S. A., & Moe, J. C. (1989). Two-sided versus one-sided celebrity endorsements: The impact on advertising effectiveness and credibility. *Journal of Advertising, 18,* 4–10.

[18] McGuire, W. J. (1968). Personality and susceptibility to social influence, In E. F. Borgatta & W. W. Lambert (Eds.). *Handbook of personality theory and research* (pp. 1130–1187). Chicago: Rand McNally.

[19] Rogers, R. W., & Mewborn, C. R. (1967). Fear appeals and attitude change: Effects of a threat's noxiousness, probability of occurrence, and the efficacy of the coping response. *Journal of Personality and Social Psychology, 34,* 54–61.

[20] Leventhal, H., Singer, R, & Jones, S. (1965). Effects of fear and specificity of recommendation upon attitudes and behavior. *Journal of Personality and Social Psychology, 2,* 20–29.

[21] Leventhal, H., & Niles, P. (1965). Persistence of influence for varying durations of exposure to threat stimuli. *Psychological Reports, 16,* 223–233.

[22] O'Keefe, pp. 167–168.

[23] Chaiken, S., & Eagly, A. H. (1976). Communication modality as a determinant of message persuasiveness and message comprehensibility. *Journal of Personality and Social Psychology, 34,* 605–614.

[24] O'Keefe, pp. 183–185.

[25] Janis, I. L. (1954). Personality correlates of susceptibility to persuasion. *Journal of Personality, 22,* 504–518.

[26] Leventhal, H. (1970). Findings and theory in the study of fear communication, In L. Berkowitz (Ed.). *Advances in Experimental Social Psychology, Volume 5.* New York: Academic Press.

[27] Eagly, A. H., & Warren R. (1976). Intelligence, comprehension and opinion change. *Journal of Personality, 44,* 226–242.

[28] Johnston, D. D. (1994). *The art and science of persuasion.* Dubuque, IA: WC Brown, pp. 188–190.

[29] Snyder, M., & DeBono, K. G. (1985). Appeals to image and claims about quality: Understanding the psychology of advertising. *Journal of Personality and Social Psychology, 49,* 586–597.

[30] Petty, R. E., & Cacioppo, J. T. (1979). Issue involvement can increase or decrease persuasion by enhancing message-relevant cognitive responses. *Journal of Personality and Social Psychology, 37,* 1915–1926.

[31] Fisher, R., Ury, W., & Patton, B. (1991). *Getting to yes* (2nd ed.). New York: Penguin.

[32] Fisher, Ury, & Patton, pp. 3–9.

[33] These principles are adapted from the video *Negotiation and bargaining skills* (1984) produced by Alvin Goldberg and Carl Larson of the University of Denver.

[34] Fisher, Ury, & Patton, pp. 3–9.

[35] Adapted from Fisher, Ury, & Patton, pp. 7–9.

[36] Fisher, Ury, & Patton, pp. 17–94.

[37] Fisher, R., & Brown, S. (1988). *Getting together: Building a relationship that gets to yes.* Boston: Houghton Mifflin.

[38] Fisher & Brown, pp. 65–66.

[39] Fisher & Brown, p. 87.

[40] Woodward, G. C., & Denton, R. E. (1992). *Persuasion and influence in American life* (2nd ed.). Prospect Heights, IL: Waveland Press.

[41] Simons, H. W. (1986). *Persuasion: Understanding, practice, and analysis* (2nd ed.). New York: Random House, p. 227.

[42] Rogers, E. M., & Storey, J. D. (1987). Communication campaigns. In C. R. Berger & S. H. Chaffee (Eds.), *Handbook of communication science* (pp. 817–846). Newbury Park, CA: Sage.

[43] Dilenschneider, R. L., & Forrestal, D. J. (1987). The *Dartnell public relations handbook.* Chicago: The Dartnell Corporation.

[44] Jeffrey, N. (1987, December 7). Preparing for the worst: First set up plans to help deal with corporate crises. *The Wall Street Journal*, p. 23.

[45] Gregory, J. R., & Wiechmann, J. G. (1991). *Marketing corporate image: The company as your number one product.* Lincolnwood, IL: NTC, pp. 179–182.

[46] Marra, J. L. (1990). *Advertising creativity: Techniques for generating ideas.* Englewood Cliffs, NJ: Prentice Hall, pp. 52–63.

[47] Horton, C. (1990, January 1). TV commercial of the decade: Apple's bold "1984" scores on all fronts. *Advertising Age*, pp. 12, 38.

Quotations

Beck, E. M. (Ed.). (1980). *Bartlett's familiar quotations* (15th ed.). Boston: Little, Brown.

Gregory, J. R., & Wiechmann, J. G. (1991). *Marketing corporate image: The company as your number one product.* Lincolnwood, IL: NTC.

Marra, J. L. (1990). *Advertising creativity: Techniques for generating ideas.* Englewood Cliffs, NJ: Prentice Hall.

Wujec, T. (1988). *Pumping ions.* Toronto: Doubleday.

Index